D1144613

GUIDE TO
BASIC SEWING

*A guide to the basic skills for successful
dressmaking and homemaking*

CAVENDISH HOUSE

Consultant editor: Sheila Brull
House editor: Ethne Rose
Designed by Judith Robertson

Published by
Marshall Cavendish Books Limited
58 Old Compton Street
London W1V 5PA

© Marshall Cavendish Limited 1970,
1971, 1972, 1973, 1974, 1975, 1976,
1977, 1978, 1979, 1981

Some of this material has previously
appeared in other Marshall Cavendish
publications.

Printed in Hong Kong

First printing 1979
This printing 1981

ISBN 0 85685 152 3

Introduction

Have you ever longed to be able to turn your hand to making a whole range of useful sewn items, from clothes for all the family to curtains, cushions, chair covers, table and bed-linen—and much more besides? Then *Basic Sewing* is the book for you. How satisfying it is to know that you can create beautiful and useful things for your home and family simply by following the straightforward instructions and step-by-step illustrations in this book, and save on the household budget at the same time.

Basic Sewing contains everything you need to know about the equipment required: needles, thread, sewing machines, shears and other basic tools of the craft. All those tricky jobs you may dread doing—like making buttonholes or putting in zip fasteners—are clearly and simply explained. How to work with different textured and patterned fabrics, how to tack and sew different kinds of seam are made easy in *Basic Sewing*.

You'll be surprised at how soon you'll be ready to make all the lovely things in this book. You want to give your husband a shirt, you need a new skirt, your small daughter wants a pretty dress and your young son a pair of knockabout dungarees—here's how to do it all, from measuring up and making the paper patterns to perfecting every trimming on the finished garment.

Perhaps you are thinking of redecorating but are worried about changing the colour scheme in case it clashes with the furnishings. Well, *Basic Sewing* tells you how new curtains and covers can easily be made in whatever shade you want. If your bed-linen looks worn out, it's no problem—you can make duvet covers, fitted sheets, a valence and frilly pillow cases, all with the help of *Basic Sewing*. Maybe you thought that lampshade-making was difficult—not at all. Make a pretty tiffany shape or striking lined empire shade as described in this book, and see the room light up with colour and style.

You don't have to stop here either because this book gives all the basic skills required to make other items from commercial patterns—or from ideas of your own. *Basic Sewing* is an indispensable guide which the experienced needlewoman will find useful as a work of reference, while the less experienced will be introduced to all the essential techniques and ideas which go into good sewing.

Contents

Sewing Basics

Know Your Tools

A sewing machine

There are three main types: straight stitch, swing needle (zig-zag), and swing needle automatic.

Straight stitch This type will sew only in a straight line. It is the least expensive and is perfectly adequate for basic sewing. It is also possible to buy attachments, such as a piping foot for stitching close to a zip.

Swing needle As well as straight stitching this machine does zig-zag stitching which is useful for neatening seams and hems, for making buttonholes, for stitching stretch fabrics, and for sewing on buttons. It is also possible to do simple embroidery stitches. Swing needle machines are in the medium price bracket.

Swing needle automatic This machine does embroidery as well as the stitches which the other two types offer. But this type of machine is the most expensive and rather a luxury unless you intend to do a good deal of decorative stitching and embroidery. Electronics have added a new refinement to automatic sewing machines. There are various models now on the market with electronically regulated motors. These enable the sewing speed to be very precisely controlled with no sacrifice of power even when sewing only one stitch at a time. Electronic models are especially good whenever exact stitching is needed, e.g. for turning corners, inserting zips, for decorative applications or for sewing through several layers of thick fabric.
Note Make sure that the machine you buy has a clear instruction book. It is also important, particularly with a more complex machine, to have it explained by an expert and if possible to take a few short lessons in its use in order to get the best possible results.

Machine needles Use size 70-90 (11-14) for lightweight fabrics, size 90

(14) for medium weight fabrics and size 90-110 (14-18) for heavy weight fabrics. Continental sizes are given first here followed by British sizes in brackets.
Ballpoint machine needles should be used for jersey fabrics to prevent cutting the thread and laddering.
Sewing needles Use size 8 or 9 for most fabrics, size 6 or 7 for fabrics such as heavy linen and for stitching on buttons, and size 10 for very fine work.

Tools you will need

Pins Use steel dressmaking pins, at least 2·5 cm (1 in) long.

Tape measure The fibreglass type is the best as it will not stretch. One with a metal strip attached at one end is useful, especially when taking up hems. Tape measures are now marked with centimetres and millimetres on one side and inches on the other. For an approximate comparison simply look on the other side of the tape measure.

Thread For man-made fibres use a synthetic thread, such as Drima. Linens and cottons require mercerized cotton, either 40 or 50. For woollen fabrics use either a synthetic or silk thread.
With all types of thread the higher the number given on the label, the finer the thread.

Scissors Large shears are advisable when working with heavy fabrics. The handles should comfortably fit the hand (left-handed shears are available). Small shears, 18-20 cm (7-8 in) long, are best for cutting out most fabrics as they are heavier than scissors and glide through the cloth more easily.
Small sharp scissors are useful for clipping seams and threads. Never use your dressmaking scissors for cutting paper patterns as they will quickly become blunt!

Unpicker This is better than scissors for cutting machine-made buttonholes, and for removing buttons and snap fasteners, as well as being useful for unpicking. Various types of unpicker are available at most haberdashers.

Iron It is necessary to have a good medium-weight iron with thermostatic controls. If you use a steam iron you must use distilled water.

Ironing board An essential item for pressing seams flat. It should stand firmly and have a smooth-fitting cover. A sleeve board is useful.

Pressing cloth A piece of finely woven wool such as nun's veiling (for woollen fabrics), cotton or muslin through which you can see details, 61 cm (24 in) square. Your cloth should not have holes, frayed edges or prominent grains, as these can leave an impression on the fabric being pressed. Nor should the cloth contain any dressing as this will stick to the iron.

Tailor's ham An egg-shaped, firmly stuffed cushion, this is useful for pressing curved areas of a garment. A pressing roll is also useful for pressing seams in narrow areas e.g. sleeves. You can make one by covering a piece of wooden dowelling with blanketing tightly rolled and stitched round.

Tailor's chalk Have two pieces for marking your fabric, white for dark fabrics and dark for light fabrics. A dressmaker's pencil is also useful.

Tracing wheel Use this for marking pattern outlines on to fabric. One made from steel with sharp points is best.

Thimble This should fit the middle finger of your sewing hand. Choose a metal one as the needle can penetrate through a plastic one while sewing.

Needle & Thread Chart

This chart is to help you select the correct machine needle and thread for your fabric.

Natural fabrics are derived from fibres, animals or plants (wool, silk, cotton or linen). Synthetic fabrics are derived from man-made fibres made from material such as wood pulp (viscose) or chemicals (polyester – Terylene or acrylic – Courtelle). Many fabrics which were traditionally woven from natural fibres are now blends of natural and man-made fibres in various proportions. In this case the choice of thread is optional. Synthetic thread is stronger and has more give than cotton thread and should always be used if the fabric is mainly composed of synthetic fibre or if it is knitted or stretchy.

Coats Drima offers the best properties of natural and synthetic fibres and can be used to sew both types of fabric.

Fabric weight	Thread		Machine Needle	
Light	*Natural fabrics*	*Synthetic fabrics*	*Continental*	*British (Milwards)*
cotton lace	Coats Satinised cotton (50)		70-90	11-14
lawn, gingham, poplin	Coats Satinised cotton (50)	Drima	70-90	11-14
silk	pure silk (if available), Drima	Drima	70-90	11-14
blends (natural and synthetic)	Drima	Drima	70-90	11-14
Medium				
tweed, corduroy, linen	Coats Satinised cotton (40)		70-90	11-14
coating, worsted	Coats Satinised cotton (40)	Drima	90	14
jersey	pure silk (if available), Drima	Drima	ballpoint needle, size suitable to fabric	
wool	Coats Satinised cotton (40)			
blends (natural and synthetic)		Drima	70-90	11-14
Heavy				
coating	Coats Satinised cotton (40)		90-110	14-16
sailcloth, canvas	Coats Satinised cotton (40)		90-110	14-16
leather	Coats Satinised cotton (40)	Drima	spearpoint needle	
plastics		Drima	spearpoint needle	
top-stitching	Drima Bold Stitch	Drima Bold Stitch	100	16

Pinking shears Not essential but useful to give a neater finish to seams, particularly when working with knitted and non-fraying fabrics.

Metre or yardstick Use this for measuring hems.

Metric measurements

Instead of yards, feet, inches and fractions of an inch, metric measurements are written as metres (m), centimetres (cm) and millimetres (mm). There are one hundred centimetres in each metre and ten millimetres in each centimetre. Therefore $1\frac{1}{2}$ centimetres ($1\frac{5}{10}$) is written as 1·5 cm. Fractions of less than 1 centimetre can also be written in millimetres e.g. 'a 5 mm turning' or '0·5 cm' instead of 'a $\frac{1}{2}$ cm turning'. A $1\frac{1}{2}$ cm turning is written as 1·5 cm.

The measurements in this book are written first in metric with the *approximate* Imperial equivalents in brackets. Wherever possible both sets of figures have been worked out in round numbers. You must always work consistently with one or other set of figures. Fabric lengths are sold by the metre and cut to tenths of a metre (10 cm) e.g. 1 metre 70 centimetres is 1·70 m.

10 cm is approximately 4 in and takes the place of the Imperial $\frac{1}{8}$ yard. Fabric widths are sold by the centimetre as shown in the table below.

Metric fabric widths

90 cm (36 in)
115 cm (45 in)
120 cm (48 in)
140 cm (54-56 in)
150 cm (60 in)

The measurements in this chart comply with the standard measurements used by pattern companies. Skirt lengths can be ascertained by counting the squares downwards from waist to hem on the required graph pattern then multiplying by the given scale of 2·5 cm (1 in) per square.

How to take your measurements

Bust Make sure that you keep the tape measure well up over the shoulder blades at the back, and measure across the fullest part of the bust (fig. 1).

Waist Tie a piece of tape or straight binding round the waist to establish the true waistline. Then run tape measure around your waist over tape so that it is comfortable but not loose (fig. 2). Keep tape on as a guide for other measurements.

Hips This measurement should be taken around the fullest part of the hips, usually 15-20 cm (6-8 in) below the waistline (fig. 3).

Back neck to waist Measure from the small bone at the back of the neck to the waistline (fig. 4).

Back neck to hem Measure from the same bone to the hemline. Remem-

Metric measurements used on dressmaking patterns						
Size	8	10	12	14	16	18
	cm (in)	cm (in)	cm (in)	cm (in)	cm (in)	cm (in)
Bust	80 (31½)	83 (32½)	87 (34)	92 (36)	97 (38)	102 (40)
Waist	61 (24)	64 (25)	67 (26½)	71 (28)	76 (30)	81 (32)
Hips	85 (33½)	88 (34½)	92 (36)	97 (38)	102 (40)	107 (42)

1   2   3   4   5

ber to allow extra for a hem (fig. 5).

Sleeve With arm bent, measure from arm top to the wrist around the bent elbow (fig. 6).

Depth of bust It is important to have the bust dart or fullness in the correct position for a good fit. Measure from centre of one shoulder to bust point (fig. 7).

Inside leg Measure from inside top of leg to length required (fig. 8).

Outside leg Measure from side of waist to length required. You must take both of these leg measurements wearing shoes with your usual heel height (fig. 9).

Depth of crotch The easiest way to take this measurement is to sit on a chair with your back straight and measure from the side of waist to the chair. Allow 1·3-2·5 cm (½-1 in) for ease of movement (fig. 10).

It is important to take your measurements correctly to help in choosing the proper pattern size. Then you will achieve a well-fitting garment.

Patterns and pattern sizes

If your measurements do not correspond with the body chart it is advisable to select the pattern according to your bust size and adjust the hips and waist as necessary.

How to use graph patterns

Graph patterns can seem rather complicated if you haven't used them before, but they are really quite simple. Graphs are a way of giving readers full-sized garment patterns but scaled down so that they fit into a book or magazine page. They are designed in exactly the same way as the paper patterns which you buy. The only difference is that a graph is a plan from which you draw up the pattern yourself. Graph patterns can be very useful too in that you can make minor adaptations to style or improve on body fit as you are drawing the pattern out.

To make a paper pattern from a graph pattern, you will find it best to work on a flat surface; the floor will do if you haven't a large enough table. You will need the following equipment:

Sheets of squared paper This is called 'dressmaker's pattern paper'

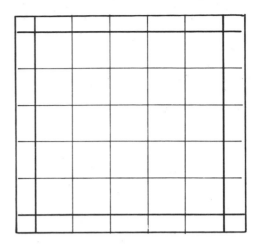

1. Pattern paper is divided into 5 cm (2 in) squares and 1 cm (⅜ in) squares.

and is obtainable from the dress fabric departments of stores. The sheets usually measure 90 by 62 cm (36 by 24 in) and are sold in packets of three, enough for a dress pattern.

Metre rule This is a wooden ruler measuring 1 metre (39½ in) long.

Soft pencil B or 2B.

Drawing out the pattern Check the scale given with the pattern. Sometimes this will be marked on the graph itself, sometimes you will find it in the instructions. It will read something like, 'one square equals

6   7   8   9   10

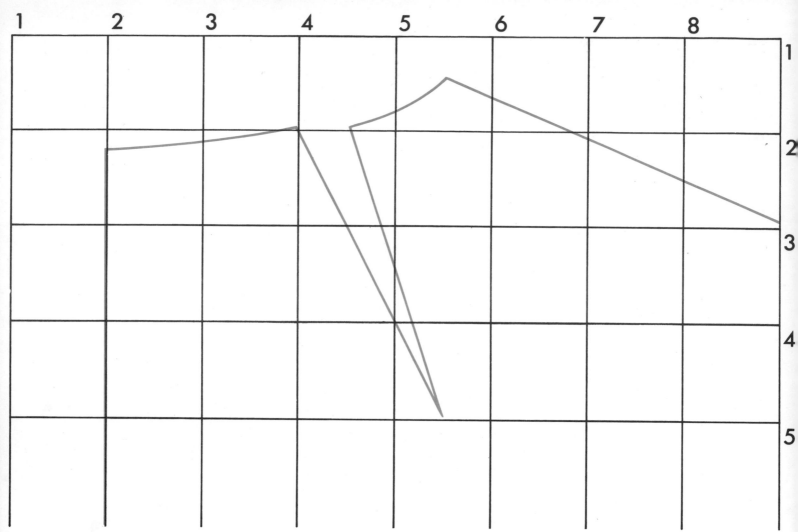

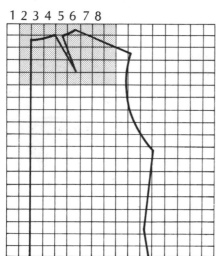

2

5 cm (2 in)' but the scale will vary, sometimes one square will equal 2·5 cm (1 in). Your squared paper will be marked off into 5 cm (2 in) squares in thick lines and into 1 cm (⅜ in) squares in a lighter toned line. For the purpose of this exercise, use the heavy, 5 cm (2 in) square lines (fig. 1).

Number the graph pattern squares, first across the top and then down the

side as shown in the diagram (fig. 2).
Draw out the area of the graph pattern on your squared paper and number the 5 cm (2 in) squares in the same way, first across the top and then down the side (fig. 3).

You now have a perfect reproduction of the area you are going to work within, scaled up from the graph pattern.

To make it clear, we have tinted the area of the graph pattern we have enlarged.

Draw in any straight lines, such as the line indicating Fold.

Study the line in the square 2 across and 2 down. You will see that it starts just below a line and curves up slightly as it touches the square next to it. Reproduce as faithfully as you can the direction of the line on your graph paper. Don't worry if your line looks a bit wobbly, you can always straighten it up later.

Compare your shoulder to waist, waist to hip and sleeve length with the graph you are copying. If you need to make any adjustments, do these before

cutting out your pattern. To alter a bodice, follow a horizontal line 10 cm (4 in) above the waist and add or subtract the necessary length. To adjust a skirt pattern, follow a horizontal line just above the hipline of pattern and on a sleeve follow horizontal lines above and below the elbow. Alter as described for bodice. Adjust skirt and sleeve lengths slightly at hem. (Also see Basic pattern alterations.)

The graph pattern given may be multi-sized, in which case the outline for each size is marked with a different colour or broken line. Simply follow the outline for the size you want.

Add all marks and words given on the graph pattern. You have now made your master pattern.

First steps before cutting out
If you are making a garment for the first time, pick a fabric that is easy to work with and not too expensive in case of catastrophe! A plain cotton or one with a small all-over print is ideal. Large patterns, checks or stretchy jerseys should not be used by begin-

10

ners, nor should those such as velvet or lace that need special making-up techniques.

Some technical terms
Selvedges The edges of the fabric, usually tightly woven and non-fraying.
Grain The straight threads running the length (warp) and width (weft) of woven fabrics. If the pattern piece has an arrow, this indicates that it should follow the direction of the grain.
Nap Any fabric with a piled surface e.g. velvet. Pattern pieces must all run in the same direction or there will be a shaded effect on the finished garment.
One-way Designs that are printed or woven in one direction. Pattern pieces must be placed accordingly. Special pattern layouts are usually

1. To straighten fabric, pull a thread across the width and then use the line as a guide to cut the fabric evenly.

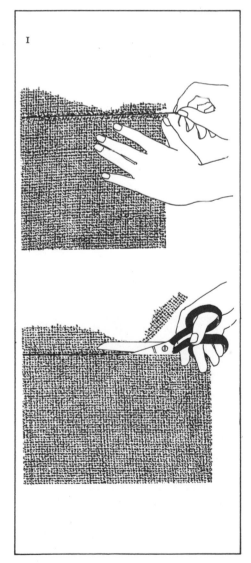

provided for 'with nap' or 'one way' fabrics.
Ease (or tolerance) Extra width included in patterns to allow for the movement of the body, so that the garment is comfortable to wear. Usually about 5 cm (2 in) on bust and hips and 2·5 cm (1 in) for the waist.
Notches and balance marks Small marks at side edges of pattern pieces to show which parts join to which.

Preparing the fabric
Before laying out a pattern make sure that the fabric lies flat when both selvedges are together, as the fabric often becomes slightly warped when wound on to the roll, or can be stretched at the selvedge on knitted fabrics such as jersey. If the cloth has a stripe or horizontal pattern trim the cut edge until it is at right angles to the selvedge: with cotton or heavy linen it is usually possible to pull a thread across the width as a guide (fig. 1).
Place the two selvedges together and providing the weft is even the material should lie flat; if it appears wrinkled pull on the cross at regular intervals down the complete length of the cloth. Then with the material held lengthways gently pull on the selvedge edge and on the fold line. Sometimes the fabric has been folded badly and it is necessary to press it.
Where possible cut out on a large table or the floor as the complete pattern should be placed on the fabric at the same time. When a delicate fabric is being used it is advisable to use a heavy blanket underneath and pin the cloth to it at the edges. It is also necessary to use fine pins or fine needles on this type of fabric as ordinary pins will mark and leave

holes.
All alterations such as shortening or lengthening pattern pieces should be made before placing them on the fabric.

Testing fabrics
To find out whether a washable fabric is colourfast wash a small square about 8 cm (3 in) square. Press while still damp on to some white fabric. The colour will run on to the white fabric if it is not colourfast.
To test for shrinkage measure a similar square of fabric, or tack mark the outline of an 8 cm (3 in) square on to it, before washing; measure again when dry and then compare the two measurements.
Fabrics in synthetic fibres do not shrink and many others are preshrunk by the manufacturer. If the test square shrinks you must preshrink the fabric before cutting out. Wet a strip of sheeting the width and length of the fabric. Wring out any excess moisture. Place sheet over fabric and roll up. Leave for several hours. Remove sheet and press fabric using a dry pressing cloth. Always work on the straight grain of the fabric, never diagonally, until fabric is dry.

Laying out a pattern
Layout instructions and diagrams are usually provided with both commercial and graph patterns (fig. 2). Follow these carefully as they will show you the best and most economical way to arrange your pattern pieces on the fabric before cutting out. Alternative versions are usually given for different

2. All patterns include layout diagrams to show you how to arrange the pieces in the best economical manner.

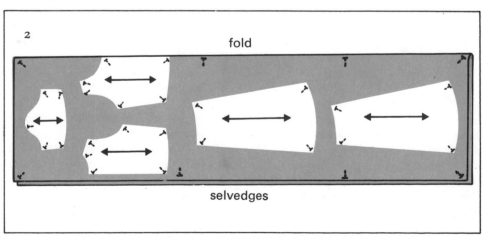

fold

selvedges

fabric widths or for 'with nap' fabrics. Note whether seam and hem allowances have been provided on the pattern or whether you must allow extra space between the pattern pieces to provide for them. Also note if any pattern pieces have to be reversed, cut on a fold of the fabric and whether they are cut on a double or single layer. Sometimes, because of unusual widths of fabric, difficult stripes, or a big pattern repeat, it is necessary to place the paper pattern in a different way from the one suggested. Once you are more experienced you will be able to adapt layouts for yourself.

Always check that the straight grain mark on every pattern piece runs parallel to the selvedges.

When pinning the pattern on to the fabric place pins so that the points lie towards the centre. This positioning of pins holds the fabric firmly and there is less risk of scratching hands when smoothing out pattern pieces. Pin fabric round edges to hold layers together on folded fabric.

Do not leave facings to be cut out later as these smaller pattern pieces can easily be mislaid.

Count all pattern pieces to ensure that none have been forgotten. Note whether any parts, such as pockets or collars, have to be cut twice.

Cutting out

Before starting to cut out the fabric make sure you have the necessary tools: a large pair of dressmaking shears for long, straight seams and a smaller sharply pointed pair for all the awkward corners and for cutting around notches.

The shears will have a pointed blade and a rounded blade. The pointed blade is used downwards when cutting out patterns to ensure that the two thicknesses of cloth are cut at the same time. The rounded blade is used downwards for such things as trimming large areas and layering (trimming turnings to different widths) so that there is no sharp point to cut the second layer of cloth.

Fabrics made from man-made fibres often blunt shears very quickly. A very light spray from an aerosol silicone polish will help to prevent this. But allow it to dry thoroughly before using the shears.

Notches may be marked on patterns

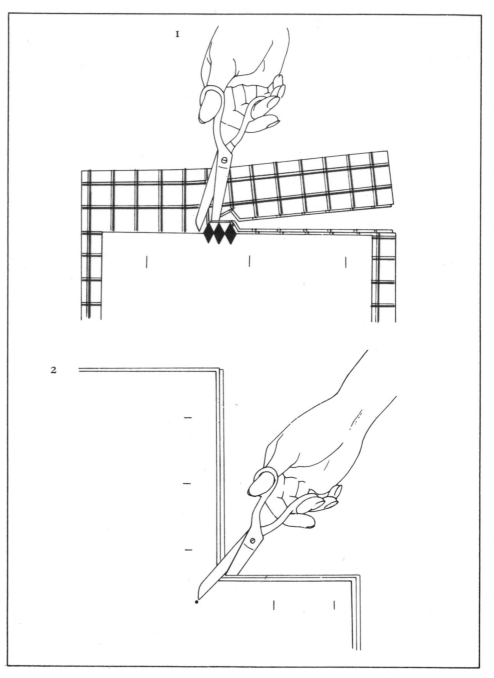

as diamonds or triangles and are often difficult to cut. Bypass these when using the big shears and go back to them using small pointed scissors. It is not practical to cut into each individual notch when there are two or three together but to cut straight across the top of them (fig. 1).

Often in a corner of a pattern piece there is a large dot and the word 'clip' (fig. 2). Do not cut this until you are ready to tack to avoid fraying and stretching.

Using the large shears, with points towards the table, make long clean cuts into the fabric. When using a patterned fabric check that both thicknesses of fabric are matching on all edges. It is sometimes advisable to cut each layer

1. Cut notches carefully, they help to match pattern pieces. 2. Clip corners when you are ready to tack.

separately as some types of cloth slip very easily. It is essential to cut fur fabric separately as only the backing must be cut, not the pile.

Cutting bias strips These are required for making bindings or rouleau ties. To find the bias of the fabric, fold so that the straightened edge is parallel to the selvedge (fig. 1). The fold is on the bias or crosswise grain.

Use a metre rule and tailor's chalk to mark out strips of the width required parallel to this fold (fig. 2). These may have to be stitched together later to make up the length required.

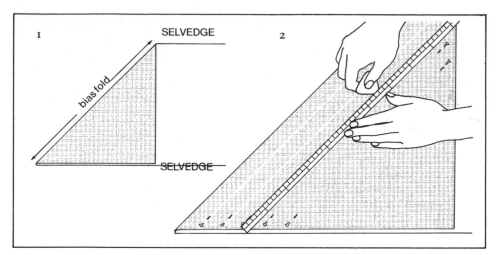

It is essential to transfer all markings on the pattern to the fabric before removing pattern. Markings are made

Left. 1. To cut bias strips, fold over a corner of fabric and 2. mark the cutting lines with tailor's chalk.

Below. 1. Making tailor's tacks.
2. Marking darts with tailor's tacks.
3. Thread tacking along the centre back.
4. Trace tacking along centre back and side seams.
5. Cutting through the tailor's tacks.

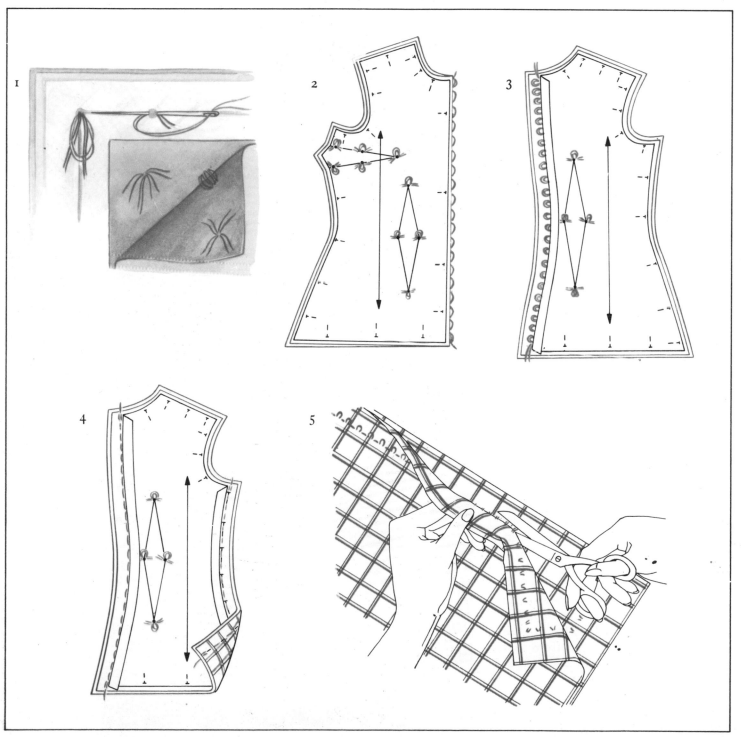

with tailor's tacks, which are large looped stitches for marking pattern details, thread tacks, for quick marking of grain or stitching lines and trace tacks, for marking centre front, centre back or stitching lines.

Tailor's tacks Using double thread, without a knot, work a small stitch through the pattern and both thicknesses of the fabric, leaving about 2·5 cm (1 in) of thread free (fig. 1). Work another stitch in the same place leaving a loop of thread of about 4 cm (1½ in), cut off the thread about 2·5 cm (1 in) from last stitch. To mark darts with tailor's tacks, take a large needle and make a hole in the pattern where the dots of the darts are marked. (With graph patterns make holes at the point of the dart, on the stitching line and halfway between the point and the stitching line.) Work the tailor's tacks as described (fig. 2). Pocket positions, notches and balance marks are also marked with tailor's tacks. On cotton and heavy fabrics use tacking cotton, which grips the cloth better than most other threads and is less likely to fall out when handling tailor's tacks. With delicate fabrics use lightweight thread such as pure silk and a needle no larger than Sharps number 10, otherwise permanent marks or holes may appear in the garment.

Thread tacking Fold pattern back at stitching line. Using double thread, without a knot, work a continuous line of small tacking stitches through the two thicknesses of fabric, leaving a loop of thread about 4 cm (1½ in) between each stitch (fig. 3).

Trace tacking Fold back pattern at stitching line. Using single thread, without a knot, work a row of small tacking stitches through single fabric (fig. 4). Place a row of pins on this line of tacking through both thicknesses of cloth. Turn fabric over and work another row of trace tacking between the pins.

It is essential when marking stitching lines to continue right to the end so that the lines of tacking cross at the corners. It is advisable when working thread tacking for stitching lines to use a different coloured thread from that used for the notches to avoid confusion.

The simple unbroken lines of this garment makes good use of stripes.

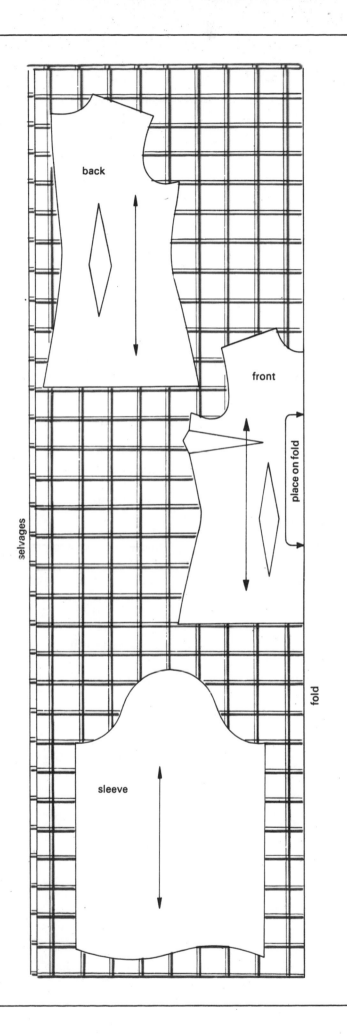

back

front

place on fold

selvages

fold

sleeve

Do not use a very dark thread on a light coloured fabric as it could leave marks.

Centre front or **centre back** Place on a fold of the cloth, and mark out with trace tacking stitches through the single fabric on fold. Start and finish with back stitches.

Fold lines Use for such things as pleats, marked with thread tacking or trace tacking.

A very simple pattern can usually be transferred on to the fabric by working tailor's tacks on each corner where the stitching lines cross each other and at about 10 cm (4 in) intervals on the stitching lines.

Tailor's chalk Use to save time in marking out a pattern but remember that it contains a certain amount of grease and can sometimes leave a permanent mark.

When all markings have been transferred to the fabric remove pattern and cut through tailor's tacks and thread tacking (fig. 5). This is done by gently pulling the two pieces of fabric apart and, with small scissors, cutting through the centre of the stitch. Some patterns do have a great many pieces. To avoid confusion it often helps to pin a small piece of paper at the bottom edge, and write on it the name of the piece of pattern after you have cut it out.

Special cutting directions
Patterned fabrics or those with a pile need more attention at the cutting out stage. Designs with simple unbroken lines are best for all these fabrics.

Stripes and checks
These must be in line on each piece of the garment, including the sleeves. It is often easiest to place the centre back body piece on to the fabric, then, matching the bottom edge of the other pieces, work round to the centre front. The sleeves must match at the underarm point so that the pattern runs in a continuous line round the arm (fig. 1). When a side bust dart is used it is not always possible to match the pattern at the underarm but this usually affects only 5-8 cm (2-3 in). It is not always possible to match vertical and

1. On patterned fabrics it is important that the design of the fabric matches when cutting out.

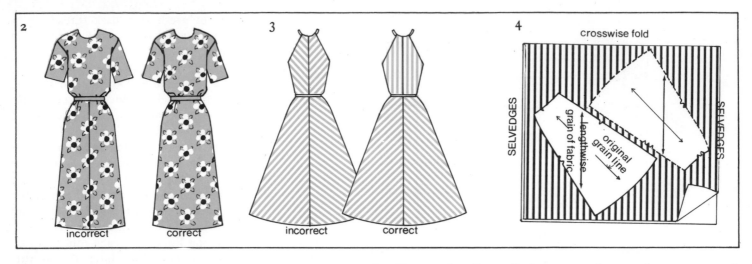

2. Large motifs should not lie over obvious figure features. 3. Diagonal stripes are best on centre back or front openings and 4. a new grain line should be placed parallel to selvedges.

horizontal stripes on the shoulder line as there is usually about 1·3 cm (½ in) of ease on the back. Match at armhole edge as often the neck edge is covered by a collar.

Pockets, tabs and flaps must also line up in the pattern unless intended otherwise. Sometimes these are cut on the cross of a checked fabric as a design feature, or on a cloth striped or ribbed vertically these may be cut with the lines running horizontally.

Avoid using designs with too many pieces to be matched or widely flaring skirts. Uneven checks and plaids are particularly difficult to work with, but even the tiniest check looks better when it is perfectly matched.

Flower prints and unusual patterns
If these have a one-way motif, lay out the pattern accordingly to be sure that the pattern runs in the right direction on all the pieces. As with checks, avoid too many pattern pieces. You may find problems, too, with patterns that have really large motifs. The least complicated way to use these is with large flowing designs such as caftans or full-length skirts. On other garments try to arrange the pattern pieces so that motifs are in the same position on back and front and on the sleeves. Make sure that really large motifs do not lie directly over the bust or seat (fig. 2).

Pile fabrics
Velvet, corduroy and fake fur come into this category. In all cases the pile of the fabric must lie in the same way on each piece. Test by smoothing the surface in one direction with your hand. Always use a 'with nap' layout.

Using diagonal stripes
To do this choose a pattern with a centre seam or front or back opening (fig. 3). Mark a new grain line on the pattern pieces at 45° to the straight grain line. To cut out, fold the full width of the fabric crosswise, with right sides together. Lay the pattern pieces on the fabric with the new line parallel to selvedges (fig. 4). Notches to be joined must be on the same stripe.

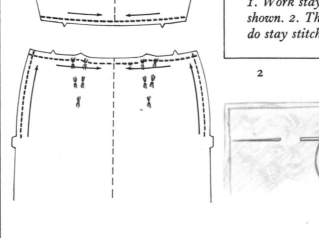

Stripes must also match at centre and side seams *on the same line*, not the seam edge. For accurate stitching use slip tacking to hold the pieces together (see Preparing for fitting). If the stripes are uneven, lay the pattern pieces on the fabric in one direction.

Preparing for fitting
The garment is now ready to be put together. Here are some useful preliminaries.

Stay stitching   Use to keep the shape of necklines or waistlines to prevent them stretching during making-up. A line of machine stitching is made in the seam allowance 1·3 cm (½ in) from the raw edge. Work with thread to match the fabric. Stitch in the directions shown (fig. 1).

Tacking stitches   Temporary stitches which are used to hold the garment sections together. Make even stitches by hand, about 6 mm (¼ in) long (fig. 2). Always work on a flat surface such as a table. Before you begin tacking

1. Work stay stiching in the direction shown. 2. This diagram shows how to do stay stitching.

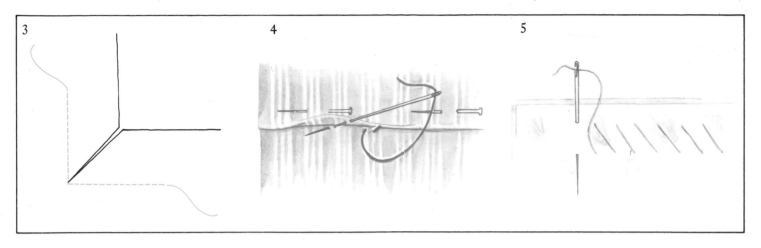

place the seam edges together, pin at each end and in the centre and match any notches. Place pins at right angles to the seam line. Once you are more experienced you can pin, then stitch simple garments together without tacking.

Tack all darts and main seam lines, centre front, sides and shoulders. Use single thread without a knot. Start and finish each line with three back-stitches as knots can cause permanent holes or damage when pulled whilst trying on the garment. It is important that the garment is tacked well to achieve a good fitting. Any alteration is made during the fitting. The garment is then re-tacked to the correct line, tried on again, and if it is then satisfactory it is ready to be machined. All tailor's tacks are removed at this stage as they could be machined in.

Reinforcing This is often necessary to strengthen seams on a corner. It is done before the seam is stitched. Stitch about 2·5 cm (1 in) either side of the point. Inward corners are clipped as shown (fig. 3).

Slip tacking This is used for matching stripes, checks or patterns accurately, also for attaching curved pattern sections or to secure fitting adjustments that have been made on the right side. Working on the right side, turn under the seam allowance. Position on corresponding section and pin carefully. Using single thread, slip needle through upper fold, then lower section, taking small stitches. When finished the seam will be tacked on the wrong side (fig. 4).

Diagonal tacking This is used to keep separate layers together e.g.

3. Reinforcing is used to strengthen corner seams. 4. Working slip tacking. 5. Working diagonal tacking.

securing interfacings firmly against fabric during making up or holding facing edges in place ready for pressing. Make slanting stitches about 6 mm (¼ in) long and the same distance apart, working at right angles to the edge of the fabric through all layers (fig. 5).

All about seams
Basic seams
There are many types of seam all of which serve the same purpose but have individual advantages The seam must be chosen to suit the fabric and the design of the garment, which means considering whether or not the fabric will fray and if the seam is to show. Always remember to press seams well after stitching and before neatening.

Plain seam This is the most commonly used seam in dressmaking as it is suitable for most fabrics.

With right sides together and notches matching, tack and stitch on the seam line. To join a bias edge to a straight edge pin, tack and stitch with the bias

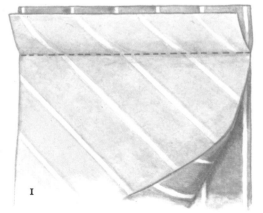

1

side upwards (fig. 1). If joining two bias edges stretch fabric slightly as you stitch over tissue paper.

Seam finishes Your dressmaking will be neater, stronger and more professional-looking if you finish off each line of stitching firmly. Start and finish each seam with a back stitch, either by hand or by running your machine backwards for 6 mm (¼ in). Thread ends should be knotted and the ends cut off. If the stitching line ends before the edge of the fabric, pull one of the thread ends through to the other side. Tie both thread ends together and cut off surplus.

Useful hand stitches
Back stitch This stitch is used for starting and finishing most hand stitching and is useful for repairing broken machine lines (fig. 1).

Using single thread, and with right sides of work together, insert needle into fabric and make a small stitch on the wrong side. Put needle back into the hole where the thread first entered the fabric. Make another stitch through the fabric twice the length of the first. Insert the needle back in the hole where it came out for the previous stitch. Continue in this way until the row of stitches is complete.

Blanket stitch Useful as a decorative finish on a raw edge. The thread loops underneath the needle which lies vertically in the fabric. Make a button loop or bar for a hook by working blanket stitches close together over a foundation of tacking stitches (fig. 2).

Hemming Used to hold all types of

1. A plain seam.

hems in place. Take a tiny stitch in the garment, bring the needle diagonally up through the hem edge. Make stitches about 6 mm ($\frac{1}{4}$ in) apart (fig. 3).

Herringbone stitch Useful for holding two layers of fabric together e.g. attaching raw edges of facings or making hems on stretchy fabrics. Work from left to right taking a small stitch in hem, then one in the fabric (fig. 4). (Catchstitching is similar, but only one thread is picked up.)

Oversewing (overcasting) Used to prevent raw edges from fraying. Make diagonal, evenly-spaced stitches over the edge of the fabric (fig. 5).

Prick stitch A version of back stitch, worked over a single thread of fabric, forming a tiny surface stitch (fig. 6).

Running stitch Used for easing i.e. gathering a slightly longer piece on to a smaller one such as for putting in a sleeve. For making gathers and, worked in even rows, for shirring. Weave needle in and out of fabric before pulling through. Make stitches an even size 2-6 mm ($\frac{1}{16}$-$\frac{1}{4}$ in) long. Several stitches can be made on the needle at same time. Draw up stitches if gathers are required (fig. 7).

Slipstitch Used to attach one piece of fabric to another when one edge is turned under as in hems, bias binding, linings or to hold trimmings in place. Slide the needle through the folded edge of the fabric, then directly opposite and barely outside the fold, pick up a thread of the under fabric. Continue in the same way, spacing the stitches evenly, from 3 to 6 mm ($\frac{1}{8}$ to $\frac{1}{4}$ in) apart (fig. 8).

Neatening seams
When each seam is finished remove the tacking, fasten the thread ends and press seam. The method of neatening depends on the type of fabric used.

Oversewing (overcasting)   This can be done separately on each pressed-open seam allowance or both seam allowances can be pressed together and oversewn as one e.g. on waists or armhole seams (fig. 1).

Zig-zag stitch This is a useful machine finish for many types of fabric with a tendency to fray. Use a small stitch on a fine fabric, a larger zig-zag on a heavier fabric (fig. 2).

Turned under Thin fabrics can be turned under for 3 mm ($\frac{1}{8}$ in) and machine stitched close to the fold (fig. 3).

Bound Thick fabrics that fray can have seam edges bound with bias or

These hand stitches are useful for neatening raw edges, and their use will add a couture finish to a garment. They are: 1. back stitch. 2. blanket stitch, 3. hemming, 4. herringbone stitch, 5. oversewing (overcasting), 6. prick stitch, 7. running stitch and 8. slipstitch.

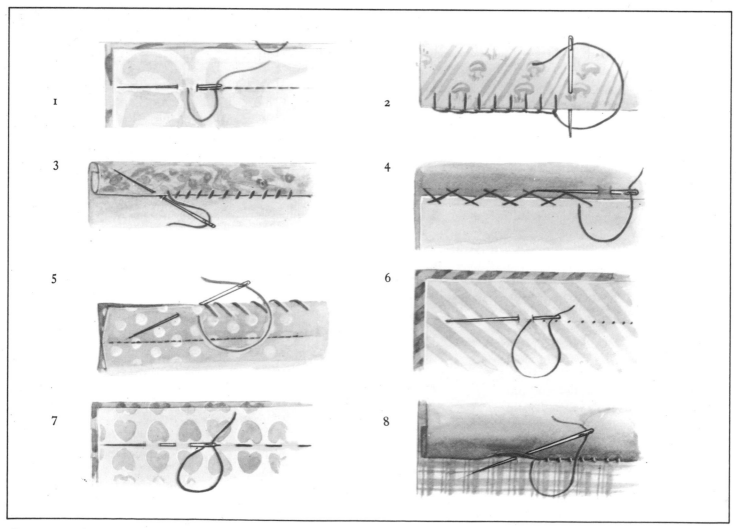

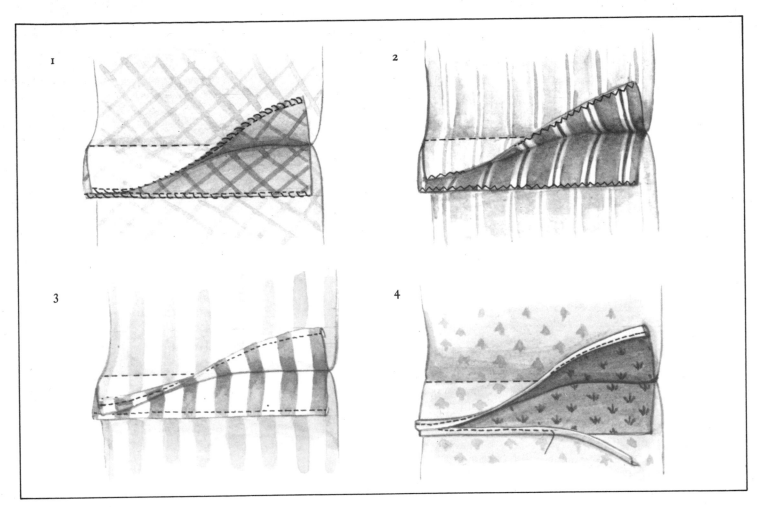

Seams can be neatened using one of these methods: 1. oversewing (overcasting), 2. zig-zag stitch, 3. edge turned under, 4. edge bound.

seam binding. Fold the binding round the edge of the fabric and stitch close to the edge (fig. 4).

Useful seams and processes

Channel seam A decorative seam to use on dresses and blouses. Turn under 1·5 cm ($\frac{5}{8}$ in) on both seam lines. Tack. Place both folds with edges touching, on to a separate strip of the same fabric the same length as the seam and cut on the same grain (fig. 1). Tack and stitch the distance of the machine foot from the fold line on either side. Remove the tacking, and turn to the wrong side. Neaten inside edges.

Double top-stitched seam This is an ordinary open seam with the turnings top-stitched down. It is flat and decorative and can be used on dresses, skirts, jackets and coats. With right sides together and notches matching, tack and stitch on the seam line. Press open on the wrong side. If the fabric frays, neaten the turnings before top-stitching. Working on the right side, machine stitch the required distance along each side of the seam (fig. 2).

Flat fell seam This seam can be worked on the inside or outside of a garment on thick or thin fabrics.

1. Channel seam
2. Double top-stitched seam.

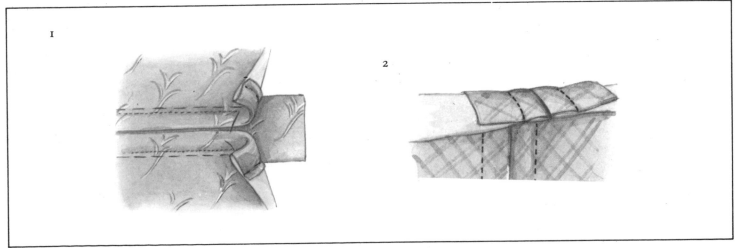

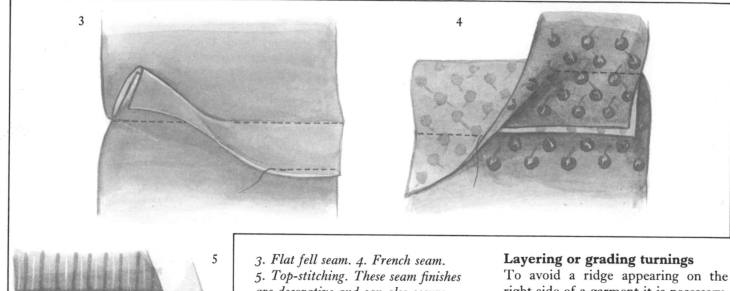

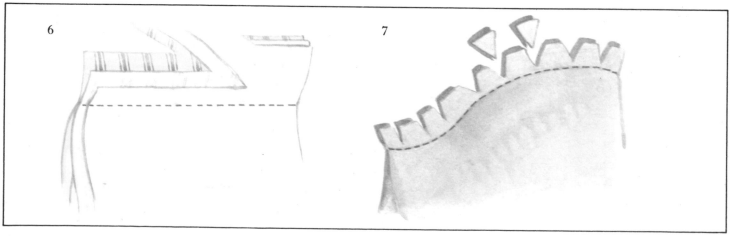

Stitch a plain seam and press, it towards one side. Trim the lower seam allowance to 6 mm (¼ in). Turn under the edge of the other seam allowance 6 mm (¼ in) and place over the trimmed seam allowance. Stitch close to the folded edge (fig. 3).

French seam This is used on sheer fabrics, baby clothes and underwear. It looks like a plain seam on the right side but the raw edges inside are neatly enclosed.

With wrong sides together and notches matching tack on the seam line 1·5 cm (⅝ in) in. Stitch at 6 mm (¼ in) out-

3. Flat fell seam. 4. French seam. 5. Top-stitching. These seam finishes are decorative and can also secure turnings.

side the seam line. Remove the tacking and trim the turning to just under 6 mm (¼ in). Press the turnings together to one side. Turn so that the right sides are together. Tack and stitch on the seam line, enclosing the raw edges (fig. 4). Press all French seams towards the back of the garment.

Top-stitching This is used to emphasize design details or to keep seam edges flat (fig. 5). Stitch a plain seam, then press it to one side. Work another row of stitching, called top-stitching, on the right side of the fabric, keeping a constant distance from the seam (the machine foot is a useful guide). Use buttonhole twist in the machine. When you reach a corner, stop before the edge with the machine needle through the fabric. Raise the presser foot and turn the fabric at a right angle so the stitching line continues the same distance away from the edge.

Layering or grading turnings

To avoid a ridge appearing on the right side of a garment it is necessary, especially where an interfacing has been used, to trim the turnings to different widths. These are usually: interfacing 2 mm ($\frac{1}{16}$ in); first turning 3 mm ($\frac{1}{8}$ in); second turning 6 mm (¼ in) (fig. 6).

Slash, cut, clip or notch

It is necessary on an inward curved seam, such as a neckline, armhole or shaped stitching line, to cut (slash or clip) almost to the machine line to enable the turning to spread out and press flat (fig. 5). On an outward curve, such as a circular cushion, it is necessary to cut V-shaped notches to reduce the bulk of the seam allowance (fig. 7).

Understitching

This is a line of machine stitching used to prevent neck facings from rolling outwards. It is done after the facing is stitched in place and the seam allow-

So that seams lie correctly, either: 6. layer or grade turnings, 7. slash, cut clip or notch curves.

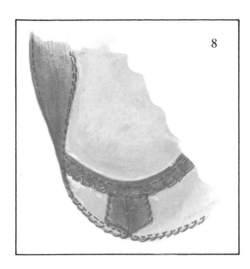

8. Facings should be understitched.

ances have been layered. Turn facing and seam allowances away from the garment. Stitch from the right side, through facings and seam allowances, close to the seam line (fig. 8).

The art of pressing

Pressing is a very important part of dressmaking. It improves the appearance of the garment and also helps you to work neatly and accurately. It is essential to press each seam after it has been stitched. It is easier to press on an ironing board, but a table well-padded with a blanket and covered with a cloth is quite adequate for flat seams. A thickly padded glove is useful for pressing small areas.

Basic pressing rules

A. Always check that the base of the iron is clean. If not, clean with a specially-made cleaning agent. Always polish the base after cleaning by rubbing with a clean soft cloth. Check that vents are not blocked.
B. If using a steam iron it is essential to use distilled water as tap water leaves a deposit in the iron. Distilled water can be purchased from a chemist.
Do not over fill the iron as the water can splash and mark the fabric.
C. Always test on a piece of fabric from which you are making the garment. Test fabric's reaction to temperature, steam and moisture.
D. When using a damp cloth, use a piece of linen if possible. The highest setting on the iron is for linen and this therefore prevents scorching.
E. Set the iron to the correct setting.
F. Remove all tacking or pins in the seams before pressing.
G. Press on the wrong side of the garment.
H. Pressing is not ironing. With pressing the iron is placed gently down on to the garment, lifted and placed down again. The iron is not moved backwards and forwards as in ironing. Press with the grain of the fabric, take care not to stretch edges or curves by pulling fabric. Delicate fabrics which do not require steam pressing should be pressed with a piece of muslin between iron and fabric.
I. Do not over-press by holding the iron on one part of the garment too long. This can leave an imprint of the iron permanently showing on the right side.
J. Do not press plastic coated fabric with an iron. If open seams are required, they must be glued down.

Pressing for a perfect finish

Seams Press either open or towards the centre-back or centre-front if to be neatened together. Always press a seam before it is neatened; this prevents ridges on the right side of the garment.

Darts Darts are always pressed towards the centre of the body: front towards the centre-front; back towards the centre-back; side bust darts towards the waist; and sleeve elbow darts down. On thick fabric the dart may have to be cut and pressed open. Be careful not to stretch this type of dart and do not cut right to the point.

Facings Have the garment flat on the ironing board or table and, where the facings have been attached, press lightly on the very edge. Remove the tacking stitches and press again to remove any stitch marks. It is advisable to insert a cloth or piece of paper between the facing and the garment when pressing the edge (fig. 1). This prevents ridges on the right side. This is sometimes also advisable for seams and hems.

Pleats When pressing pleats, it is essential to have the edge of the pleat fold on the wrong side parallel with the edge of the ironing board. Press on the folds, remove tacking stitches and press again to remove stitch marks (fig. 2). After pressing in pleats with a damp cloth hang up the garment straight away to let the pleats dry completely before doing any more work on the garment.

Pressing a shoulder seam Using a pressing glove, turn your hand upwards and place it under the shoulder join, with the glove extended about 1·3 cm (½ in) beyond the join into the sleeve (fig. 3). Place the tip of the iron gently on to the seam line with the turnings towards the sleeve and at the same time slightly lift the tips of the fingers in the mitt. This will round the top of the sleeve in the armhole and

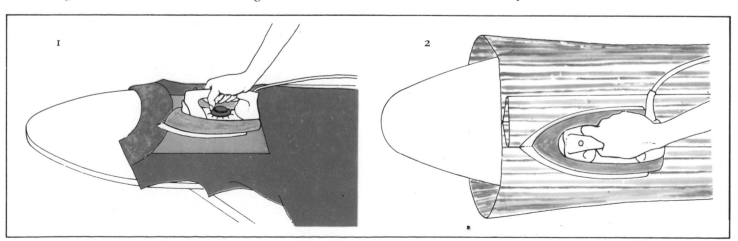

help to remove any wrinkles. Continue in this way until the top of the sleeve has become smooth and moulded. Do not over-press by holding the hot iron and damp cloth on one spot for too long. You can also use a tailor's ham for this purpose.

Pressing a hem Place the garment on the ironing board and gently press. Lift the iron and press again. The nose of the iron should be pointed towards the waistline of the garment (fig. 4). Do not move the iron backwards and forwards, or from side to side as this will stretch the fabric. Also avoid seam edge of hem.

Shrinking When there is excess fullness on a garment such as at the hemline on a flared skirt, or a tight fitting sleeve without elbow darts, a natural fabric can be shrunk to avoid pleats or creases on the right side. Work a gathering thread on the stitching line, pull up to the required length and press with a damp cloth a little at a time. After each press gently pat the fabric, this helps to flatten any bulges. Continue in this way until all the fullness has been eliminated. Remove the gathering thread.

Collars With under collar facing upwards press on the very edge. Remove tacking stitches and press again (fig. 5).

Pressing gathers Gathers should never be pressed flat. Place the garment on to the ironing board and, with wrong side of fabric upwards, press from the lowest edge, on the straight grain, up towards the gathers. Nose the tip of the iron into the gathers then move the garment around the board and press the next section in the same way (fig. 6). When complete hang up the garment immediately.

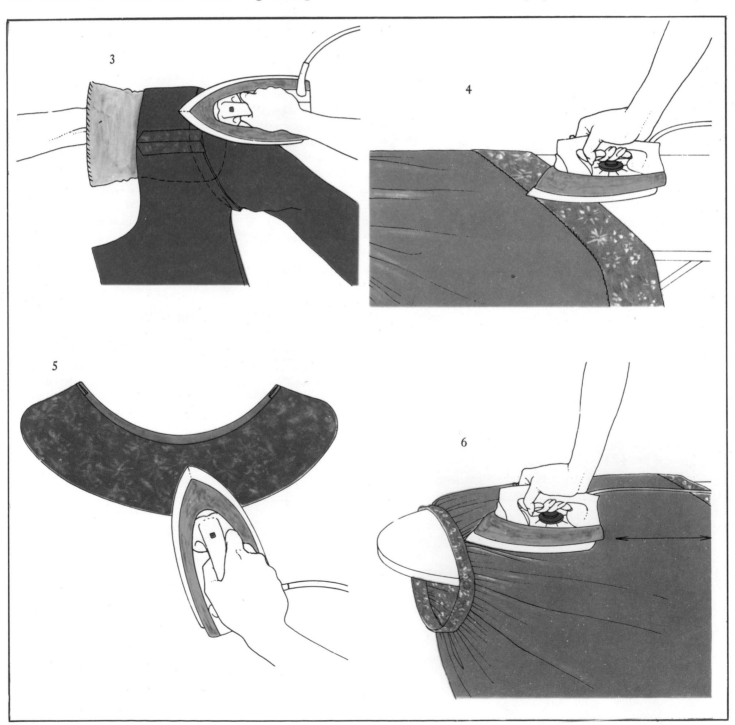

Dressmaking

Pinafore Sundress

More basic know-how

Included in this section are hems, facings, gathering and all kinds of fastenings. Some of the information is given in more detail than is needed for the first dressmaking projects in this book, but is grouped together for convenient reference later.

Buttons and buttonholes

Hand-worked buttonholes These should be made on all soft or delicate fabrics. Button and buttonhole positions are usually marked on the pattern and these markings should be transferred to your fabric before the pattern is removed. If you have had to alter the pattern by lengthening or shortening, alter the buttonhole positions accordingly. Do not cut the actual buttonholes until you are ready to sew them.

The buttonhole stitch that is used is often confused with blanket stitch, but the thread is placed at the back of the needle for buttonhole stitch (fig. 1). This forms a knot on the very edge of the buttonhole which gives strength and longer wear. Horizontal buttonholes have one rounded end and one square end. Vertical buttonholes (used where there is less 'pull') have two rounded ends.

Always make a test buttonhole on a piece of double fabric first.

To establish the buttonhole size, measure the length of the button by placing it on the fabric. Place a pin at either side. The thickness of the button must also be considered as a thick button needs a larger sized buttonhole. An extra 6 mm ($\frac{1}{4}$ in) is sometimes allowed to take this into account.

Work a row of stitching around the edge of the cut and oversew, before buttonholing to prevent fraying (fig. 2). For closely woven fabrics use ordinary sewing thread, for heavier or fraying fabrics use buttonhole twist. When stitching buttonholes the general rule is that nine stitches are worked at the rounded end and nine stitches at the square end (fig. 3a, b). Have about 68 cm (27 in) of thread in the needle so that it will be sufficient to complete the whole buttonhole.

Machine-worked buttonholes These can be made with a machine that can produce a close zig-zag stitch or has an automatic buttonhole-making device (full instructions will be found in the machine manual).

Buttons These should be selected with care as they can add an individual look to a very simple garment. The size and the thickness of the buttons must be suitable for the garment. For example, heavy rough-faced ones should not be attached to a fine fabric as they will tear the threads. Most cards of buttons have instructions stating whether or not it is safe to use an iron near them, as they may have a synthetic content like nylon. Most large stores have various types and sizes of button moulds, to which you can attach your own fabrics. Some stores have a button covering service. It is advisable to buy one or two extra buttons in case of loss or breakage. When sewing on the buttons, use a suitable thread for the fabric and work at least four stitches through the same place on the fabric. If using a button without a shank insert a pin or matchstick between the button and the fabric and work the stitches over it. Then wind the thread several times around the stitches between the button and fabric. Take the thread to the wrong side and fasten off with three very small backstitches.

Some other fastenings

Metal press studs These are usually silver or black, in various sizes, and are used at the top of an opening. The studs are in two parts, convex and concave. The convex part is always attached to the top part of the opening on the wrong side, as near to the edge as possible and invisible from the right side (fig. 1). The stud is sewn on with about four stitches to each hole, and the thread taken just beneath the fabric into the next hole. The stitches must not show on the right side.

1. The thread is kept behind the needle to work buttonhole stitch, 2. Oversew the cut to stop fraying, 3a – 3b. Make nine stitches at each end of buttonhole.

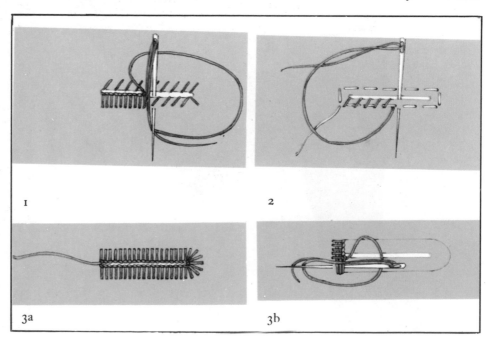

Fasten off with three back stitches. The convex part is attached first, then the concave part of the stud placed in the correct position by either of two methods: (a) by pushing a pin through both parts of the stud to obtain the correct position on the other edge of the garment, then marking, (b) by pressing the two parts of the stud together and rubbing the concave half with tailor's chalk and pressing on to the garment in the correct position. Sew on in the same way as for convex part, this time letting the stitches go through the fabric, fasten off on the wrong side with three back stitches.

Nylon press studs These are in one size only and are used for baby clothes or fine fabrics. They are attached in the same way as metal press studs.

Hooks and eyes These are in silver and black. They are usually sewn a short distance from the actual opening and are mostly used for extra strength on waistbands. They are sewn on with the hook pointing towards the opening with the flat side to the fabric. After sewing through the holes, the needle is then slipped just beneath the fabric and three back stitches worked under the tip of the hook (fig. 2).
The eye should also be facing the opening and after sewing through the holes, three back stitches should be worked just above the hole on each side to help keep the eye flat.

Hooks and bars These are usually attached very near the edge of the fabric. Sometimes the bar can be replaced by a buttonhole-stitched loop made in a thread which matches the fabric, so that it is practically invisible (fig. 3).

Touch and close fastener This is made of two layers of strong tape, either 1 cm ($\frac{3}{8}$ in), 2 cm ($\frac{3}{4}$ in) or 3 cm ($1\frac{1}{4}$ in) wide, available in black or white. One layer is faced with a strip of small nylon hooks and the other a strip of soft piled nylon. The hooked side is always placed on the underwrap with the hooks facing outwards. The piled

1. Position for press studs.
2. Stitching hooks and eyes.
3. Hooks and bars.
4. Touch and close fastening.

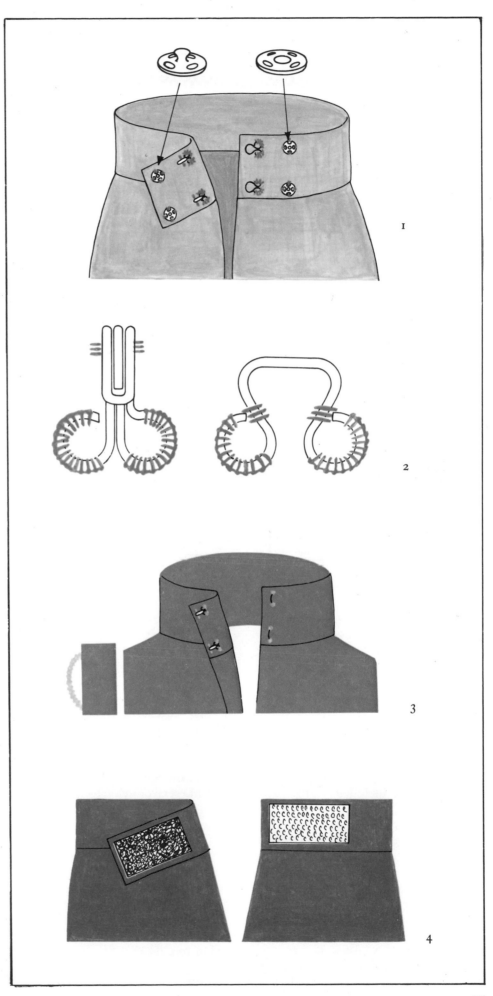

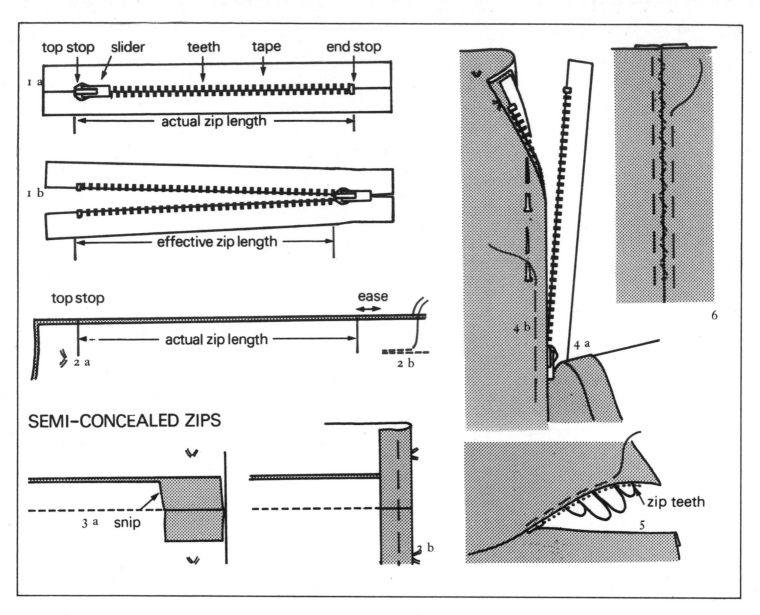

1a, 1b, The parts of a zip fastener.
2a. Determining length of zip needed.
3 to 9. Putting in centred seam zip.

side is placed on the overlap with the pile facing inwards (fig. 4). Cut off about 5 cm (2 in) from strip, separate the layers and machine stitch in place round the edges of each half.

Zip fasteners

*Techniques included: halfback-stitch.

A zip consists of two rows of interlocking teeth secured to two strips of tape, to which the garment fabric is sewn. The two strips of tape are secured with an end stop and the teeth are opened or closed by the slider. The slider and end stop take up about 1.3 cm ($\frac{1}{2}$ in) of the effective zip length (fig. 1a and 1b).

There are zips designed to meet every dressmaking and tailoring need. You

can also choose between metal and nylon zip teeth, both being equally good in the correct application, although care must be taken not to damage the nylon teeth when ironing.

Fabric and suitable zip type

Sheers; silks; poplin; fine crêpe: featherweight metal or nylon teeth with cotton tape.

Mediumweight wools; linen: lightweight metal or nylon teeth with cotton tape.

Heavier tweeds; where strength is required: skirtweight metal teeth.

Mand-made fibres, fine to medium-weight: nylon teeth with nylon tape.

Anoraks or jackets – any fabric: open ended with metal or nylon teeth.

All fabrics (except loose woven tweeds): 'invisible' with metal teeth or nylon teeth.

Length of zip required Before

purchasing the zip for a particular garment, consult the pattern for the suggested length and always purchase this length unless the pattern is to be shortened or lengthened. If in doubt, leave the purchase of the zip until the garment is fitted.

Do not purchase too short a zip as this causes strain and the zip might break, thus needing replacement.

The opening left in a garment for inserting a zip should always be a little longer than the actual zip teeth to allow the fabric to be eased slightly to the tape. Allow 1 mm ($\frac{1}{16}$ in) extra opening per 2.5 cm (1 in) of zip. For zips longer than 40 cm (16 in) allow a total of 2.5 cm (1 in) extra.

Also, the zip teeth should never go right up to the neck finish or waist-band so allow an extra 6 mm ($\frac{1}{4}$ in) here (fig. 2a).

Zip seams When machining the zip

seam, finish the end off very securely. This prevents strain on the zip (fig. 2b).

Snip through the waist seam allowance if any 3·2 cm (1¼ in) from the edge of the opening and press open (fig. 3a).

Tack and press the zip opening back on the seam line (fig. 3b).

Methods of sewing zips

Note When setting in a zip always work from the right side of the garment so that the sewing lines can be kept straight.

Centred seam zip This method is used on dresses with collars, either at the front or the back, medium to heavyweight tweed skirts, trousers and open ended zips.

Tack and press zip opening back on the seam line. Open the zip and place it behind the folded edges of the opening with the end stop to the end of the machining (fig. 4a).

Pin and tack one side of the zip in place, with the zip teeth just behind the fold and tacking 6 mm (¼ in) from the fold (fig. 4b). The extra length allowed for the opening is eased along the zip length by holding the zip and fabric as shown (fig. 5).

Bring up the other side of the zip and catch the two fold edges together (fig. 6), so that the two sides can be matched in length and pattern.

Tack the second side 6 mm (¼ in) away from the fold.

For a couture finish, sew in the zip by hand using a tiny half back stitch (see fig. 16). Work each side from the bottom up, angling the bottom end to the seam line (fig. 7). If you wish to machine the zip in place, use a zipper foot to allow the stitching to be closer to the zip.

Machine to within 5 cm (2 in) of the top of the zip, leave the needle in the work and lift the foot (fig. 8a).

Unpick 8 cm (3 in) of the catch tacking and ease the zip slider down past the foot (fig. 8b). Complete the machining. This method prevents the stitching line from widening at the slider. Neaten the back by stitching the zip to the seam allowance (fig. 9).

Decorative zips These are most used in pinafore dresses and pockets. Tack the zip in place as shown for the centred zip. Sew the facings in place and complete the hem.

10. A centre front decorative zip on a waistcoat.

11. Open ended zip on jacket.

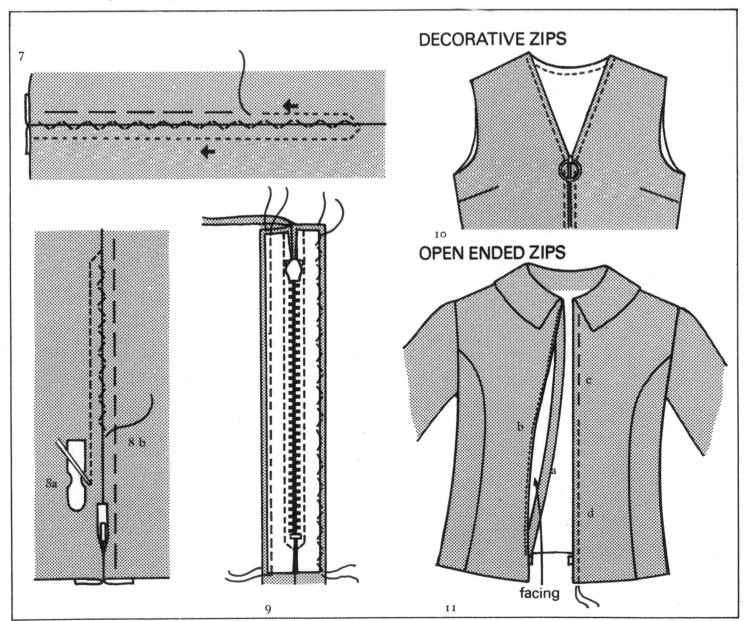

DECORATIVE ZIPS

OPEN ENDED ZIPS

facing

7

8a 8b

9

11

10

CONCEALED ZIPS

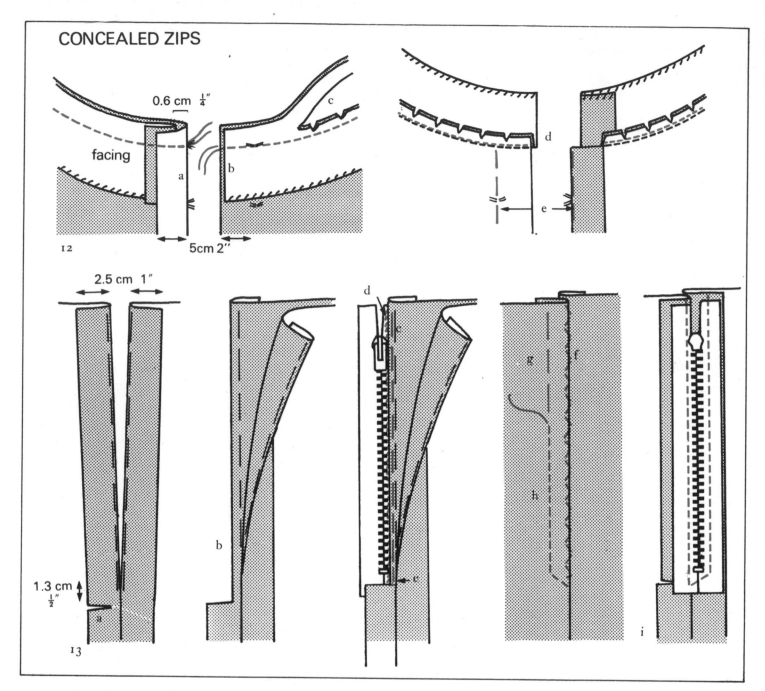

12, 13. Inserting a concealed zip.

For a pinafore dress, top-stitch round the neck and down to the hem, 6 mm (¼ in) away from all edges (fig. 10).
For pockets, top-stitch evenly all round the zip before applying the pocket bag to the garment.

Open ended zips Assemble the garment, leaving the zip opening between the facings and the fronts. Press the turnings back (fig. 11a). Separate the zip and slip the two sections in the openings, and place so that the teeth are just hidden behind the fold between garment and facing (fig. 11b). Pin and tack through the front, the zip tape and the facing (fig. 11c).

Top-stitch, using strong thread or buttonhole twist threaded on top of the machine (fig. 11d).

Concealed zips These are used on dresses without collars, lightweight fabric skirts and trousers.
Note The zip seam should be cut with a 2·5 cm (1 in) allowance.

Preparation of dress facing Place the right side of the neck facing to the right side of the dress, matching shoulder seams and centre front. On the left hand side, turn back the facing 6 mm (¼ in) from the dress sewing line. Turn the dress seam allowance back to the sewing line (fig. 12a). On the right hand side, take the facing

straight to the edge (fig. 12b).
Machine the facing in place, and trim the seam to 6 mm (¼ in). Snip at 1·3 cm (½ in) intervals (fig. 12c).
Turn the seam allowance of the left hand side of the dress to the wrong side and press flat (fig. 12d).
For all openings using this concealed zip method, work a line of tacks along the sewing lines of the opening (fig. 12e).
For side skirt or trouser zip, read 'back' for 'right hand side' and 'front' for 'left hand side'.
Snip the right hand side seam allowance to within 3 mm (⅛ in) of the seam, 1·3 cm (½ in) below the end of the opening (fig. 13a).
Fold the turning along this new line

28

so that the seam allowance projects beyond the seam line by 3 mm ($\frac{1}{8}$ in) (fig. 13b).

Place the zip right side uppermost behind this line, with the end stop just above the end of the opening. Pin and tack in place, with the fold just missing the zip teeth (fig. 13c).

Hem firmly right down to the end of the 3 mm ($\frac{1}{8}$ in) extension (fig. 13d).

Snip the remaining 3 mm ($\frac{1}{8}$ in) seam allowance (fig. 13e).

Bring the left hand side over so that the fold lies along the original sewing line on the right hand side. Temporarily stitch in place (fig. 13f). Tack 1·3 cm ($\frac{1}{2}$ in) away from the fold on the left hand side (fig. 13g).

Using a half back stitch (see fig. 16), sew up from the seam line at an angle and up the 1·3 cm ($\frac{1}{2}$ in) line, or machine taking care to stitch a straight line (fig. 13h).

Fig. 13i illustrates the wrong side of the garment and zip, showing how it should lie in position. Slipstitch ends of facing in place.

Zip guards These are used to protect underwear and sensitive skins from being rubbed by the zip teeth, and they give a very professional finish to the garment.

Measure the zip opening and add 3·8 cm ($1\frac{1}{2}$ in). Cut one piece of lining and one piece of fabric as shown (fig. 14a).

Place right sides together and stitch the curved side (fig. 14b).

Turn to the right side and tack around the stitched edge. Press flat (fig. 14c).

Place the long raw edge to the right hand side zip tape, making sure that the fabric side of the guard is towards the zip (fig. 14d). Machine through the guard, zip tape and seam allowance (fig. 14e). If the garment is unlined, neaten the raw edge (fig. 14f).

Include the top of the guard into an extended zip guard or neck facing.

Invisible zips These give an opening which looks like a seam, and are

14-16. Zip finishes: half back stitch.

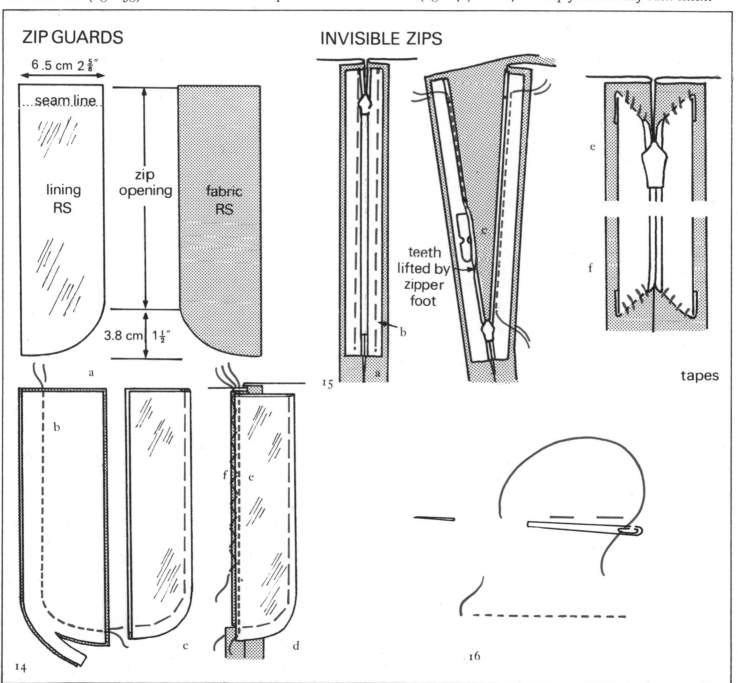

ZIP GUARDS

6.5 cm 2$\frac{5}{8}$"

seam line

lining RS

zip opening

fabric RS

3.8 cm 1$\frac{1}{2}$"

a

b

c

d

14

INVISIBLE ZIPS

teeth lifted by zipper foot

b

a

15

e

f

tapes

16

good for all fabrics except loose, bulky tweeds where the fibres might be caught by the slider.

After fitting the garment, sew the zip seam, leaving an opening 2·5 cm (1 in) longer than the zip teeth. Tack opening and press.

On the wrong side lay the closed zip centrally over the seam with the zip teeth uppermost (fig. 15a).

Pin and tack through the zip tape and seam allowance only (fig. 15b).

Remove the seam tacking and open the zip carefully. Keeping the teeth uppermost, machine through the tape and seam allowance only, stopping when the zipper foot meets the slider. Machine the other side of the zip (fig. 15c).

Close zip. Lift zip and seam allowance up and complete the seam still using the zipper foot.

Secure the zip tapes to the top by folding the ends outwards and sew to the seam turnings (fig. 15e).

The tapes at the bottom edge are also sewn to the seam turnings (fig. 15f).

*Half back stitch** Bring the thread up after fastening firmly on the wrong side. Take a tiny 1·5 mm ($\frac{1}{16}$ in) stitch back and come up 4·5 mm ($\frac{3}{16}$ in) forward (fig. 16).

Facings and interfacing

Facings are used to finish a raw edge neatly. They can be cut to the same shape as the edge of a garment, stitched round the edge and then turned to the inside e.g. to finish a neck or armhole. A facing can also be

I. Cutting new facing.

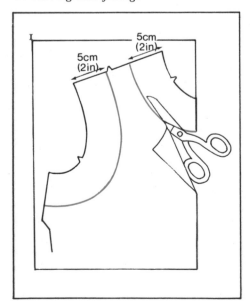

5cm (2in)
5cm (2in)

a turned-back extension of the garment e.g. down a front or back opening. When part of a garment consists of two layers e.g. a wide shoulder strap or belt the under layer can also be referred to as a facing.

To cut a facing (if this is not already part of the pattern). Take the front bodice pattern piece and place on a large sheet of paper. Draw round the outline of shoulder and area to be faced e.g. neck and/or armhole. Working from the outside edge, measure 5 cm (2 in) and draw a curve parallel to neck or armhole curve. Cut off facing pattern along drawn line. Repeat for back of bodice pattern. (fig. 1).

Interfacing Is used to add firmness to areas of a garment e.g. collars, waistbands, cuffs or facings. Either a woven or non-woven fabric (Vilene) can be used.

The interfacing is cut to the same shape as the facing and either trimmed and catchstitched to the facing seam line before it is attached or tacked to the facing and machined into the garment together with it.

Hems

*Techniques included: invisible hemming (or blindstitch).

Beautifully finished hems are most important as they provide a professional finish to a carefully made garment. The length is dictated by fashion to a certain extent, but it must be right both for the garment and for the particular figure.

To gauge the effect of the garment always wear the appropriate shoes for the outfit and add a belt if the design has one. Check the length of the garment by standing in front of a mirror, and always wear the jacket when looking at a suit skirt to see that the proportion of jacket to skirt is correct.

Hem length There are various ways to obtain the right hem length:

From the back neck, measure the length of the pattern and adjust if necessary (fig. 1a).

After cutting out, make tailor's tacks along the hemline and pin the hem up to the line when fitting (fig, 1b).

Place a dress of the right length on a hanger with the new dress over it. Pin up the new hem to match (fig. 2).

Ask a friend to measure up from the ground and mark the line with pins (fig. 3).

Use a skirt marker. Be careful here; measure 1·3 cm ($\frac{1}{2}$ in) longer than needed to avoid the possibility of the chalk marking the fabric permanently. Turn up 1·3 cm ($\frac{1}{2}$ in) above the chalk line (fig. 4).

Preparation before neatening
Trace tack along the hem fold and unpin (fig. 5).

Most hems are 5 to 6·5 cm (2 to 2$\frac{1}{2}$ in) deep, so trim evenly to the required depth (fig. 6). Exceptions are for blouses, 2·5 cm (1 in); faced hems, 1·3 cm ($\frac{1}{2}$ in); long skirts of fine fabric, 1·3 cm ($\frac{1}{2}$ in).

Trim all seam allowances to 6 mm ($\frac{1}{4}$ in) between the hemline and the hem edge (fig. 7).

Hem neatening For non-fraying fabrics oversew or zig-zag along the cut edge.

For fraying fabrics use one of the following methods:

Zig-zag 6 mm ($\frac{1}{4}$ in) away from the cut edge and trim to the machining (fig. 8a).

For straight hemlines, edge with straight binding (fig. 8b).

For curved or bias edges, ease the hem and edge with bias binding (fig. 8c).

For fine cottons (mainly children's clothes and summer dresses), fold under the raw edge for 1·3 cm ($\frac{1}{2}$ in). For pleats which are seamed, the seam turnings are snipped the hem depth above the hemline and pressed open below the snip. Above the snip, the turnings are neatened and pressed together (fig. 9).

After neatening the raw edge, press it, making sure it is away from the body of the garment.

Fold the hem up on the tacked line, slip a piece of card or brown paper inside the fold and press well. Use a damp cloth rather than a steam iron as it is easier to control the amount of steam this way. Tack through the folded edge to keep it firmly in place.

Types of hem

Plain This is used for absolutely straight hems i.e. skirts and trousers. Tack the hem 1·3 cm ($\frac{1}{2}$ in) below the neatened edge. Sew in place using

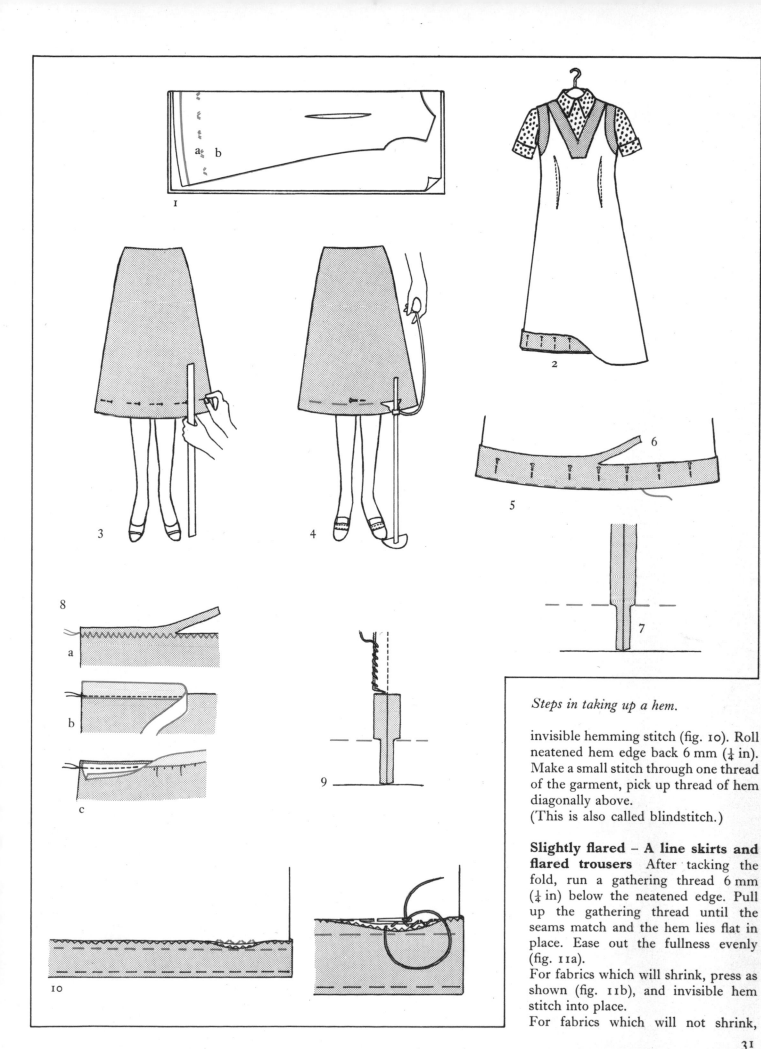

Steps in taking up a hem.

invisible hemming stitch (fig. 10). Roll neatened hem edge back 6 mm ($\frac{1}{4}$ in). Make a small stitch through one thread of the garment, pick up thread of hem diagonally above.

(This is also called blindstitch.)

Slightly flared – A line skirts and flared trousers After tacking the fold, run a gathering thread 6 mm ($\frac{1}{4}$ in) below the neatened edge. Pull up the gathering thread until the seams match and the hem lies flat in place. Ease out the fullness evenly (fig. 11a).

For fabrics which will shrink, press as shown (fig. 11b), and invisible hem stitch into place.

For fabrics which will not shrink,

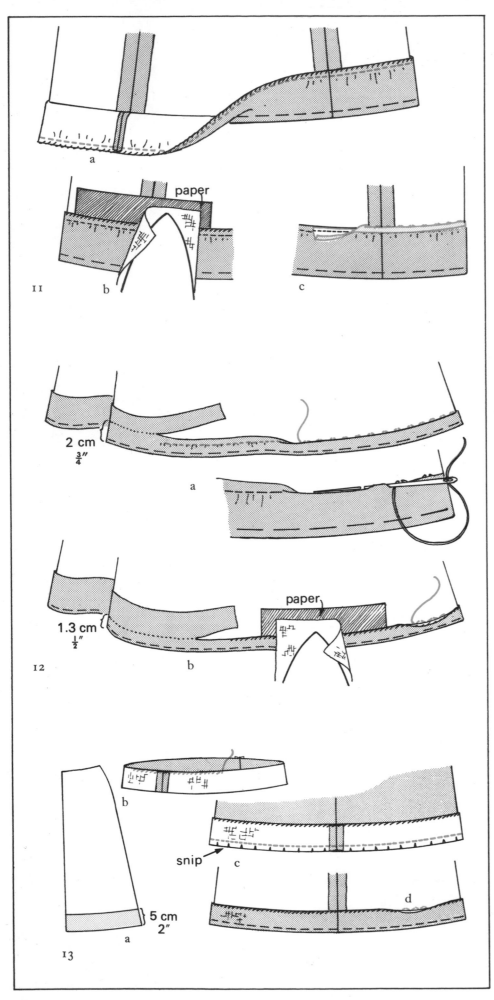

attach bias binding, stretching it slightly. Fold the binding over the raw edge and slipstitch in place (fig. 11c).

Very flared skirts It is not easy to make a deep hem for these, so they are usually finished either with a narrow or a faced hem.

Narrow hem for lightweight fabrics Cut the hem depth to 2 cm ($\frac{3}{4}$ in). Do not neaten the edge. Run a gathering thread 6 mm ($\frac{1}{4}$ in) from the cut edge. Turn under 6 mm ($\frac{1}{4}$ in) and pull the gathering thread so it lies easily against the skirt. Slipstitch the hem through the fold (fig. 12a).

Narrow hem for heavier fabrics Cut the hem depth to 1·3 cm ($\frac{1}{2}$ in) and neaten the edge by oversewing or zig-zag stitch. Press the hem up over paper and stitch with invisible hemming stitch (fig. 12b).

Faced hem for all fabrics If extra bulk is not desirable, then lining or net can be used for the facing fabric. Cut a 5 cm (2 in) facing from the skirt pattern (fig. 13a).
Sew the facing seams together and neaten the shorter edge (fig. 13b).
Place the facing to the right side of the skirt hem and stitch (fig. 13c).
Snip if necessary, turn to inside and press. Sew the facing to the skirt with invisible hemming stitch (fig. 13d).

Rolled hem for sheer fabrics Trim the hem to 6 mm ($\frac{1}{4}$ in). Turn under 3 mm ($\frac{1}{8}$ in) (fig. 14a) and either slipstitch hem (fig. 14b) or machine (fig. 14c).

Tailored hem for jackets, coats and sleeves A strip of canvas is used to support the weight of a coat or jacket hem and to give a good line.
Cut 5 cm (2 in) strips of canvas on the true cross grain of the fabric (fig. 15a). Lay the canvas above the hemline and catchstitch to the garment (fig. 15b). Turn up the hem and sew it to the canvas with invisible hemming stitch (fig. 15c).

Lining hem finish for jackets and coats Finish the coat or jacket and

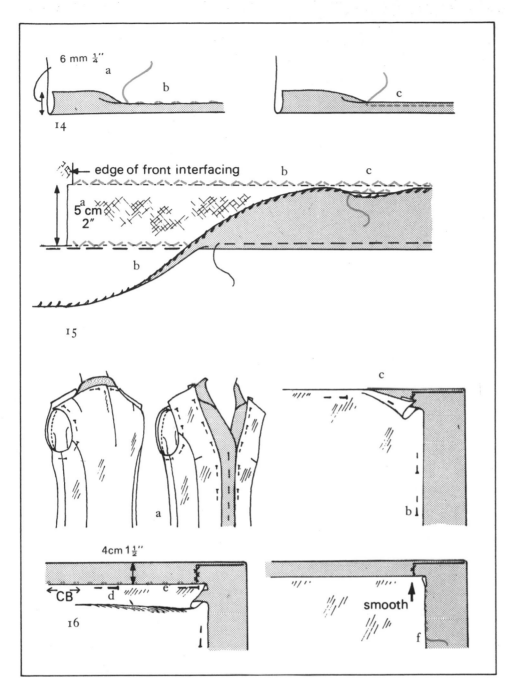

14. *Rolled hem.*
15. *Tailored hem.*
16. *Lining hem finish.*

press it well. Make up the lining and press this too. (A lining pattern has extra width included in the centre back and also in the length. This is to allow for ease in wear and to prevent the lining pulling the outer fabric.)

Pin the lining to the jacket, matching seam lines, armholes and style lines (fig. 16a).

Fold under and pin the front edges (fig. 16b).

Fold and pin the hem turning to the exact length of the jacket or coat (fig. 16c).

Lift up the folded edge 2·5 to 4 cm (1 to 1½ in) and re-pin (fig. 16d). Slipstitch the hem along the fold (fig. 16e).

Fold down the pleat at the front edges and finish slipstitching (fig. 16f).

Gathering and shirring

Gathering This produces soft folds in light fabrics. Gathering enables a larger piece to join on to a smaller one e.g. a gathered skirt joined to a plain top. Gathers also add fullness on shoulders and sleeves, or are used on frills.

Shirring This is a form of gathering where several rows of equally spaced gathers are used to produce a decorative effect.

Gathering by hand Use single thread on lightweight fabrics and double thread on heavyweight fabrics. Start with three back stitches and work small straight running stitches. Do not fasten off at the end of the row but leave the thread hanging. With right sides together, pin centre of gathering to centre of part of garment to which it is to be attached, and pin together at each end. Pull up gathering thread to fit. Wind thread round a pin in a figure-of-eight. Put in more pins before tacking. Pins should be placed vertically to enable tacking to be done on the gathering line without pins scratching fingers.

By machine Loosen top tension on machine slightly, and turn stitch length adapter to the longest stitch. Working from the right side of the fabric, machine on the stitching line. Pull up gathering from both ends. Wind thread round pins in figures-of-eight.
Tighten top tension when you have finished gathering.

Ease This is extra fullness in one pattern piece e.g. on a sleeve head. One section is slightly larger than the other and the surplus is reduced by gathering for a short distance (marked on the pattern) until the two pieces fit exactly.

Joining gathered skirt to bodice Gather skirt with two rows of gathering stitches for extra strength and pull

Below. An example of shirring or gathering by hand.

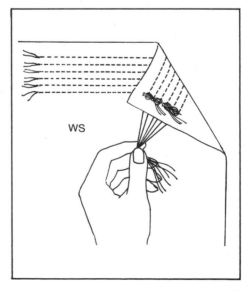

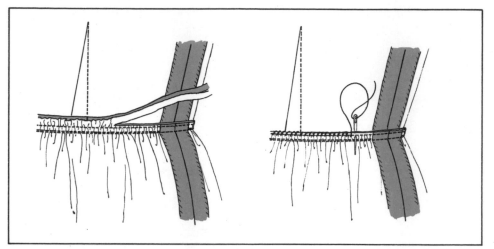

Top right. Two diagrams show how to join a gathered skirt to a bodice.

up gathers until skirt fits bodice (use synthetic thread for gathers to avoid thread snapping). With right sides together, pin the bodice to the skirt, matching centre front and back and side seams. Tack and stitch with gathered side upwards. Make a second row of stitching 6 mm ($\frac{1}{4}$ in) from the first in the seam allowance. Press the seam upwards, taking care not to flatten gathers. Neaten by oversewing seam allowances together.

Girl's sun or pinafore dress

This sun dress can also be teamed with sweaters and shirts to be worn as a pinafore dress on duller days. Stripes used vertically give no matching problems but the design looks just as good made up in a plain fabric. The pattern is cut from a simple diagram.

*Techniques included: patch pockets.

Measurements

The pattern and instructions are given to fit a child 6, 8, 10 or 12 years of age. Chest sizes 63.5 cm (25 in), 69 cm (27 in), 72.5 cm (28$\frac{1}{2}$ in) and 76 cm (30 in).

Making the pattern

The measurements given for the pattern pieces are for a size 6. For the larger sizes the measurements given in the chart must be added to the basic size 6 measurements when cutting the pattern.

Suggested fabrics

Cotton, denim, corduroy, lightweight wool, ticking.

You will need:

115 cm (45 in) wide fabric with or without nap, all sizes, 1.60 m (1$\frac{3}{4}$ yd).
90 cm (36 in) wide interfacing, all sizes, 30 cm ($\frac{1}{4}$ yd).
Sewing thread to match fabric.
Two 1.3 cm ($\frac{1}{2}$ in) buttons.
15 cm (6 in) zip fastener.
Hook and eye.
Squared or plain paper for pattern.

Cutting out

A 1.5 cm ($\frac{5}{8}$ in) seam allowance has been allowed on all edges except the dress centre front and the front and

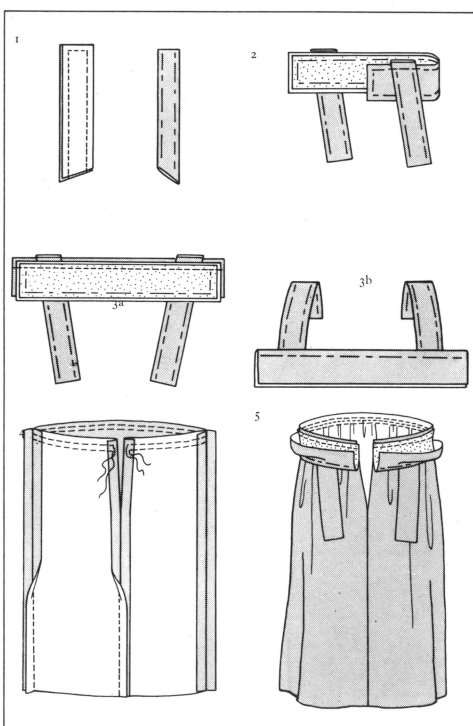

back band centre front. 6·5 cm (2⅝ in) seam allowance has been included on the lower hem edges. The positions for the back shoulder straps move to- wards the centre back by the same amount that is graded up for the larger sizes and the side on the front and back band by half this amount.

To make the dress

Shoulder straps   1. With right sides together, tack and stitch the shoulder strap facings to the shoulder straps round the outer edges, leaving the slanted edge open. Trim seams and cut across corners. Turn straps right side out. Tack close to stitched edges and press flat.

Band   2. Tack interfacing to the wrong side of the front and back band. With right sides together, matching raw edges, tack the shoulder straps to either side of the centre back in posi- tions marked.

3. With right sides together, tack and stitch the band facing to the band along the top edge, securing the straps when doing so. Trim interfacing close to stitching and layer seam. Press seam towards band. Turn facing to the inside and tack close to the stitched edge. Press flat.

Centre back and side seams   4. With right sides together, tack and stitch the centre back of the dress to within 12 cm (4½ in) of the top edge. With right sides together, tack and stitch the side seams. Press seams open. Work two rows of gathering stitches around the top edge of the dress.

Joining the dress to band   5. With right sides together, matching centre fronts, sides and centre backs, pin the dress to the band, pulling up the gathers to fit. Tack, speading the gathers evenly. Stitch entire seam, having the band facing free. Trim interfacing close to stitching and layer seam. Press seam towards band. Insert the zip fastener into the centre back opening.

6. On the inside, turn under the seam

This cool and comfortable sundress for a young girl makes use of the more basic sewing skills and is, therefore, a good dress for beginners. With it you make buttonholes, attach a gathered skirt, and make a plain hem. You will also learn how to make patch pockets.

allowance of the band facing and slip-stitch to the stitching line and to the zipper tape.

*Patch pockets 7. Tack the inter-facing to the wrong side of the pocket band. Catchstitch to the fold line. Turn under the seam allowance of the other edge and tack. With right sides together, tack and stitch the pocket band to the pocket. Trim interfacing close to the stitching. Press seam towards band.

8. With right sides together, fold band along fold line and stitch the side edges as shown. Trim interfacing close to stitching and cut across corners. Turn band right side out. On the inside, slipstitch the band facing to the stitching line. Turn in seam allowance round outer edge of pocket and tack. On the outside, top-stitch band 6 mm ($\frac{1}{4}$ in) away from seam line.

Repeat steps 7 and 8 for second pocket.

9. Tack the pockets to the dress front in positions marked on the pattern. Top-stitch 6 mm ($\frac{1}{4}$ in) in from outer edge of pockets. Press flat.

Hem 10. Try dress on child and mark the hem. Turn up the hem and tack close to the folded edge. Trim hem to an even width. Neaten the raw edge by hand overcasting or machine zig-zag. Sew the hem to the dress using invisible hemming stitch.

To finish 11. Check length of shoul-der straps and make worked or machine buttonholes on the front band in positions marked. Sew buttons to the shoulder straps in positions marked. At the centre back, sew a hook and eye to the top edge of the band.

Follow the diagram below when laying the pattern pieces on the fabric.

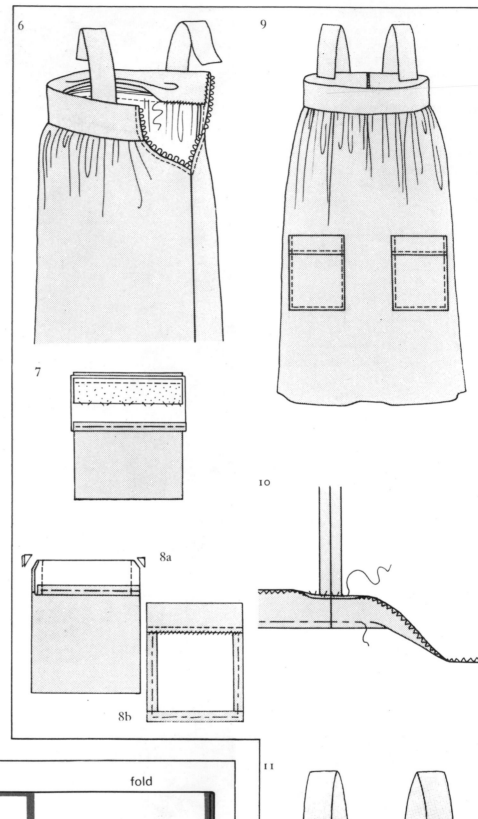

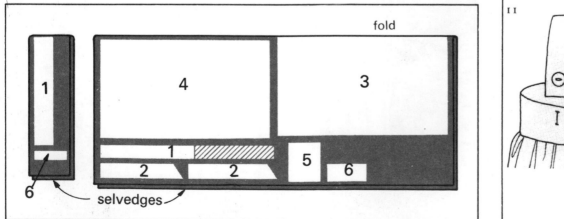

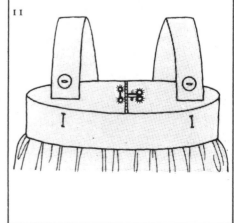

Additional measurement chart in centimetres
(inches given in brackets)

Size	8	10	12
Front and back band (length)	2·5 (1)	4·5 (1¾)	6.5 (2½)
Shoulder straps (length)	1·3 (½)	2·5 (1)	3·8 (1½)
Side seams front and back	1·3 (½)	2·5 (1)	3·8 (1½)
Hemline	5 (2)	10 (4)	15 (6)

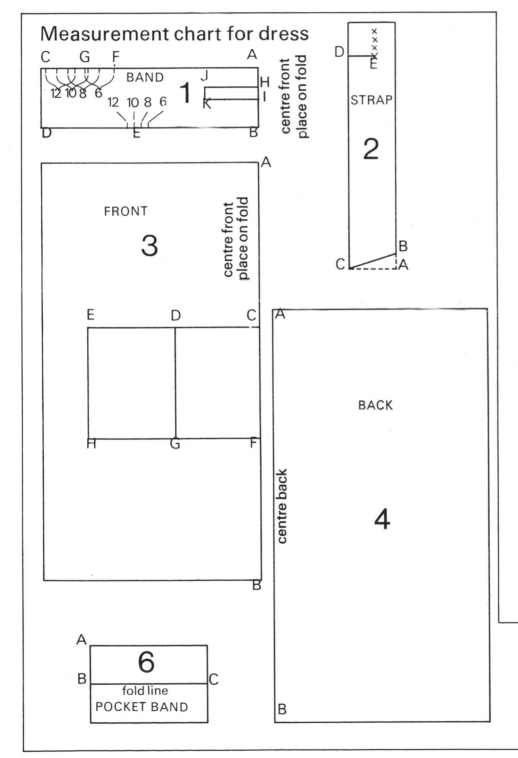

Measurement chart for dress

Diagram 1 BAND, Diagram 2 STRAP, Diagram 3 FRONT, Diagram 4 BACK, Diagram 5 POCKET, Diagram 6 POCKET BAND

Measurement instructions for drafting the pattern

Front and back band (diagram 1)
Draw a rectangle measuring 35 cm by 8 cm (13¾ in by 3¼ in).
A to B = centre front
C to D = centre back
B to E = 15·3 cm (6⅛ in) – match to side seams.
A to F = 19 cm (7½ in)
F to G = 4·7 cm (1⅞ in)
F to G = back shoulder strap position
A to H = 3·2 cm (1¼ in)
A to I = 5 cm (2 in)
H to J and I to K = 8 cm (3¼ in)
J to K = buttonhole position

Shoulder straps (diagram 2)
Draw a rectangle measuring 7·5 cm by 36·5 cm (3 in by 14⅜ in)
A to B = 2·2 cm (⅞ in)
C to D = 31 cm (12¼ in)
D to E = 3·8 cm (1½ in)
E = button position

Dress front (diagram 3)
Draw a rectangle measuring 31·8 cm by 63 cm (12½ in by 24¾ in)
A to B = centre front
A to C = 26·8 cm (10½ in)
C to D = 11·5 cm (4⅝ in)
D to E = 15 cm (6 in)
A to F = 44·3 cm (17½ in)
F to G = 11·5 cm (4⅝ in)
G to H = 15 cm (6 in)
E to H and G to D = pocket position

Dress back (diagram 4)
Draw a rectangle measuring 33·3 cm by 63 cm (13⅛ in by 24¾ in)
A to B = centre back

Pocket (diagram 5)
Draw a rectangle measuring 18·5 cm by 16·3 cm (7¼ in by 6½ in)

Pocket band (diagram 6)
Draw a rectangle measuring 18·5 cm by 12 cm (7¼ in by 4¾ in)
A to B = 6 cm (2⅜ in)
B to C = fold line – this line being horizontal

Mother and Daughter Aprons

More basic know-how
Frills and flounces

Frills can give a pretty finish to many garments and they are not difficult to apply. Frills can be straight or bias-cut. To produce the fullness needed for a frill, cut the fabric two to three times longer than the finished length then gather up to required size. Wide frills need more fullness than narrow ones. A long length of frill may have to be joined before it is applied. Any seams should be pressed open before gathering the frill. Neaten the outer edge of the frill with a narrow machine-stitched seam.

Frill on a straight edge With right sides together, pin the gathered frill to the edge, leaving 1·3 cm (½ in) of the hem edge extending. Stitch with frill side up (fig. 1). Trim the seam allowance on the frill to 3 mm (⅛ in). Fold the hem edge under for 3 mm (⅛ in) then fold it over the trimmed seam and stitch in place (fig. 2). Press seam towards garment.

Frill in a seam Prepare frill and pin and stitch to one seam edge of garment as described for frill on a straight edge. With right sides together place section with frill attached on to second section. Pin and tack. Make a second line of stitching to enclose frill. Turn right sides out and press, taking care not to flatten frill.

Frills on collars and cuffs Prepare narrow frill as previously described. With right sides together, pin frill to outer edge of top collar or cuff.

When corner is reached ease gathers round, pushing them closer together to give extra fullness. Stitch with frill side up (fig. 3) leaving neatened outer edges free. Press carefully. With right sides together, pin, tack and stitch under collar or cuff on to outer section enclosing frill. Trim seam allowances to 6 mm (¼ in). Turn to right side and press carefully.

Frill with heading Neaten both long edges of frill and make line of gathering below the top edge to depth

Matching aprons for mother and daughter have a frill-decorated yoke.

1, 2. Frill on a straight edge.
3. Frill on collar or cuff. 4. Frill with a heading and frill in a seam.

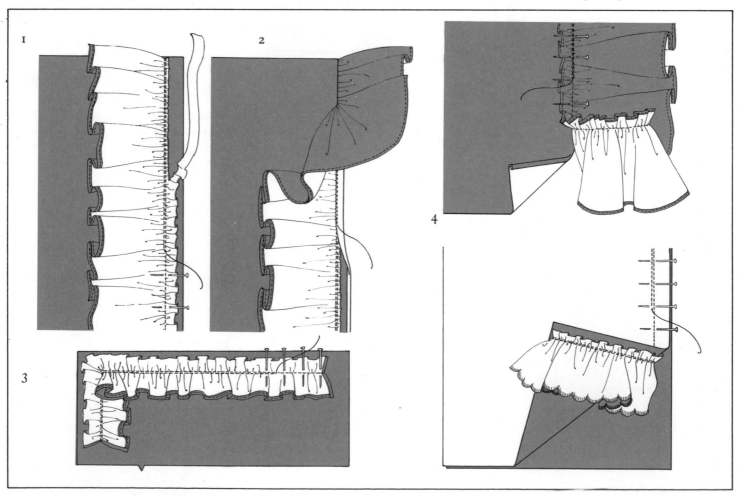

required for heading (fig. 4). Press a 3 mm ($\frac{1}{8}$ in) double fold on edge of garment. Pin frill on right side with gathering line close to folded edge. Stitch along this line to attach frill to garment. This technique can be used to add a flounce to the hem of a skirt.

Mother and daughter aprons

These frilled aprons are both practical and feminine.
*Techniques included: applying frills to yoke, bias binding.

Measurements

The mother's apron is given in sizes 10, 12, 14 and 16 and the daughter's apron is given to fit chest sizes 61 cm (24 in), 66 cm (26 in), 71 cm (28 in) and 76 cm (30 in). Each size is indicated on the graph pattern by a cutting line of a different colour.

Making the pattern

Draw up the pattern to scale from the graph pattern given here. One square represents 2·5 cm (1 in) square.

Suggested fabrics

Mix and match cottons, broderie anglaise.

You will need:

To make the mother's apron:
90 cm (36 in) wide fabric without nap in main colour, 2·75 m (3 yd) all sizes.
90 cm (36 in) wide fabric without nap in contrast colour, 1·20 m (1¼ yd), all sizes.
Two 1·5 cm ($\frac{5}{8}$ in) buttons.
To make the daughter's apron:
90 cm (36 in) wide fabric without nap in main colour, 1·80 m (1¾ yd), all sizes.
90 cm (36 in) wide fabric without nap in contrast colour, 1·10 m (1⅛ yd), all sizes.
One 1·5 cm ($\frac{5}{8}$ in) button
For both aprons you will need:
Sewing thread to match fabric.
Squared paper for pattern.

Cutting out

There are no seam allowances included on the pattern. When cutting out, allow 1·5 cm ($\frac{5}{8}$ in) seam allow-ance on all edges.
Note No pattern pieces are given for the apron ties or the underarm bias strips, so cut the following pieces from the main colour fabric as indicated on the cutting layouts.

Mother's apron

For ties cut two pieces measuring 91·5 cm by 8·5 cm (36 in by 3¼ in) and for the armhole bias strips cut two pieces measuring 30·5 cm by 2·5 cm (12 in by 1 in).

Daughter's apron

For ties cut two pieces measuring 66 cm by 6·5 cm (26 in by 2½ in), and for the armhole bias strips cut two pieces measuring 23 cm by 2·5 cm (9 in by 1 in).
Note All the above measurements for ties and bias strips include seam allowance.

To make both aprons

Frills 1. With right sides together, notches matching, join the front frill between back frill pieces. Press the

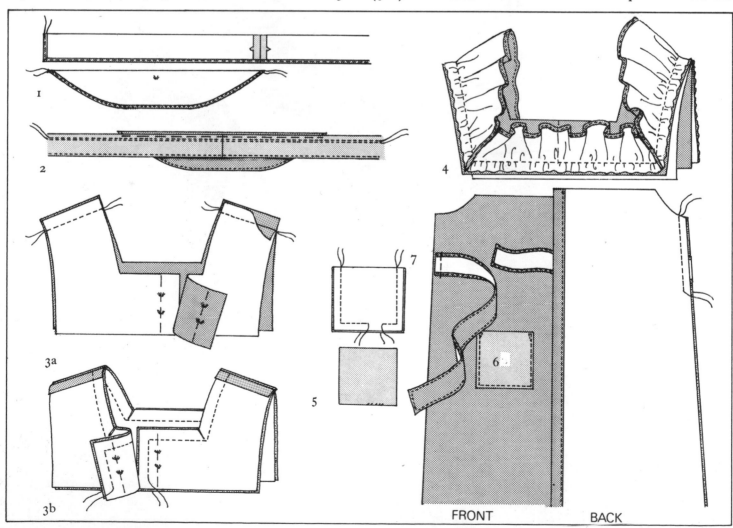

FRONT   BACK

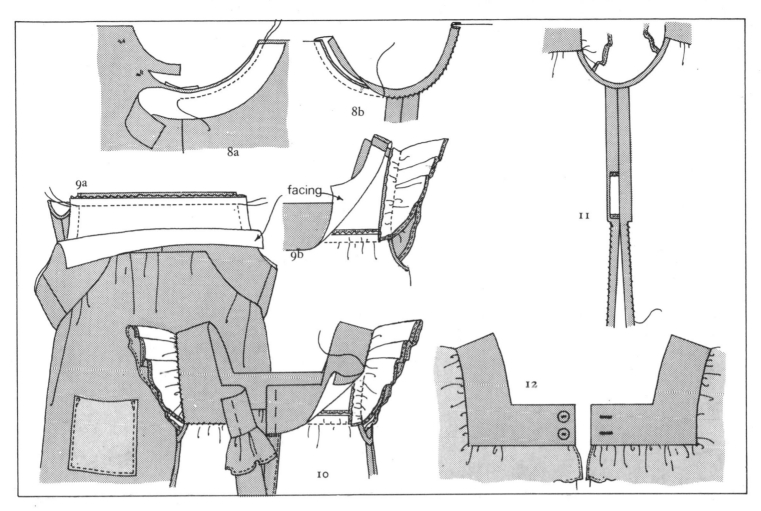

seams open.

To neaten the outer frill edges turn under 3 mm ($\frac{1}{8}$ in) and press flat. Turn under another 6 mm ($\frac{1}{4}$ in) and machine stitch.

Neaten the curved edge of the under frill in the same way. Press flat.

2. With the right side of both frills facing upwards, place the under frill beneath the main frill, matching the dot to the shoulder seam, and tack in place. Work two rows of gathering stitches the length of the main frill.

Yoke 3. With right sides together, stitch the back yokes to the front yoke at the shoulder seams. Press the seams. Repeat for the yoke facing.

With right sides together, stitch the yoke facing to the yoke at the neck edge, and down the centre back as shown. Clip the corners and turn the yoke right side out. Tack around the stitched edges and press flat.

Applying frills to yoke 4. With right sides together, pin the prepared frill to the yoke edge, matching the entire front and the shoulder seams. Pull up the gathering threads, distribute the gathers evenly and stitch.

Pockets 5. With right sides to-gether, fold the pocket in half and stitch around three sides leaving a small opening for turning the pocket to the right side.

Layer the seams and turn the pocket right side out. Tack around all edges and press flat. Slipstitch the opening to close. Repeat for second pocket.

6. Place the pockets in the positions indicated on the front skirt. Tack and top-stitch in place.

Skirt and ties Neaten the centre back skirt edges and three edges of the ties (leaving one short edge raw), as instructed in step 1.

7. With right sides together, tack the ties to the front skirt as indicated on the pattern.

With right sides together tack and stitch the skirt backs to the skirt front at the side seams, from the armhole to 1·3 cm ($\frac{1}{2}$ in) below the tie. Press the seams open.

8. Trim the armhole seam allowance to 6 mm ($\frac{1}{4}$ in). *With right sides to-gether, stitch the bias strip to the armhole. Press the bias strip away from the armhole and then turn under 6 mm ($\frac{1}{4}$ in) and press flat. Hem the fold edge of the binding to the line of stitching around the armhole. Press flat. Ready-made bias binding is applied in the same way (seam allowances on bought binding are ready-pressed).

Joining skirt to yoke 9. Work two rows of gathering stitches across the top of skirt and back. With right sides together, pin the front skirt to the front yoke and the back skirts to the back yokes. Pull up the gathers and distribute them evenly.

Stitch, being careful not to catch yoke frill edge in seam. Press towards yoke.

10. Turn under the seam allowance of the yoke facing and hem to the line of stitching as shown. Press flat.

Side and hem edges 11. Turn under 6 mm ($\frac{1}{4}$ in) on the side seam and hem edges and press flat. Turn under the rest of the seam allowance and stitch by hand. Clip the seam allowance 1·3 cm ($\frac{1}{2}$ in) above the end of the side seam to allow the seam to lie flat. Press side and hem edges flat.

Buttons and buttonholes 12. Work one buttonhole on the child's apron and two on the mother's apron on the back yoke as shown. Stitch on buttons to correspond.

Graph pattern for mother's apron

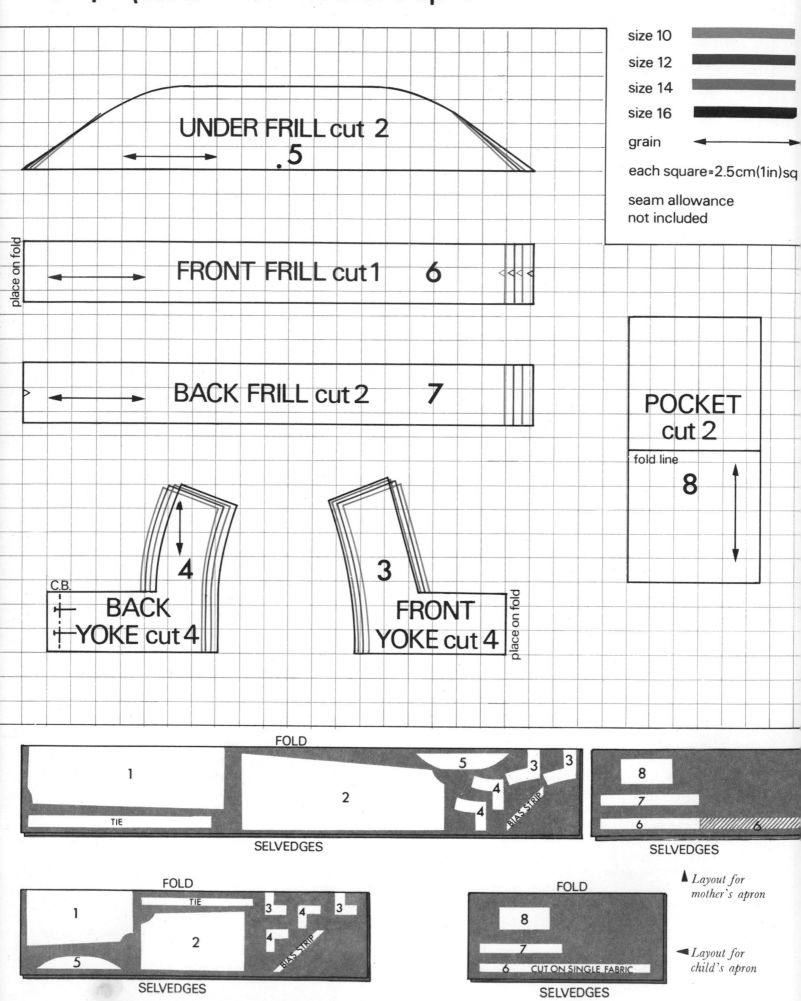

UNDER FRILL cut 2

.5

FRONT FRILL cut 1   6

place on fold

BACK FRILL cut 2   7

POCKET
cut 2

fold line

8

C.B.

BACK
YOKE cut 4

4

3

FRONT
YOKE cut 4

place on fold

size 10
size 12
size 14
size 16

grain

each square=2.5cm(1in)sq

seam allowance
not included

FOLD

1

TIE

2

5

3   3

4

4

BIAS STRIP

SELVEDGES

8

7

6   6

SELVEDGES

FOLD

1

TIE

2

5

3   4   3

4

BIAS STRIP

SELVEDGES

FOLD

8

7

6   CUT ON SINGLE FABRIC

SELVEDGES

▲ Layout for
mother's apron

◄ Layout for
child's apron

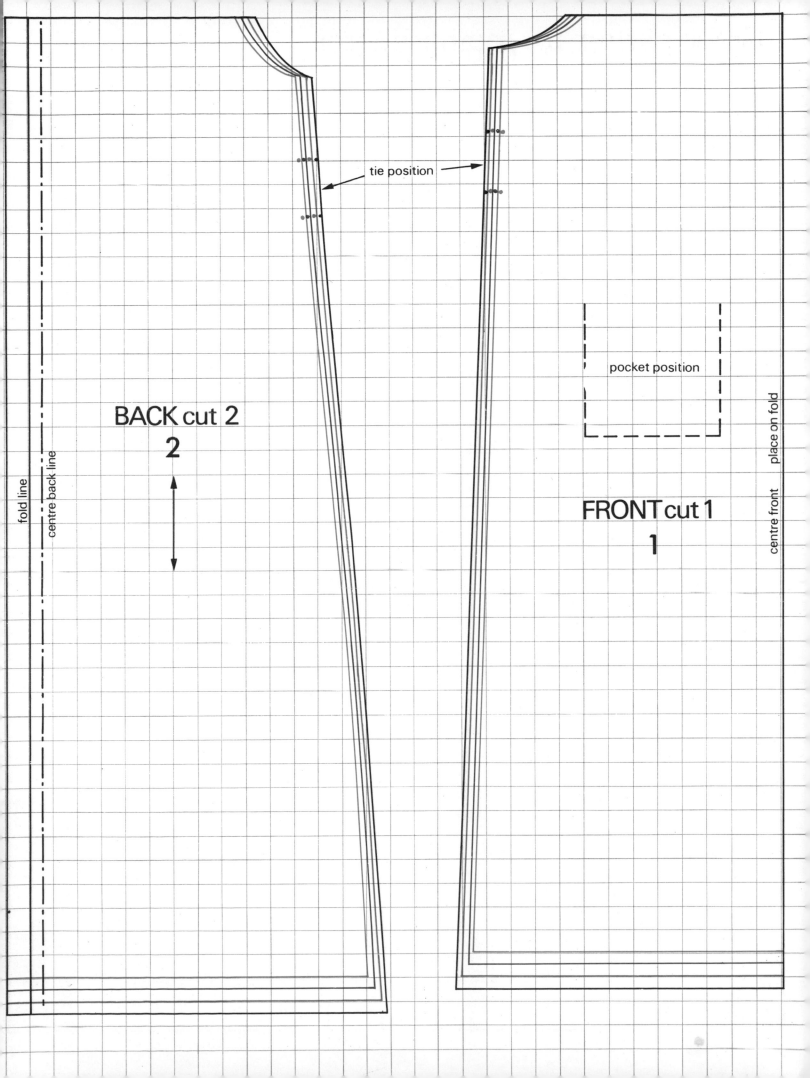

fold line

centre back line

BACK cut 2

2

tie position

pocket position

place on fold

centre front

FRONT cut 1

1

Graph pattern for daughter's apron

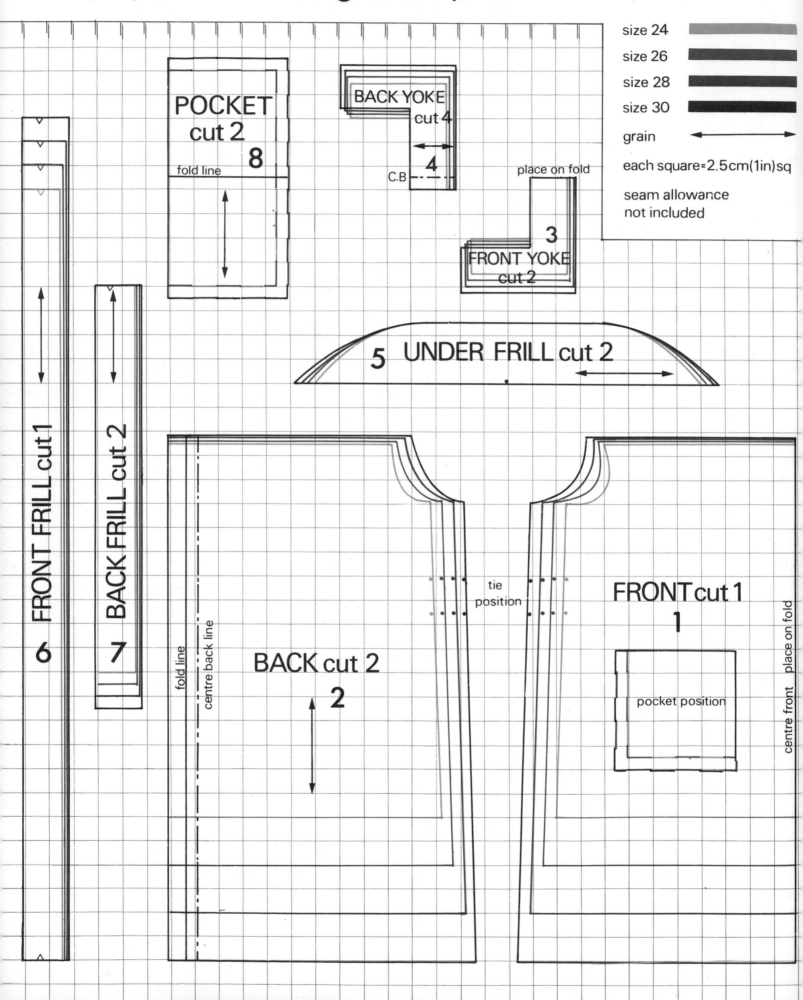

POCKET cut 2

8

fold line

BACK YOKE cut 4

4

C.B

place on fold

3

FRONT YOKE cut 2

size 24
size 26
size 28
size 30

grain

each square=2.5cm(1in)sq

seam allowance not included

5 UNDER FRILL cut 2

FRONT FRILL cut1

6

BACK FRILL cut 2

7

fold line

centre back line

BACK cut 2

2

tie position

FRONT cut 1

1

pocket position

centre front   place on fold

Toddler's Party Dress

A simply charming dress to make for a toddler. It takes very little fabric and could be made up from quite small remnants with yoke, main dress and collar and cuffs in different fabrics, chosen to mix and match. The yoke edge could also be trimmed with lace for a party dress. The design could also be adapted without the yoke insertion as a pinafore dress.

*Techniques included: attaching collar and neck facing, faced sleeve opening, setting in sleeves.

Measurements

The pattern and instructions given here are to fit a child of 1, 2 or 3 years of age. Chest sizes 51 cm (20 in), 53 cm (21 in) and 58·5 cm (23 in). Each size is indicated on the graph pattern by a cutting line of a different colour.

Making the pattern

Draw up the pattern to scale from the graph pattern given here. One square represents 2·5 cm (1 in) square.

Suggested fabrics

Viyella, cottons, cotton blends, lightweight woollens and woollen blends.

You will need:

90 cm (36 in) wide fabric, without nap, all sizes 1·20 m (1¼ yd) main fabric.
90 cm (36 in) wide fabric, without nap, all sizes 30 cm (¼ yd) contrast fabric.
90 cm (36 in) wide non-woven iron-on interfacing, all sizes 30 cm (¼ yd).
15 cm (6 in) zip fastener.
Five 1 cm (⅜ in) buttons.
Sewing thread to match fabrics.
Squared paper for pattern.

Cutting out

A seam allowance of 1·5 cm (⅝ in) has been included on all seam edges and a hem allowance of 4 cm (1½ in).

To make the dress

Yoke 1. With right sides together, matching notches, ease and pin the yoke to the front dress to fit yoke.

Tack and stitch.
Neaten the turnings together by overcasting and press seam towards yoke. On the right side work a row of topstitching in contrast thread 6 mm (¼ in) from yoke seam on the yoke, through all thicknesses of fabric.

Centre back, side and shoulder seams 2. With right sides together, matching notches, tack and stitch the centre back seam to end of zip opening. Neaten raw edges by overcasting. Press the seam open. Insert the zip fastener in the centre back opening.

With right sides together, matching notches, tack and stitch the front to the back at the side and shoulder seams. Press the seams open and neaten the raw edges by overcasting.

Collar 3. Iron-on the interfacing to the wrong side of two collar pieces.

With right sides together, matching notches, tack and stitch the collar facings to the collar sections. Trim and notch the seam allowance. Turn through to the right side and tack close to stitched edges. Press flat.

*Attaching collar and neck facing to dress 4. Matching notches and the dot to the shoulder seam, pin the two collar sections to the neck edge of the dress, having the front edges meet. Tack.

5. With right sides together, tack and stitch the front and back neck facings together at the shoulder seams. Press seams open.

With right sides together, matching

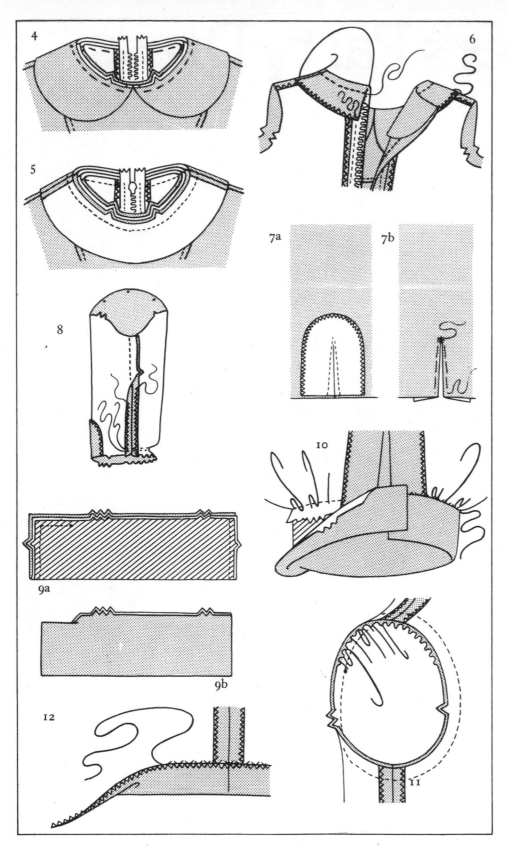

4

5

6

7a   7b

8

9a

9b

10

11

12

facing to the lower sleeve edge as indicated on the pattern. Stitch, taking 6 mm ($\frac{1}{4}$ in) seam, tapering to dot. Slash opening almost to the point.

Turn facing to inside and tack close to stitched edge. Press flat. Catchstitch facing to sleeve.

8. With right sides together, matching notches, tack and stitch the underarm seam of sleeve. Press seam open and neaten raw edges by overcasting. Work two rows of gathering stitches round lower edge of sleeve.

Repeat steps 7 and 8 for second sleeve.

Attached cuffs 9. Iron interfacing on to the wrong side of the cuff piece with one edge to the fold line.

With right sides together, fold the cuff on the fold line. Tack and stitch across the ends and to dot as shown. Trim the turnings and clip to the dot. Turn cuff to right side. Tack close to stitched edges and press flat.

10. With right sides together, matching notches, pin the interfaced half of the cuff to the lower sleeve edge, pulling up the gathers to fit evenly. Stitch. Trim turnings and press cuff. Turn under the seam allowance on the remaining edge of the cuff and sew to the stitching line. Press flat.

Repeat steps 9 and 10 for second cuff.

*Setting in sleeves 11. Work two rows of gathering stitches between the dots at the top of the sleeve. With right sides together, matching notches and underarm seams, pin the sleeve into the armhole, pulling up gathers to fit evenly. Stitch the seam with the sleeve uppermost. Press the seam towards the sleeve and neaten the raw edges together by overcasting.

Repeat for second sleeve.

Hem 12. Try the dress on the child and mark the hemline. Turn up the hem and tack close to the fold line. Trim the hem to an even width and neaten the raw edge by overcasting. Sew the hem to the dress using invisible hemming stitch. Press flat.

To finish Work a hand or machine buttonhole on each cuff as indicated on pattern. Sew buttons to underwrap of cuff immediately under buttonholes. On the centre front of the yoke, sew three buttons 2·5 cm (1 in) apart, with the top button 2·5 cm (1 in) below neck edge.

Make this sweet little dress and learn how to set in sleeves and use facings.

notches and shoulder seams, tack and stitch the neck facing to the neck edge over the collar. Trim turnings and clip on curves where necessary.

6. Neaten the raw edge of the facing by overcasting. Turn the facing to the inside and tack close to the stitched edge. Catchstitch the facing to the shoulder seams. Turn under the ends

at the centre back and slipstitch to the zip tape.

On the right side work a row of topstitching close to the collar and facing neck edge through all thicknesses.

*Faced sleeve opening 7. Neaten the outside edge of the sleeve opening facing by overcasting.

With right sides together, tack the

Graph pattern for dress

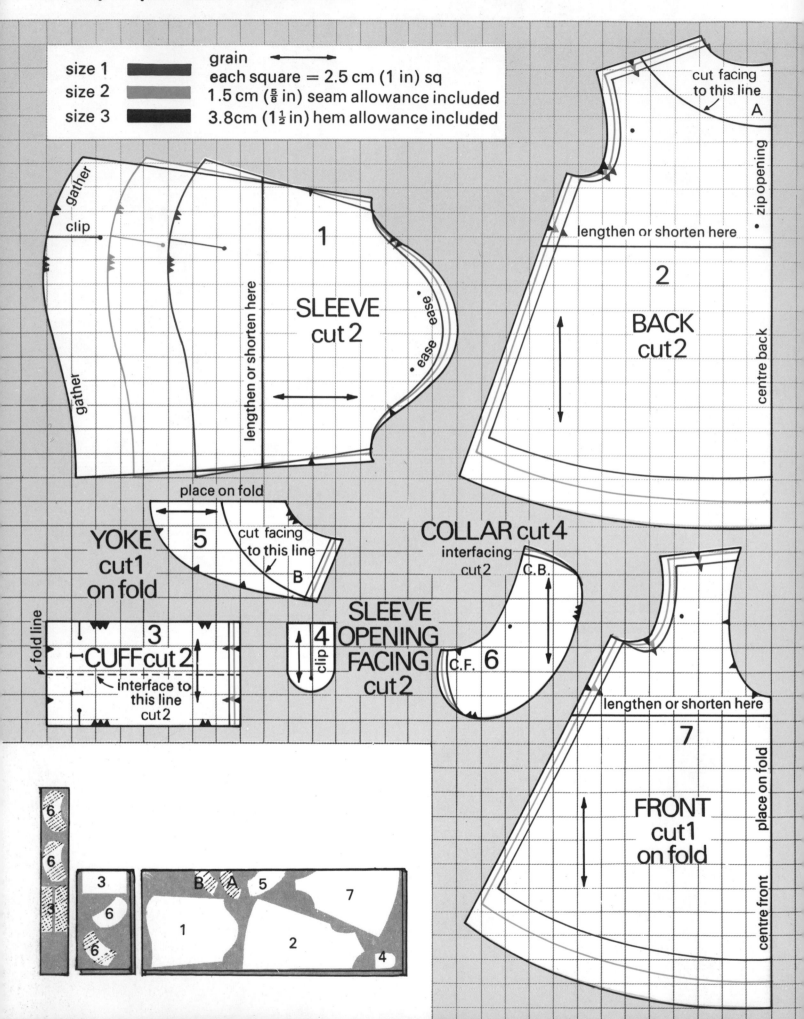

size 1 ▬
size 2 ▬
size 3 ▬

grain ←→
each square = 2.5 cm (1 in) sq
1.5 cm (⅝ in) seam allowance included
3.8cm (1½ in) hem allowance included

gather
clip
gather

1

SLEEVE
cut 2

lengthen or shorten here

ease
ease
ease
ease

cut facing
to this line

A

zip opening

lengthen or shorten here

2

BACK
cut 2

centre back

place on fold

YOKE
cut 1
on fold

5

cut facing
to this line

B

COLLAR cut 4

interfacing
cut 2

C.B.

fold line

3

CUFF cut 2

interface to
this line
cut 2

SLEEVE
OPENING
FACING
cut 2

4

clip

C.F.

6

lengthen or shorten here

7

FRONT
cut 1
on fold

place on fold

centre front

6
6
3
3
6
6

B A 5
7
1
2
4

Long Evening Dress

More basic know-how
Darts

Although their use is influenced by the vagaries of fashion (darts are not found in loose, unfitted clothes) these are essential whenever shape is required in a garment. Darts give fullness at the bust, hip, shoulder or elbow and always point towards the fullest curve of the body. Darts are generally made on the wrong side of the garment, their size and position can be adapted if alterations are needed. Bust dart points should be in line with the point of the bust and should be altered if necessary. Dart positions should be marked with tailor's tacks (they can be shown either as lines or dots on the pattern).

Working on the wrong side, fold the dart so that the markings coincide exactly. Pin and tack as shown, working from the seam edge to the point of the dart, tapering the stitching line to nothing at the point (fig. 1). Pull out the tailor's tacks then stitch the dart in the same direction as the tacking, taking the last stitches just past the folded edge of the fabric so that the thread forms a chain, cut off thread and knot close to fabric (fig. 2). Press each dart after stitching (details are given in section on pressing). If using a thick fabric e.g. tweed, slash the dart down the centre and press open (fig. 3). Shoulder and elbow darts are narrower than darts on a bodice or skirt but are stitched in the same way.

Basic pattern alterations

Because figures vary so much in height and general proportions, pattern companies make patterns for various figure types, ranging from teen, junior miss, miss petite and half size for the short sturdy figure, to women's for the tall, mature figure.

These figure type designations do not necessarily relate to age; a tall, well-built girl may require a women's size or a petite older woman can use an adapted teen pattern; the important thing is to know your figure.

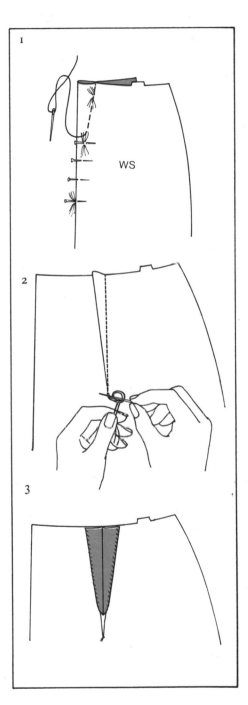

1. Pin and tack the dart before sewing.
2. Stitch toward dart point and then knot securely. On heavy fabrics the darts should be slashed as shown.

Details of the various figure types are to be found in the pattern books in department stores, where there are usually trained assistants to advise customers.

Taking accurate measurements

It is most important to have your own proportions accurately measured. The specific measurements given on the pattern envelope are actual body measurements.

The patterns do include a built-in allowance for ease, and where necessary they also include any extra fullness demanded by current fashion. There are fashion trends in fit and figure as well as in length and styling. Pattern manufacturers follow fashion trends very closely, so if you select a pattern that is right for your figure size, very little alteration should be necessary to give the correct fit and fashionable look.

General rules for altering patterns

When shortening or lengthening a garment, try to keep all the main lines of the pattern intact (i.e. style lines and hip, bust and elbow).

Try to preserve the proportions of the pattern and to disturb the outline as little as possible.

Remember that an alteration to one part of a garment affects the pieces adjacent to it.

An alteration which entails an addition to a pattern must be made before the garment is cut out.

Testing patterns

Remember to take account of current fashion trends, both of style and fit, when testing patterns for length and width.

With the exception of the sleeves, the best method of testing a pattern is to pin up one half and try it on in order to determine the length in relation to the figure.

A sleeve pattern would tend to tear if pinned up for fitting: instead, take the outer arm measurement from shoulder to elbow and down to the wrist, with the arm bent. Compare this measurement with the pattern, taking into account any extra style fullness.

Most patterns give instructions for

lengthening or shortening bodices, sleeves and skirt. These are repeated here with diagrams, followed by some of the less common alterations which are often necessary.

Shortening and lengthening

Bodice too long This causes creases above the waistline (fig. 1a).

To shorten, make horizontal tucks on the pattern and pin it down on paper (fig. 1b and c). Straighten the seam lines as shown (fig. 1b and c).

Bodice too short This causes creases at the side seams and the bodice rides above the waistline (fig. 2a).

To lengthen the bodice, crease and cut across the pattern horizontally. Spread it by the required amount and pin the pattern to paper (fig. 2b and c). Remember that if the style allows for a bloused effect in the bodice or sleeve this fullness must be retained.

Sleeve too long Make horizontal tucks on the pattern and pin it down on to paper (fig. 3).

Sleeve too short To lengthen, crease and cut across the pattern horizontally. Spread it by the required amount and pin the pattern on to paper (fig. 4).

Skirt too long To shorten, make a horizontal tuck in the pattern and pin it down on paper (fig. 5).

Skirt too short To lengthen, crease and cut across the pattern horizontally. Spread the required amount and pin the pattern to paper (fig. 6).

Alterations for unusual figure variations

Square shoulders Square shoulders cause creasing across the neckline (fig. 7a and b).

Pin the bodice down on paper to armhole level. Cut the new shoulder line allowing the required amount, 1·3 to 2 cm ($\frac{1}{2}$ to $\frac{3}{4}$ in) at the armhole tapering to nothing at the neck (fig. 7c and d).

Raise the line at the underarm to maintain the original size of the armhole (fig. 7e and f).

Note: this type of figure often requires a larger armhole, in which case omit the addition at the underarm but in-

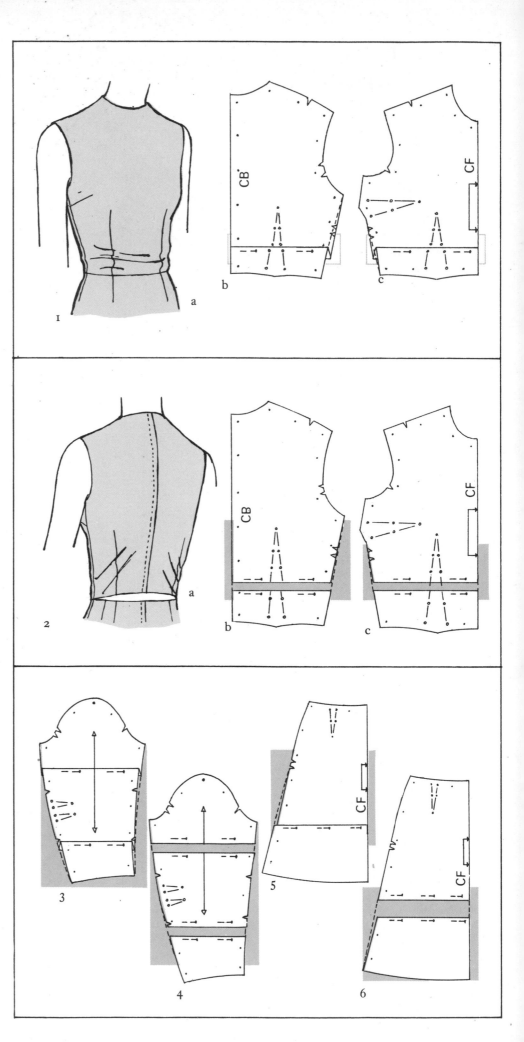

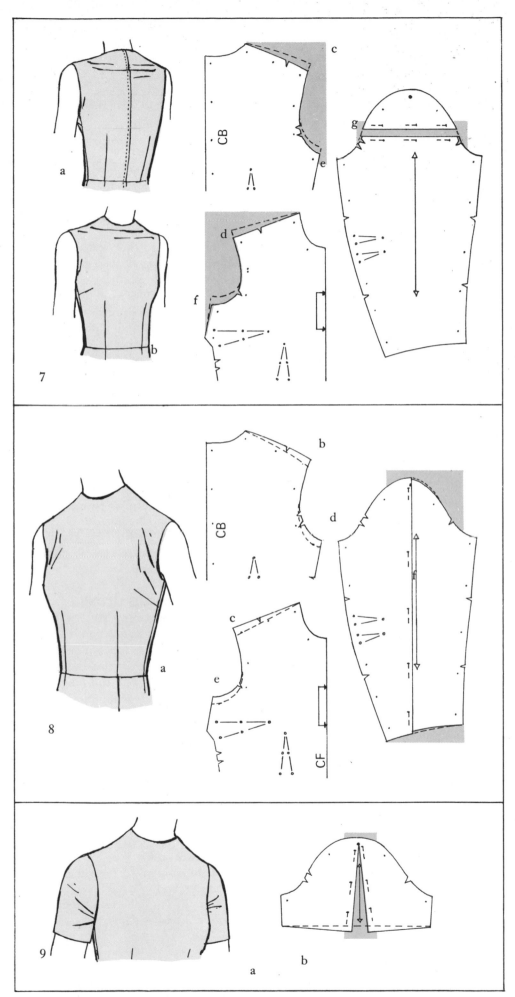

crease the sleeve head as shown to make it fit into the larger armhole with the correct amoung of ease (fig. 7g).

Sloping shoulders These cause folds at the armhole (fig. 8a).
Draw a line from the armhole tapering to nothing at the neckline and cut away the required amount (fig. 8b and c).
Cut away the same amount at the underarm to retain the original arm-hole size and sleeve head (fig. 8d and e).
Note: this type of figure often has thin arms so it may be necessary to decrease the sleeve width by making a lengthwise fold down the centre of the sleeve (fig. 8f).
In this case do not cut away at the bodice underarm.

Large upper arm This causes creas-es at the underarm and across the crown (fig. 9a).
Slash the pattern through the centre from the hem to the top of the crown. Pin the pattern to a sheet of paper, spreading the pattern pieces apart by the required amount. Draw around the spread-out pattern to give the new sleeve shape (fig. 9b).

Round shoulders This causes the neckline and the collar to stand away from the back neck (fig. 10a).
Slash the pattern about 11·5 cm (4½ in) down from the neck at the centre back to the armhole. Do not cut away (fig. 10b). Raise the neck the required amount, 2 to 2·5 cm (¾ to 1 in) (fig. 10c) and pin to paper.
Restore the neck to its original meas-urement using the lengthened, curved line if the design has a centre back seam (fig. 10d), or using the straight line if the pattern is cut to a fold (fig. 10e), taking the extra fullness into a dart at the neckline (fig. 10f).
Alternatively, slash across from the centre back to the armhole, then slash down from the centre of the shoulder. Raise the back neck and spread the shoulder to make a shoulder dart (fig. 10g).

Hollow or sway back This causes horizontal wrinkles below the waist (fig. 11a).
On the back skirt pattern, cut away about 2 cm (¾ in) from the centre

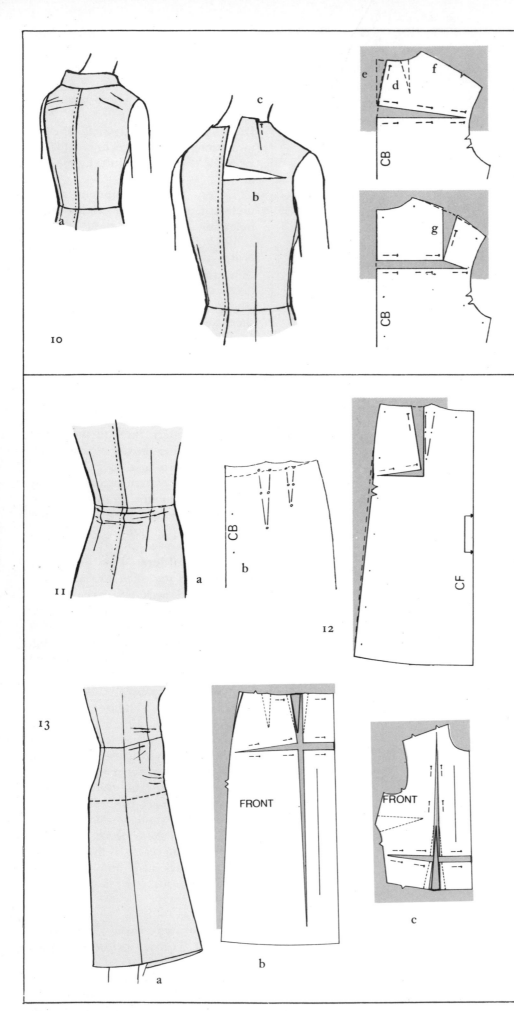

back, sloping to nothing at the side seam (fig. 11b). This alteration can be done at the fitting stage if preferred.

Large waist For some designs it is not practicable to alter the side seams, for example:

A. In a design which has no side seams.

B. Where a design has a one-sided effect.

C. Folds coming from a side seam, or a pocket or other style feature crossing it.

To increase the front waist measurement, slash the skirt pattern down from the centre of the waistline and across to the side seam at approximately hip level. Spread the pattern to give the required amount at the waist and pin to paper (fig. 12).

High abdomen This figure type causes the skirt to kick up at the hem and the skirt to crease horizontally around hip level (fig. 13a).

Slash down from the centre of the waistline and across to the centre front line of the pattern at approximately hip level (fig. 13b). Do not cut away. Spread the pattern as shown to give extra width and height. Pin to paper. Re-draw the waistline and the centre front line. A bodice can be enlarged similarly (fig. 13c).

Long evening dress

This figure-skimming style is flattering to all age groups and easy and comfortable to wear. It can be dressed up for formal occasions or left simple and uncluttered. The full-length version shown here is made up in luxurious pure silk with a fully mounted lining to add a beautiful finish. You can add a belt if you wish. The dress is easily adaptable and can be worn either day length or as a tunic over trousers.

*Techniques included: inset tab fastening, mounting.

Measurements

The pattern is given in women's sizes 10, 12, 14 and 16. Each size is indicated on the graph pattern by a cutting line of a different colour.

The fully mounted lining in this evening dress is what gives the garment its professionally made appearance.

Making the pattern

Draw up the pattern to scale from the graph pattern given here. One square represents 2·5 cm (1 in) square.

Suggested fabrics

Silk, poplin, linen, wool and cotton mixtures, fine wool, wool crêpe.

You will need:

90 cm (36 in) fabric, with nap, all sizes 3·50 m (3⅞ yd).
90 cm (36 in) underlining fabric, all sizes 3·50 m (3⅞ yd) or 120 cm (48 in) fabric, with nap, all sizes 3·50 m (3⅞ yd).
120 cm (48 in) underlining fabric, all sizes 3·50 m (3⅞ yd).
90 cm (36 in) interfacing (optional), all sizes 70 cm (¾ yd).
Eight 1 cm (⅜ in) buttons.
Sewing thread to match fabric.
Squared paper for pattern.

Cutting out

No seam allowance is included on the pattern so add 1·5 cm (⅝ in) for seams and 6·5 cm (2½ in) hem allowance.
Note If using wool crêpe do not mount. If you are mounting the dress cut out each pattern piece in underlining fabric. The underlining fabric should relate well to the main dress fabric e.g. jap silk for pure silk; lawn or marquisette are also suitable for the suggested fabrics above. The colour of the underlining should not be deeper than the top fabric. Underlining can also be used to give body to loosely woven fabrics.
If you do not wish to mount the dress, cut out and apply interfacing to the tab, wrap facing and collar sections (see Facings).

To make the dress

*Mounting the fabric Tack each underlining piece to the corresponding dress piece with wrong sides together, raw edges level; the facings are not mounted. First work a row of tacking through the centre then tack all round each piece, close to the edge. Then make up as one piece of fabric (all pattern markings should be indicated with tailor's tacks).

*Inset tab fastening 1. Pin and tack the tab to the tab facing with right sides together and with the facing uppermost. Starting at the top, stitch down the right side, turn and stitch to the point. Fasten off securely at the point. Trim the seam allowance to 6 mm (¼ in). Turn the tab to the right side and tack firmly along the stitched edge, rolling the facing under slightly to avoid it showing. Carefully press this edge on the wrong side of the tab taking care that the tacking stitches do not make impressions on the fabric.
2. Pin, tack and stitch the centre front seam of the dress from the pointed end of the tab stitching line to the hem. Clip into the seam allowance, neaten the seam by overcasting and press open. Pin, tack and stitch the raw edge of the tab to the right dress front on the tab stitching line. Do not stitch along the neckline. Spread the corner on the dress so that you can stitch comfortably towards the pointed end of the tab. Take care that the point of the tab is in line with the centre front seam. Trim seam and press carefully. Fold under the seam allowance on the facing and pin it over the seam line on the point of the tab. Slipstitch in place. Remove the tacking and press the tab.
3. Pin and tack the facing to the wrap extension on the left side of the dress, with right sides facing. Stitch along the front edge of the wrap extension

Follow the pattern layout below when placing the pieces on the fabric.

but leave the lower edge and the neck edge unstitched. Trim the seam allowance and turn the facing inside the dress. Tack along the stitched edge and press.
4. Top-stitch the tab 6 mm (¼ in) from the seam line, pivoting the machine needle carefully at corners and point. Oversew the raw lower edge of the wrap extension and sides of facing to neaten.

Darts, shoulder and side seams
5. Pin and tack the shoulder and bust darts, shoulder and side seams, matching balance marks and seam lines. Tack waist darts if using. Try on dress and adjust fit if necessary.
Stitch and press darts.
Stitch shoulder and side seams. Press and neaten seams.

Armholes 6. Cut 4 cm (1½ in) wide bias strips to length of armholes, plus 8 cm (3 in). Curve the bias strips to follow the curve of the armholes by placing the bias strip on an ironing board and pressing round the outer edge, gently stretching this into a curve. Press in the fullness on the inner edge of the curve so that the binding will be flat. Turn in 1·3 cm (½ in) seam allowance at one end of the bias strip. With right sides facing, starting at the armhole seam line pin the inner curved edge of the bias strip around the armhole seam line. Ease the fullness of the bias into the underarm curve. Overlap the other end of the bias strip as shown, but do not trim and stitch until the binding is complete to avoid it dragging. Tack and stitch the bias binding in place along the seam line. Snip into the seam allowance on the dress only, then turn binding to the inside. Roll the seam edge slightly to the inside to prevent the bias showing and tack in place.
Turn under the raw edge of the binding and slipstitch to the dress. Slipstitch the ends of the binding. Press carefully.
Repeat for second armhole.

Collar 7. Interface one section of collar if fabric requires it. Place the top and under collar pieces together, with right sides facing. Pin, tack and stitch along the upper curved edge. Trim the seam allowance to 6 mm (¼ in) and turn to the right side. Tack along the stitched edges and press.
Tack the front facings to the dress

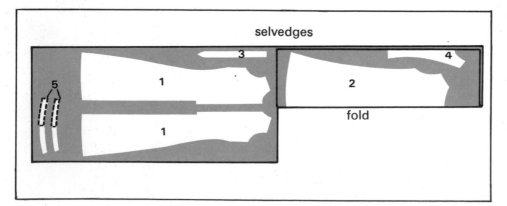

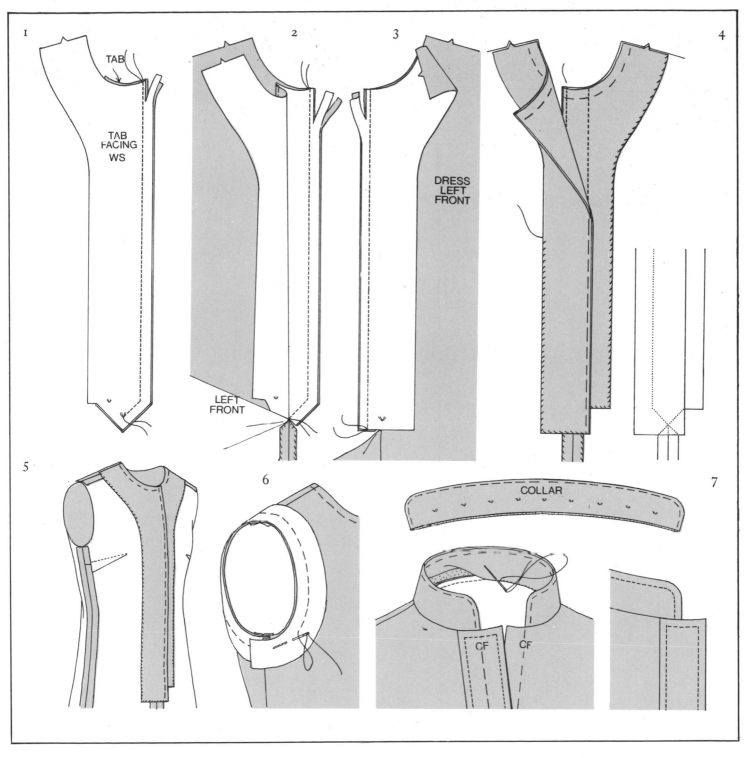

along the neckline. With right sides together, raw edges level, pin and tack the outer collar band to the neckline. Tack, stitch and trim the seam allowance. Turn under the seam allowance on the inner collar band, lay it over the stitching line to cover the machine stitches and slipstitch in place. Make tiny stitches as the inner edge of the band will show if you wear the neck of the dress unbuttoned. Top-stitch around the outer edge of the collar taking care that the stitches line up with the top-stitching on the tab.

Fastenings 8. Mark the position for the first buttonhole 1 cm ($\frac{3}{8}$ in) down from the neck edge of the tab. Position the remaining buttonholes in pairs and at evenly spaced intervals down the tab. Leave a space at belt position. Work vertical buttonholes either by hand or machine in positions marked. Stitch on buttons to correspond.

Finishes with mounted under-linings Seam allowances should be oversewn by hand. Catch facings lightly to seam lines by hand. To stop the underlining folding up inside the

hem, prick stitch fabric and lining together just below the hem line before the hem is turned up and finished. When sewing the inner edge of hems and bias facings to the mounted dress make sure that you do not sew through to the outside fabric but only catch the underlining fabric to give the outside a smooth finish.

Hem 9. Check that the length of the dress is correct and that the hem is level. Trace tack along the finished hemline. Turn up and stitch hem (see Hems).

Graph pattern for long dress

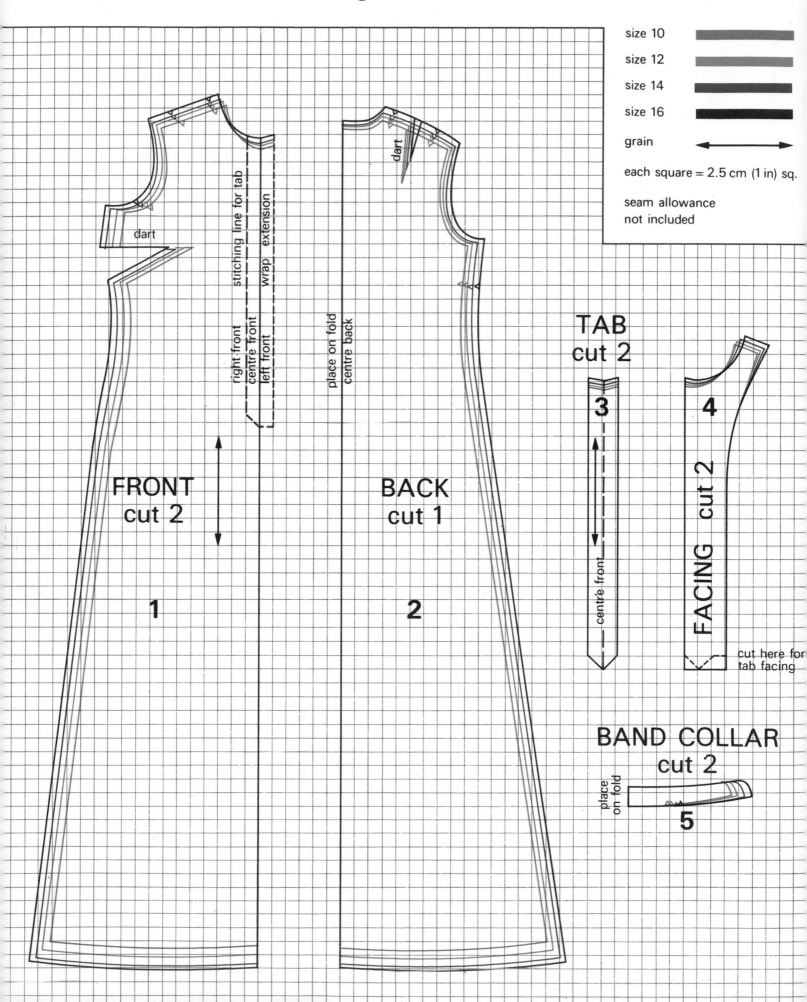

size 10
size 12
size 14
size 16
grain
each square = 2.5 cm (1 in) sq.
seam allowance not included

dart

stitching line for tab
wrap extension
right front
centre front
left front
place on fold
centre back

dart

TAB
cut 2

3

centre front

FRONT
cut 2

1

BACK
cut 1

2

4

FACING cut 2

cut here for tab facing

BAND COLLAR
cut 2

place on fold

5

Skirt with Flare

More basic know-how
Waistbands and belts
*Techniques included: stab stitch, catchstitch, ladder stitch.

Waistbands

A properly sewn and fitted waistband never stretches, wrinkles or folds over, nor is it too tight or so loose that it slips down to the hips.

Personal preference and the style of the garment determine the width and type of waist finish and all waistbands need to be interfaced to prevent stretching, particularly where loosely woven fabrics are being used. Knits need an elastic section to ensure a proper fit. Petersham can be used for interfacing; this comes in various widths and is either plain or stiffened with small 'bones' of plastic. If used in a washable garment, it should be pre-shrunk by washing and left to drip dry.

Unless the garment is gathered at the waist, the skirt is eased to the band to fit the curve of the body directly below the waist. For this reason the skirt waist measurement must be 2·5 cm (1 in) bigger than the waistband, which itself must be a comfortable fit. This is where personal preference comes in and it must be left to the individual to decide how much ease to allow. If the design has an overlapping waistband, the ends of the waistband should overlap by 3·8 cm to 5 cm (1½ in to 2 in) with the back extending under the front for side openings, the left extending under the right for front openings and the right extending under the left for back openings.

The waistband is applied after the zip and zip guard, if used, and before the lining. If a waistband is not required, then the waist is finished by the addition of a shaped facing which should be interfaced with a firm non-woven or woven interfacing. This is applied after the zip is sewn in and the lining tacked into place.

Tailored waistband Cut the waistband with one long edge to the selvedge; if this is not possible neaten one long edge by overcasting by hand or machine. Make it 8 cm (3 in) longer

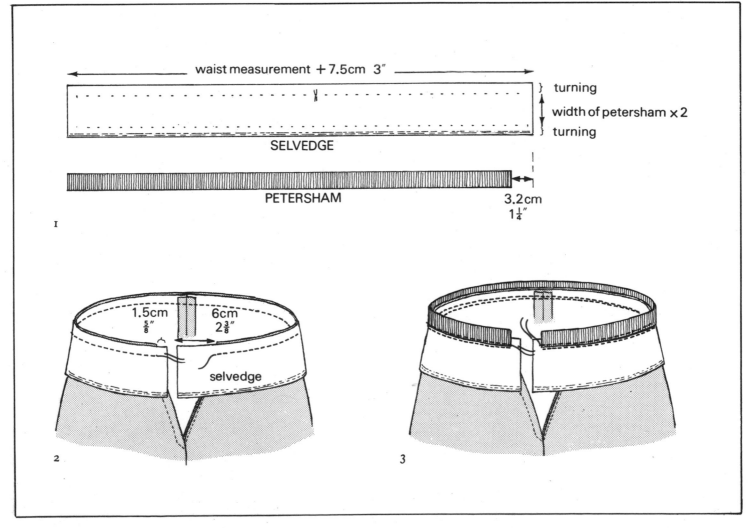

than the waist measurement and twice as wide as the petersham, plus two turnings. Cut the petersham 3·2 cm (1¼ in) shorter than the band (fig. 1). Ease the skirt on to the long cut edge of the waistband, leaving 6 cm (2⅜ in) underlap on the appropriate side. Tack through band and skirt and machine (fig. 2).

Stitch the petersham just above this line, placing it so that there is a 1·5 cm (⅝ in) turning left at both ends (fig.3). Turn in the seam allowance over the ends of the petersham and fold the band over the petersham (fig. 4). Tack.

Snip at the zip, turn under along the underlap and tack along the length of the band. Hem the extension and the front ends (fig. 5).

Machine or stab stitch (see fig. 26) along the waistband seam, stitch through the skirt and inside waistband, not through the front of the band (fig. 6). If you are lining the skirt turn in the lining waist seam allowance and hem to waistband seam allowance along the stitching line.

Elasticised waistband This is used for knitted fabrics and gives a smooth finish in front and a slight gather at the back to take up the ease and prevent stretching. Because elastic is used the back darts can be made smaller, or left out altogether, and the difference between skirt and band can be as much as 6·3 cm (2½ in), comprising of 1·3 cm (½ in) to ease in at the front and 5 cm (2 in) at the back.

Substitute the back half of the peter-

sham with elastic of the same width, cut 5 cm (2 in) shorter and stitch a 5 cm (2 in) length of petersham at the end to make the underlap (fig. 7).

Sew the waistband to the skirt as shown in fig. 2.

Sew the petersham sections as in fig. 3 but do not sew the elastic (fig. 8). Fold the waistband over and finish as shown in figs. 4, 5 and 6.

Strong machine finished waistband
This is a useful finish for children's clothes, denims etc., and where the machined effect adds to the style of the garment.

Lay the petersham to the wrong side of the band and shape end if required. Catchstitch all round (fig. 9). See fig. 27 for technique.

Fold the band with right sides together along the centre fold and machine each end. Do not stitch through the petersham. Trim the corner (fig. 10). Turn to the right side and press.

Using the un-interfaced side, lay the right side of the band to the wrong side of the garment, easing as before (fig. 11a).

Machine and press the seam into the band (fig. 11b).

Turn in the remaining long edge over the petersham and tack over the seam. Machine round band.

If required, make a buttonhole by machine or hand.

Faced waistline using fabric Some trousers or skirts are finished with a shaped facing, when comfort or style

call for it. When there is a yoke to the garment, this is interfaced and the facing cut to match the yoke and not itself interfaced. Otherwise the facing is interfaced before being sewn to the skirt. Use the weight of interfacing suitable for the garment fabric. The garment is completed before the facing is sewn in, any lining is tacked in and any yoke seams pressed towards the waist.

Cut out the facing pieces, separate and place the wrong side to the interfacing. Tack all round inside the sewing line and cut out. This ensures that the pieces match exactly (fig. 12).

Join the seams and trim back the interfacing, press open (fig. 13).

Finish the lower edge by oversewing the raw edge to the interfacing (fig. 14a), or trim the interfacing back 6 mm (¼ in), turn facing over interfacing and machine down (fig. 14b).

Place the right side of the facing to the right side of the skirt, matching seams and easing garment to fit. Machine (fig. 15).

Layer the seam (fig. 16a).

Snip through to the stitching line (fig. 16b).

Understitch the facing to the seam allowance to stop it rolling back (fig. 16c). Turn the facing to the wrong side and press well. Fold under the end seam allowances, mitring slightly to avoid the zip, and hem to the zip tape (fig. 17a).

Catch the facing to the seams and darts (fig. 17b).

Sew hook and eye to the top of the facing to keep it in place and to prevent

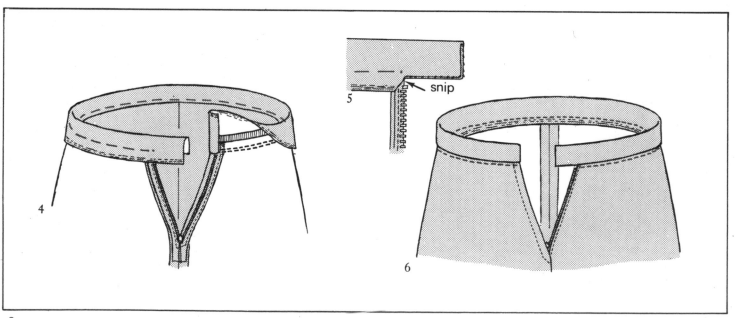

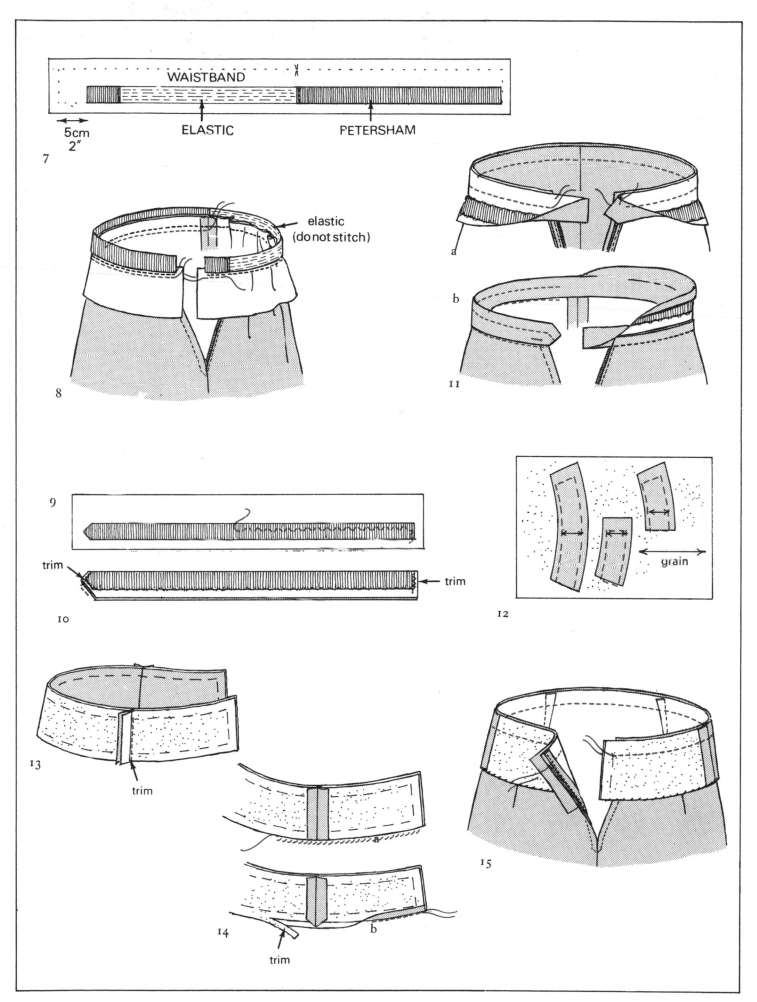

WAISTBAND

ELASTIC

PETERSHAM

5cm
2"

7

elastic
(do not stitch)

8

a

b

11

9

trim

trim

10

grain

12

13

trim

14

trim

b

15

strain on the zip (fig. 17c).

For a yoke facing, proceed as above but hem it all round the yoke seam to provide a neat finish (fig. 18).

Faced waistline using shaped petersham It is possible to purchase shaped petersham but if this is not available then shape a straight piece by pulling it under a medium hot iron, stretching one side slightly (fig. 19).

When attaching the petersham, great care must be taken to make sure that the inside diameter is sewn to the garment.

Fit the petersham to the body allowing 1·3 cm ($\frac{1}{2}$ in) extra at each end. Finish the garment as for the faced waistline and trim the waist seam to 1·3 cm ($\frac{1}{2}$ in), neatening the edge by oversewing (fig. 20).

Place the inside curve of the petersham on the waist seam line on the right side as shown. Ease the skirt and tack. Sew one line of machining along the edge of the petersham and a second line 3 mm ($\frac{1}{8}$ in) away (fig. 21).

Turn to the wrong side, fold under the petersham turnings and finish as fig. 17).

Belts

A belt made of fabric is a good alternative to a purchased one in that it does not 'break' the line of the garment. This can be disastrous if the figure is not all it should be, as the eye is drawn to the waist instead of taken away from it.

There are various interfacings which can be used to stiffen belts: petersham, boned petersham, buckram, commercial belt stiffening. The latter is not suitable if the belt is to be finished by top-stitching.

Cut the interfacing 15 cm (6 in) longer than the waist measurement, shaping the end to a point or curve as required (fig. 22a).

Cut two pieces of fabric the length and width of the interfacing plus turnings (fig. 22b).

Lay the petersham centrally on the wrong side of one piece of fabric and catchstitch the turnings in place, snipping the corners to enable the fabric to lie flat (fig. 23).

Press the turnings of the other piece to the wrong side and lay it over the petersham. Either tack into place if the belt is to be top-stitched (fig. 24a), or ladder stitch together for a plain belt (fig. 24b).

Make a hole for the buckle 3·8 cm (1$\frac{1}{2}$ in) from the plain end, buttonhole stitch round or apply an eyelet (fig. 25a). (Eyelet kits are available in many colours and instructions are given with each set.)

Place the prong of the buckle through the hole and hem the edge down to the wrong side (fig. 25b).

Check for the correct position of the hole at the shaped end and make a hole (fig. 25c).

*Stab stitch Working from the right side, push the needle down vertically, and pull the needle through from the wrong side. Then push the needle up vertically and pull through from the right side. The stitches should be very small and evenly spaced.

*Catchstitch Used for attaching interfacing to facings.

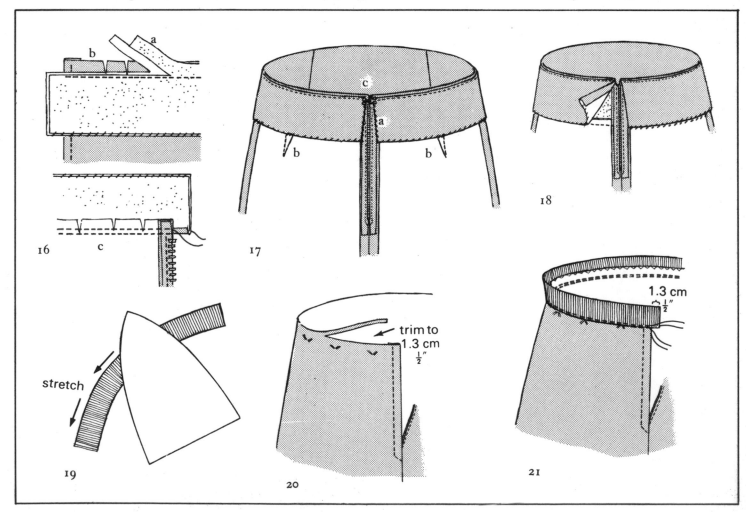

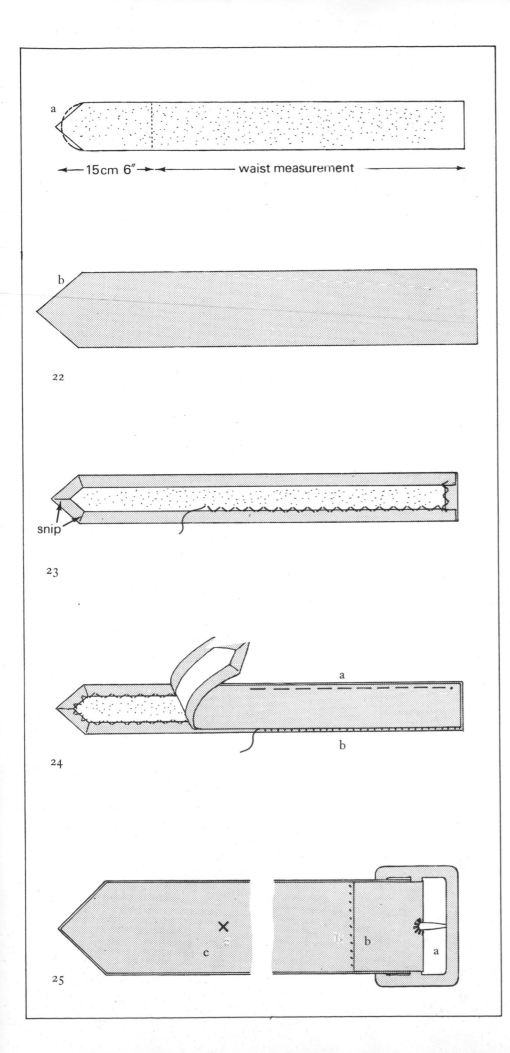

← 15cm 6″ → ← waist measurement →

a

b

22

snip

23

a

b

24

c

b

a

25

Working from the wrong side, pick up a thread of the fabric, then pick up a thread of the interfacing. The stitches must not go through to the right side.

*Ladder stitch Slip the needle through each fold of fabric in turn, creating a series of straight stitches which should be invisible.

Skirt with a flare

The line of the skirt is gently flared, emphasised by the Tootal corduroy from which it is made. The shape could not be easier to sew, just two pattern pieces and a narrow waistband. For an extra touch of luxury you can add a lining.
*Techniques included: lining a skirt.

Measurements
The pattern is given in women's sizes 10, 12, 14 and 16. Each size is indicated on the graph pattern by a cutting line of a different colour.

Making the pattern
Draw up the pattern to scale from the graph pattern given here.
One square represents 2·5 cm (1 in) square.

Suggested fabrics
Corduroy, needlecord, cotton blends, lightweight wools and wool mixtures, light tweeds.

You will need:
90 cm (36 in) wide fabric, with nap, all sizes 3·10 m (3⅜ yd).

140 cm (54 in) wide fabric, with nap, all sizes 2·40 m (2⅝ yd).
90 cm (36 in) wide lining (optional), all sizes 1·60 m (1¾ yd).
90 cm (36 in) wide woven interfacing, all sizes 30 cm (¼ yd).
20 cm (8 in) zip fastener.
Sewing thread to match fabric.
Squared paper for pattern.

Cutting out
A seam allowance of 1·5 cm (⅝ in) has been allowed on all seam edges and a hem allowance of 6·5 cm (2⅝ in).

To make the skirt
Front 1. With right sides together, raw edges level, matching notches, tack and stitch the centre front seam.

A simple flared skirt is a practical addition to any wardrobe and, depending on the fabric it is made in, will be a suitable style for any occasion. Make this skirt and learn all about fitting waistbands and making belts.

Press the seam open.

Back 2. With right sides together, raw edges level, matching notches, tack and stitch the centre back seam from the hem to the circle. Press the seam open. Tack around the opening

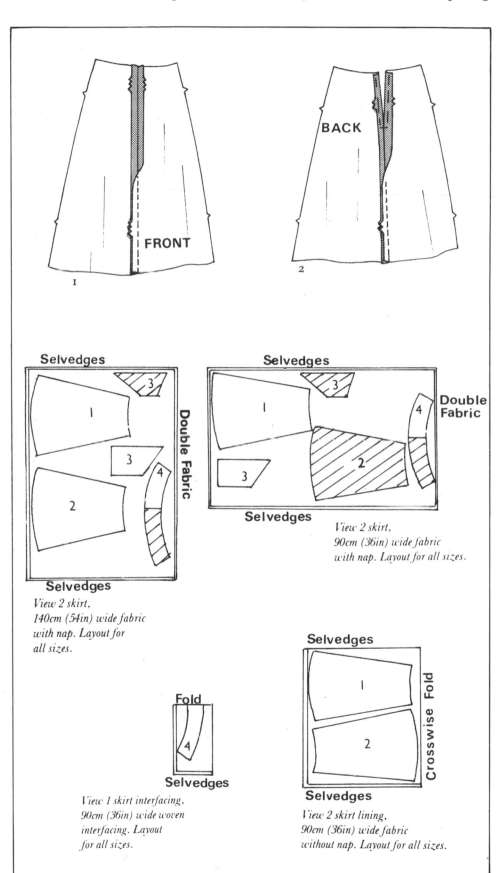

View 2 skirt,
90cm (36in) wide fabric
with nap. Layout for all sizes.

View 2 skirt,
140cm (54in) wide fabric
with nap. Layout for
all sizes.

View 1 skirt interfacing,
90cm (36in) wide woven
interfacing. Layout
for all sizes.

View 2 skirt lining,
90cm (36in) wide fabric
without nap. Layout for all sizes.

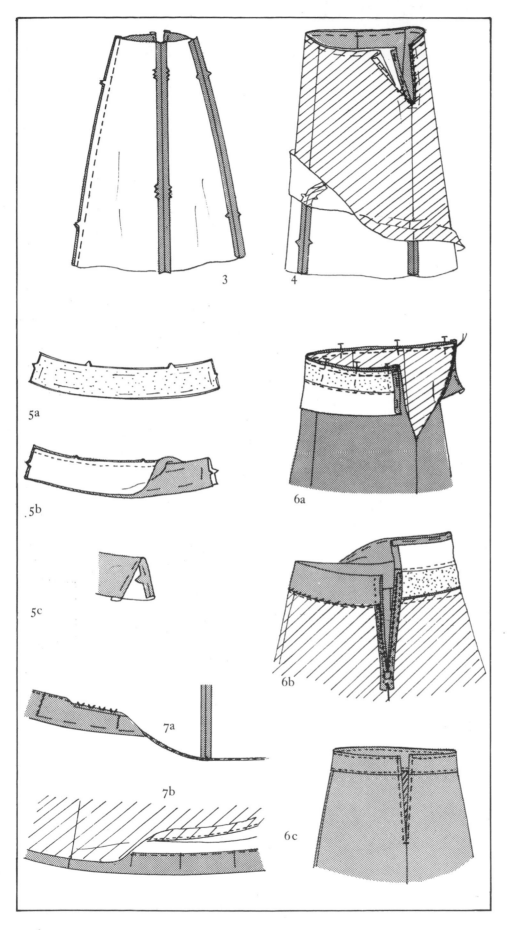

With wrong sides together, matching centre fronts and side seams, tack the lining to the skirt, round the waistline and the centre back opening. Slipstitch the lining to the skirt at the back edge opening as shown.

Waistband 5. Tack the interfacing to the wrong side of the waistband.

With right sides together, matching notches, tack and stitch the two waistband pieces together along the notched edge. Cut the interfacing close to the stitching and layer the seam allowance. Turn under 1·5 cm ($\frac{5}{8}$ in) seam allowance at the centre backs on both waistband pieces. Tack as shown and press flat.

Turn the waistband to the right side and tack close to the stitched edge. Press the stitched edge flat.

Attaching waistband 6. With right sides together, raw edges level, matching centre fronts, side seams and centre backs, pin the waistband to the skirt. Stitch the entire waist. Cut the interfacing close to the stitching and layer the seam. Press the seam flat towards the waistband.

Insert the zip fastener at the centre back opening from the circle to the top of the waistband.

Turn under 1·5 cm ($\frac{5}{8}$ in) seam allowance on the lower edge of the waistband facing. Tack and press flat. Sew the fold edge of the facing to the stitching line of the waistband and to the zip tape at the centre back, 6 mm ($\frac{1}{4}$ in) away from the teeth.

On the right side, top-stitch 1 cm ($\frac{3}{8}$ in) from the top and waistline edges of the waistband (optional).

Hem 7. Try on the skirt and mark the hem. Turn up the hem and tack close to the fold edge. Trim the hem allowance to an even width and neaten the raw edge either by overcasting or by turning under 6 mm ($\frac{1}{4}$ in) and machine stitching.

Dart out any fullness and sew the hem to the skirt using invisible hemming stitch or catchstitch. Press the hem edge flat.

Note If using wool fabrics, neaten the raw edge by overcasting, gather up the fullness and shrink out using a damp cloth.

Lining hem This is sewn separately from the skirt hem.

Mark the hem 2·5 cm (1 in) shorter than the skirt hem. Sew the hem up in the same way as the skirt.

as shown.

Side seams 3. With right sides together, raw edges level, matching notches, tack and stitch the front to the back at the side seams starting at the top. Press the seams open.

*Lining 4. Make up the lining as for the skirt following steps 1, 2 and 3.

Graph pattern for A-line skirt

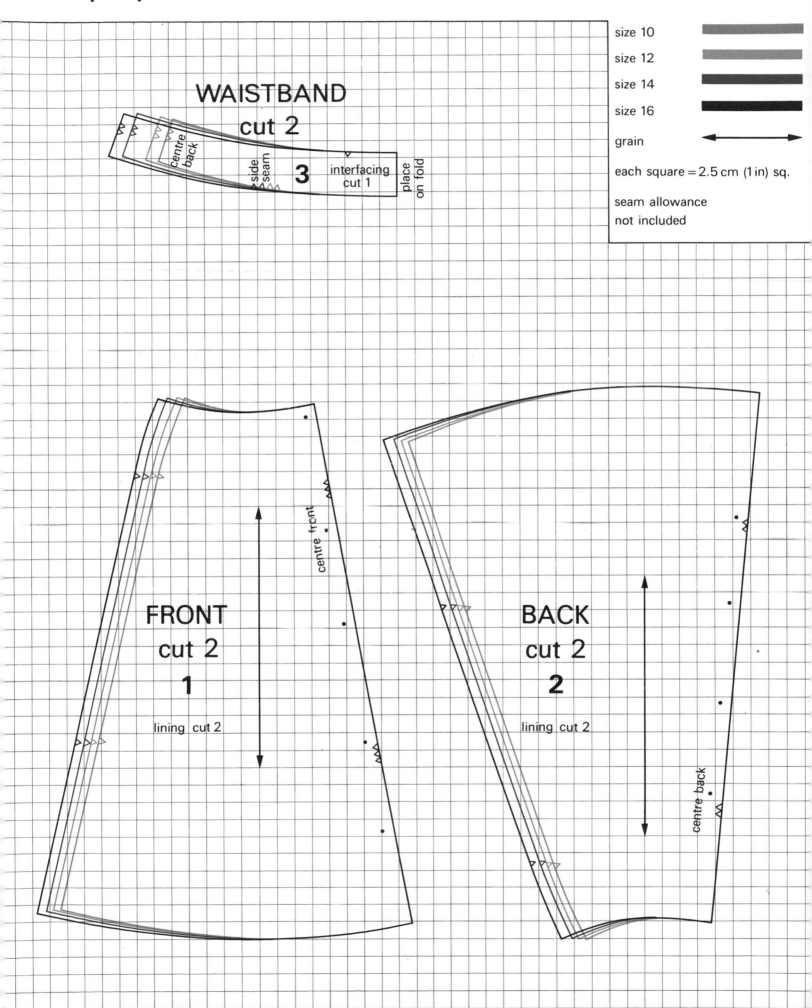

size 10
size 12
size 14
size 16

grain

each square = 2.5 cm (1 in) sq.

seam allowance
not included

WAISTBAND
cut 2

centre back

side seam

3

interfacing
cut 1

place on fold

centre front

FRONT
cut 2
1

lining cut 2

BACK
cut 2
2

lining cut 2

centre back

Man's Sport shirt

More basic know-how
Making up jersey fabrics
Some commercial patterns are designed for a fabric with a specific amount of stretch like jersey knits. This is usually indicated on the pattern pack.

Cutting out Pin and cut your fabric on a large flat surface and do not allow the fabric to hang over the edge to prevent unwanted stretching. To straighten fabric fold on a lengthwise rib, cut crosswise ends square with the end of the table. Hold ends together with tacking.

Sewing Use a ballpoint machine needle and a synthetic thread. Test your machine stitching on a scrap of spare fabric to adjust stitch length before making up your garment. A small zig-zag or stretch stitch is the best to use. Otherwise, use a medium stitch length, stretching the fabric slightly as you sew.

Taping Where stretching is undesirable e.g. on waists, necklines or shoulders use cotton seam binding to hold the seam to its original length. Tack the binding to the seam line and stitch at the same time as you stitch the seam (fig. 1).

Buttonholes Back buttonholes with a light but firm fabric.

Neatening This is often unnecessary as jersey does not fray. If seam allowances curl stitch them together with two rows of stitching (fig. 2).

Pressing Check iron temperature according to the fibre of the fabric. Always test on a spare scrap of fabric. Use a damp pressing cloth made of thin cotton. The ironing board should be softly padded to prevent impressions of seams and darts being made on the right side.
Darts should be slashed and pressed open.

Shirt
Here's a shirt that is simply made for a sporting life, or for casual week-end wear. It has a front buttoning placket opening, trim collar and neatly fitting short sleeves. This design is only suitable for use with jersey or stretch fabrics.

Measurements
The pattern and instructions are given to fit chest sizes 87 cm (34 in), 92 cm (36 in), 97 cm (38 in) and 102 cm (40 in). Each size is indicated on the graph pattern by a cutting line of a different colour.

Making the pattern
Draw up the pattern to scale from the graph pattern given here.
One square represents 2·5 cm (1 in) square.

Suggested fabrics
Cotton jersey, synthetic jerseys, stretch towelling.

You will need:
150 cm (60 in) wide fabric, with nap, all sizes, 1·30 m (1⅜ yd).
90 cm (36 in) woven interfacing; all sizes, 70 cm (¾ yd).
Sewing thread to match fabric.
Four 1 cm (⅜ in) buttons.
Squared paper for pattern.

Cutting out
No seam allowance is included on the pattern so add 1·5 cm (⅝ in) to all seam edges and 4 cm (1½ in) hem allowance.

To make the shirt
Front opening 1. Tack interfacing to wrong side of front bands on notched side and catchstitch to fold line.
On the un-notched edge, turn under 1·5 cm (⅝ in) seam allowance and tack. On the shirt front, stay stitch round inner corners of front opening.
With right sides together, matching notches, tack and stitch left front band to left front to circle and right front band to right front to circle, taking 1·5 cm (⅝ in) seam allowance. Trim interfacing close to stitching line

Working with stretch fabrics requires the use of special techniques, and this sports shirt provides the perfect opportunity to acquire these skills.

1. Tape stitched to seam to retain the original length. 2. Neaten seams by sewing turnings together and trimming.

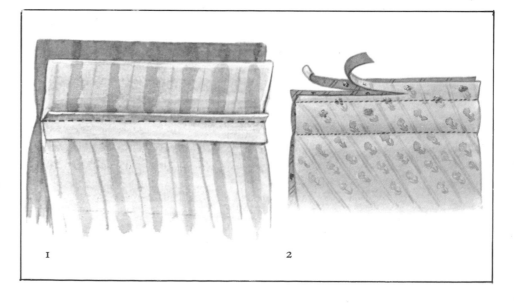

1   2

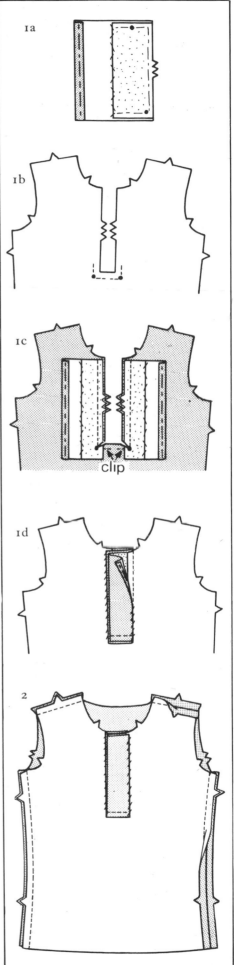

1a

1b

1c

clip

1d

2

and layer seam allowance. Clip to inner corners as shown.

Fold band to inside along fold lines, having left band over right band on the outside. Working on the wrong side, tack and stitch the bands to the shirt front across lower edges, taking 1·5 cm (⅝ in) seam allowance as shown. Slipstitch bands on the inside to stitching line.

Shoulder and side seams 2. With right sides together, matching notches, tack and stitch shoulder and side seams. Press seams open.

Collar 3. Tack interfacing to wrong side of collar and collar band. With right sides together, tack and stitch under collar to upper collar round outer un-notched edges as shown. Trim interfacing close to stitching, layer seam and cut across corners.

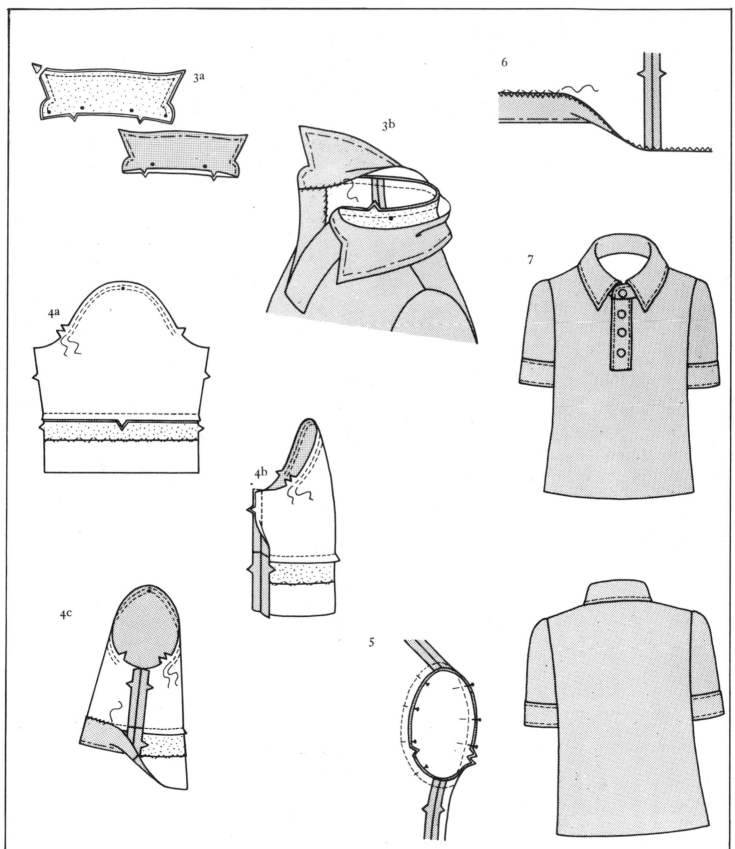

Turn collar through to right side and tack round stitched edge. Press flat. With right sides together, matching centre backs, circles to shoulder seams, notches and circles to centre fronts, tack and stitch interfaced collar section to neck edge. Trim interfacing close to stitching line, layer seam and clip curves. Press seam towards collar. On the inside, turn under seam allowance of upper collar and slipstitch to stitching line, enclosing all thicknesses.

Sleeves and sleeve bands 4. Tack interfacing to wrong side of notched edge of sleeve band and catchstitch to fold line. With right sides together, matching notches and underarm seams, tack and stitch interfaced band edge to lower edge of sleeve. Trim interfacing close to stitching line and layer seam. Press seam towards band. Work two rows gathering stitches round top of sleeve between notches. With right sides together, matching notches and seams, tack and stitch underarm seam. Press seams open. Fold band to inside along fold line and tack close to folded edge. Turn under seam allowance of band and slipstitch to stitching line. Press flat.
Repeat for second sleeve.

Setting in sleeves 5. With right sides together, matching underarm seams, notches and circle to shoulder seam, pin sleeve into armhole, easing in fullness between notches. Stitch seam having sleeve uppermost. Press seam towards sleeve and neaten raw edges together. Repeat for second sleeve.

Hem 6. Try shirt on wearer and mark hem. Trim hem to an even width. Turn hem up and tack close to folded edge. Neaten raw edge by hand or machine overcasting. Sew hem to shirt using invisible hemming stitch. Press flat. Alternatively make a double machine-stitched hem.

To finish 7. On the outside, top-stitch collar and front bands 6 mm (¼ in) in from outer edges and 6 mm (¼ in) in from inner seam line of bands. Top-stitch sleeve bands 6 mm (¼ in) from outer and seam edges. Mark buttonhole positions on left front along centre front line and on collar band as indicated on pattern. Make worked or machine buttonholes. Sew buttons on right front band directly under buttonholes.

Graph pattern for shirt

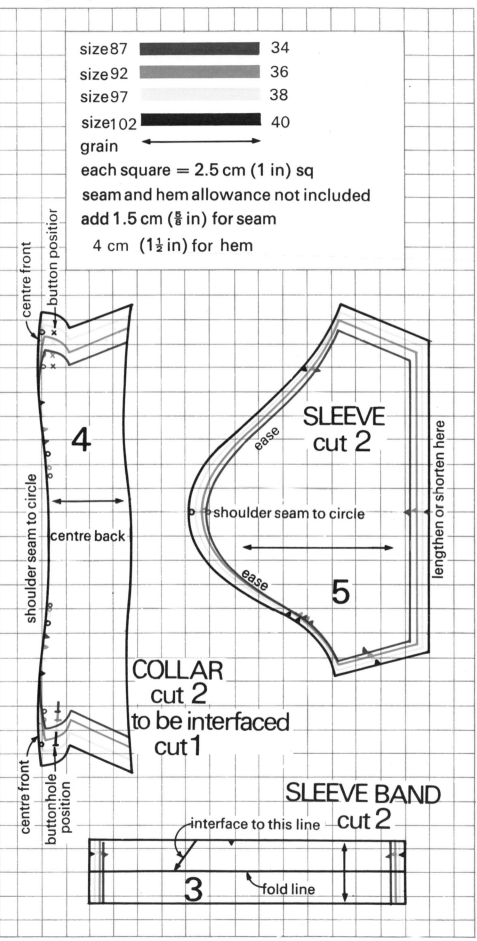

size 87		34
size 92		36
size 97		38
size 102		40

grain

each square = 2.5 cm (1 in) sq

seam and hem allowance not included

add 1.5 cm (⅝ in) for seam

4 cm (1½ in) for hem

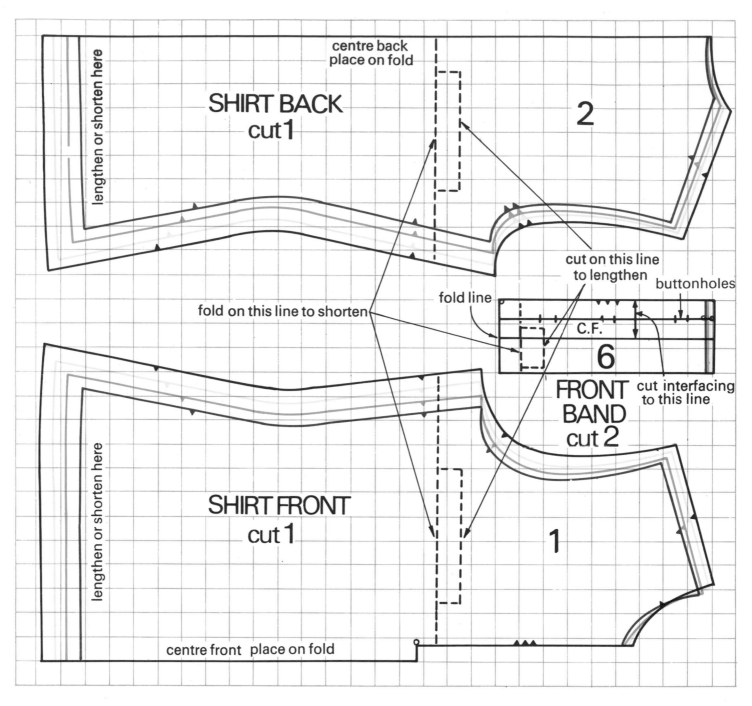

SHIRT BACK
cut 1

lengthen or shorten here

centre back
place on fold

2

cut on this line
to lengthen

buttonholes

fold line

fold on this line to shorten

C.F.

6

FRONT
BAND
cut 2

cut interfacing
to this line

SHIRT FRONT
cut 1

lengthen or shorten here

1

centre front place on fold

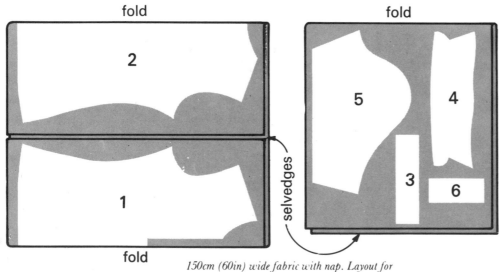

fold

2

1

fold

fold

5

4

3

6

selvedges

*150cm (60in) wide fabric with nap. Layout for
all sizes.*

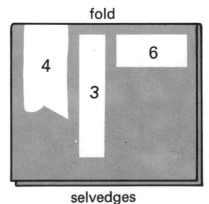

fold

4

6

3

selvedges

*90cm (36in) wide woven interfacing.
Layout for all sizes.*

Blouson Cover-up

More basic know-how
Using bias strips

To join bias strips Pull a thread at each end and cut on the straight grain. Place strips on a flat surface with right sides up and angles matching (fig. 1).

Place one strip on to the other with right sides facing and the edges cut on the straight grain together so that bias cut edges cross each other 6 mm ($\frac{1}{4}$ in) from the pointed ends. Tack and stitch strips together 6 mm ($\frac{1}{4}$ in) in from the edge (fig. 2).

Press seam open and trim off points. When joining stripes or checks join the bias strips so that the pattern is not broken.

Rouleau Made from bias strips is suitable for lacing, loop buttonholes, belt carriers, shoe-string straps and bows. Cut a strip 2·5 to 3 cm (1 to 1$\frac{1}{4}$ in) wide, from the true bias of the fabric. With right sides together, fold strip in half lengthways and stitch 6 mm ($\frac{1}{4}$ in) in from the edge (fig. 1). Do not trim the turnings as these turnings make the filling. Sew end of tube on to eye

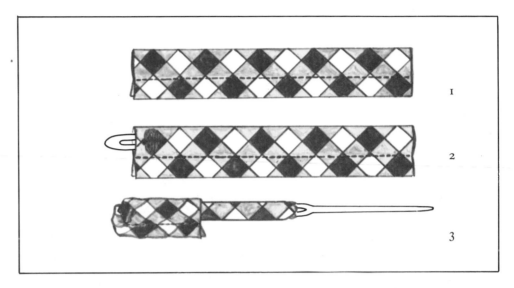

of a large bodkin, or blunt-ended tapestry needle (fig. 2). Push this through the tube until it reaches the other end (fig. 3). Cut thread from tube to needle.

Note It is quite possible to make a wider rouleau for belts by using the same method.

Loop buttonholes

Cut the length of bias fabric required for a continuous strip of buttonholes

1. Rouleau is made from a bias strip stitched to make a tube. 2. Sew a bodkin to one end and 3. pull through.

plus 3 cm (1$\frac{1}{4}$ in) extra for each loop. Make a rouleau as described above. Place the end of the rouleau to the edge of the garment on the right side. Pin into position. Make loops the size required to fit each button as shown. Leave approximately 6 mm ($\frac{1}{4}$ in) between the loops (fig. 1). Tack and stitch loops in place along the seam line before attaching the facing.

1. Join bias strips by matching the angles and stitching as shown in 2.

1. Loop buttonholes are made by sewing a length of rouleau along the opening.

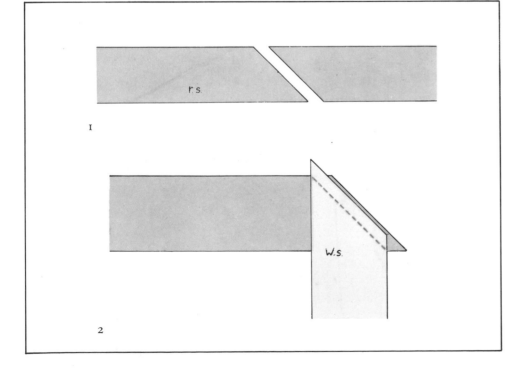

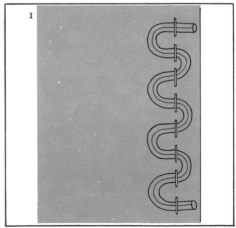

Jersey blouson

It's pretty cool! A blouson in soft jersey to wear with shorts or trousers. You can cover it with a fine layer of netting.

*Techniques included: loop buttonhole.

Measurements

The pattern and instructions given here are to fit size 10, 12, 14 and 16.

Making the pattern

The measurements given on the pattern pieces are for a size 10. For sizes 12, 14 and 16, add to the blouse front and back seams, armhole edges and lower edge and to the sleeve top, side and lower edges, the measurements given in the chart.

Suggested fabrics

Cotton jersey, jersey towelling, woollen jersey. Netting optional.

You will need:

140 cm (54 in) wide fabric, all sizes, 1·40 m (1½ yd) (for narrower widths allow an extra 90 cm (⅞ yd)).
Netting (optional), the same quantity as for fabric.
3 mm (⅛ in) wide elastic, all sizes, 2·10 m (2¼ yd).
Sewing thread to match fabric.
One 6 mm (¼ in) button.
Squared or plain paper for pattern.

Cutting out

A seam allowance of 6 mm (¼ in) has been included on the neck edges and 1·5 cm (⅝ in) on all other seam edges. A lower hem allowance of 3·8 cm (1½ in) and a sleeve hem allowance of 2 cm (¾ in) have also been included.

Note   If netting is being used, cut out the pattern pieces in the main fabric first. Then lay the netting over each piece. Pin and tack securely in place before cutting the netting to the shape. Treat as one fabric when making up.

To make the blouson top

Keyhole neckline 1. Work two rows of stay stitching 3 mm (⅛ in) apart around the keyhole shape of the front neckline, the first row just outside the stitching line. Trim the fabric close to the stitching.

2. Cut a strip of bias fabric the length of the keyhole opening by 2·5 cm (1 in) wide. (A particularly stretchy jersey fabric can be cut on the straight or crosswise grain.) With right sides together, tack and stitch the binding to the opening, taking 6 mm (¼ in) seam allowance.

Fold the binding over the opening edge, turn under 6 mm (¼ in) seam allowance and slipstitch to the line of stitching. Press flat.

Side seams 3. With right sides together, matching notches, tack and stitch the back to the front at the side seams. Work a second row of stitching 1 cm (⅜ in) away from the first and trim seam to stitching or zig-zag stitch raw edges together. Press seams towards back.

Sleeves 4. With right sides together, tack and stitch the underarm seam. Finish seam as for 3. Press seam towards back. Repeat for second sleeve.

5. With right sides together, matching notches and underarm seams, tack and stitch the sleeve into the armhole. Finish seam as described before but do not trim. Press seam towards the sleeve. Repeat for second sleeve.

Neckline 6, 7. Work two rows of

For summer wear make this jersey blouson top. It is loose fitting and has a rouleau trimmed keyhole neckline

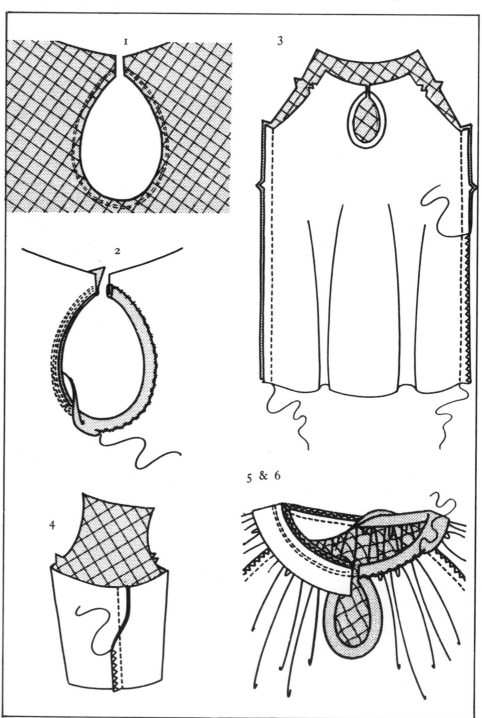

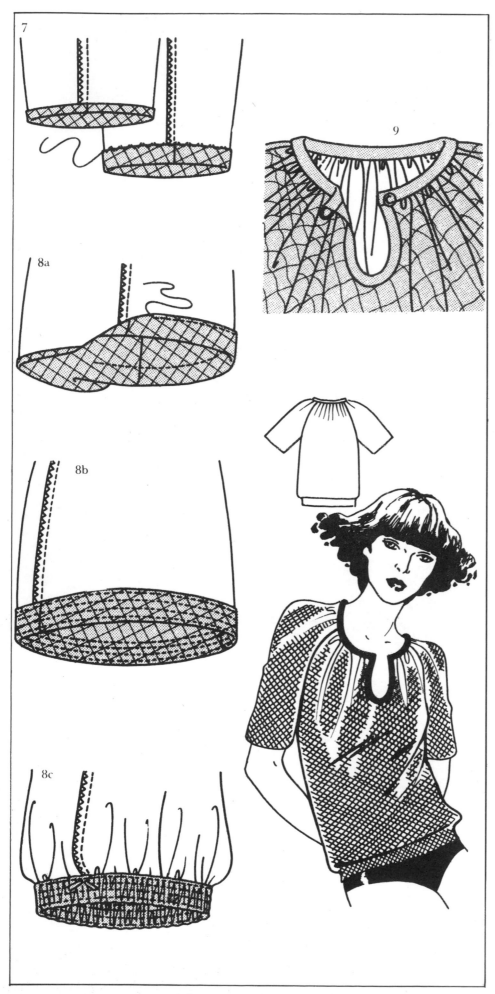

gathering stitches around the neckline. Draw the gathers up to 66 cm (26 in) for sizes 10 and 12, and 71 cm (28 in) for sizes 14 and 16.

Try on the blouse to check that the fullness is in the most becoming position.

Pin and tack a narrow strip of paper to the wrong side along the stitching line of the neck and machine stitch the gathers to this. Cut a strip of binding fabric 2·5 cm (1 in) longer than the neckline and 2·5 cm (1 in) wide.

On the short edges turn 1·3 cm ($\frac{1}{2}$ in) to the wrong side. Tack and stitch the binding to the neckline. Tear away the paper stay. Fold the binding to the wrong side, turn under 6 mm ($\frac{1}{4}$ in) and slipstitch to the stitching line. Press binding flat.

Sleeve hems 7. At the lower edge of the sleeve hem, turn under 6 mm ($\frac{1}{4}$ in) and tack. Turn under a further 1·3 cm ($\frac{1}{2}$ in) and slipstitch the hem to the sleeve. Press flat. Repeat for second sleeve.

Lower hem edge 8. Turn under and tack 6 mm ($\frac{1}{4}$ in) along the lower hem edge. Turn up the hem along the fold line, tack and press.

Machine stitch into place close to the fold, leaving an opening at one side to allow for elastic to be threaded through. Work another row of machine stitching 6 mm ($\frac{1}{4}$ in) below the first. Make a second casing for the elastic by working a further row of machine stitching close to the bottom edge and another row 6 mm ($\frac{1}{4}$ in) above.

Carefully unpick one or two stitches in the side seam of the lower casing to make an opening for the elastic to be threaded through. Cut two lengths of elastic to fit the hips comfortably plus 6 mm ($\frac{1}{4}$ in).

Thread the two lengths of elastic through the casings, overlap ends by 6 mm ($\frac{1}{4}$ in) and sew firmly to secure. Slipstitch the openings to close.

To finish 9. Sew a button to the top of the neck opening on the left side.

*Work a loop on the right side to correspond. Length of loop should be diameter plus thickness of button. Make a foundation loop from a length of thread secured with a backstitch each end. Repeat twice more. Work closely packed blanket or buttonhole stitches along this loop. (A larger version can be made for a belt.)

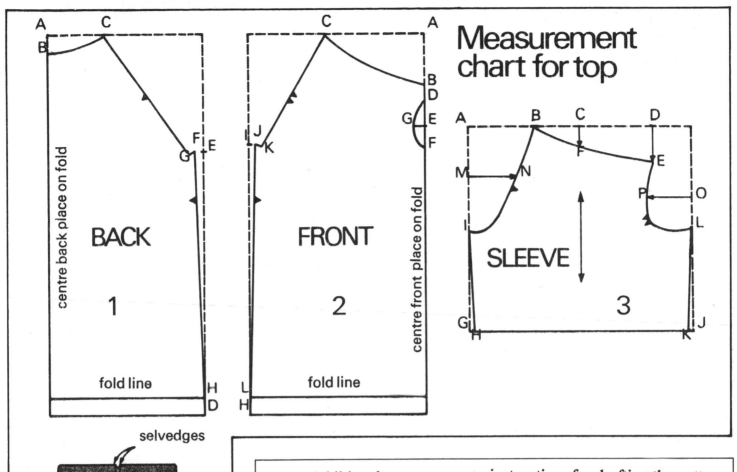

Measurement chart for top

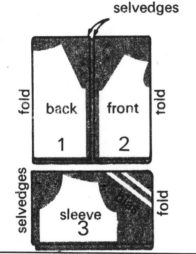

140 cm (54 in) wide fabric with nap. Layout for all sizes.

Additional measurement	**instructions for drafting the pattern**		
Additional measurement chart in centimetres (inches in brackets)			
Size	12	14	16
Blouson front and back			
Side seams (width)	1 ($\frac{3}{8}$)	2·2 ($\frac{7}{8}$)	3·5 ($1\frac{3}{8}$)
Armhole edges	0·6 ($\frac{1}{4}$)	1·3 ($\frac{1}{2}$)	2·5 (1)
Lower edges (length)	1·3 ($\frac{1}{2}$)	2·5 (1)	3·8 ($1\frac{1}{2}$)
Sleeve			
Top edge	0·6 ($\frac{1}{4}$)	1·3 ($\frac{1}{2}$)	2 ($\frac{3}{4}$)
Side edges (width)	0·6 ($\frac{1}{4}$)	1·3 ($\frac{1}{2}$)	2 ($\frac{3}{4}$)
Lower edge (length)	0·6 ($\frac{1}{4}$)	1·3 ($\frac{1}{2}$)	2 ($\frac{3}{4}$)

Measurement instructions for drafting the pattern

Back (diagram 1)
Draw a rectangle measuring 27·5 cm by 66·5 cm (10$\frac{3}{4}$ in by 26$\frac{1}{4}$ in).
A to B = 2·5 cm (1 in)
A to C = 10 cm (4 in)
Connect B to C.
D to E = 46·5 cm (18$\frac{1}{4}$ in)
E to F = 1·3 cm ($\frac{1}{2}$ in)
F to G = 1·3 cm ($\frac{1}{2}$ in)
C to G = 26 cm (10$\frac{1}{4}$ in)
D to H = 3·8 cm (1$\frac{1}{2}$ in) = fold line.
D to H = 3·8 cm (1$\frac{1}{2}$ in) = fold line.

Front (diagram 2)
Draw a rectangle measuring 30·5 cm by 64·8 cm (12 in by 25$\frac{1}{2}$ in)
A to B = 8 cm (3$\frac{1}{4}$ in)
A to C = 17 cm (6$\frac{3}{4}$ in)
Connect B to C.
A to D = 11·5 cm (4$\frac{1}{2}$ in)
A to E = 15 cm (6 in)
A to F = 19·3 cm (7$\frac{1}{2}$ in)
E to G = 2 cm ($\frac{3}{4}$ in)
Connect D to G and G to F.
H to I = 46·5 cm (18$\frac{1}{4}$ in)
I to J = 6 mm ($\frac{1}{4}$ in)
J to K = 1·3 cm ($\frac{1}{2}$ in)
C to K = 23 cm (9 in)
H to L = 3·8 cm (1$\frac{1}{2}$ in) = fold line.

Sleeve (diagram 3)
Draw a rectangle measuring 46 cm by 41·8 cm (18 in by 16$\frac{1}{2}$ in).
A to B = 13 cm (5$\frac{1}{4}$ in)
A to C = 23 cm (9 in)
A to D = 38 cm (15 in)
D to E = 8 cm (3 in)
C to F = 3·8 cm (1$\frac{1}{2}$ in)
Connect B to F, F to E.
G to H = 1·3 cm ($\frac{1}{2}$ in)
H to I = 21 cm (8$\frac{1}{4}$ in)
J to K = 6 mm ($\frac{1}{4}$ in)
K to L = 21 cm (8$\frac{1}{4}$ in)
A to M = 10 cm (4 in)
M to N = 10 cm (4 in)
Connect B to N, N to I.
L to O = 6·5 cm (2$\frac{1}{2}$ in)
O to P = 9 cm (3$\frac{1}{2}$ in)
Connect E to P, P to L.

His 'n' Her Nightshirts

This nightshirt pattern is easily adaptable to make a smart casual shirt for him or a shift dress for her.

Measurements

The woman's nightshirt is in sizes 10, 12, 14 and 16 and the man's version is in sizes 97 cm (38 in), 102 cm (40 in), 107 cm (42 in) and 112 cm (44 in).

Making the pattern

Draw up the required pattern to scale from the graph patterns given here. One square represents 2·5 cm. (1 in) square.

Suggested fabrics

Cotton, fine wool, cotton and wool mixtures.

You will need:

To make the woman's nightshirt:
115 cm (45 in) fabric, all sizes, 3·10 m ($3\frac{3}{8}$ yd).
To make the man's nightshirt:
115 cm (45 in) fabric, all sizes, 3·40 m ($3\frac{5}{8}$ yd).

For either:
Four 1·5 cm ($\frac{5}{8}$ in) buttons.
Sewing thread to match fabric.
Squared paper for pattern.

Cutting out

There are no seam allowances included on the pattern. When cutting out add 1·5 cm ($\frac{5}{8}$ in) to all edges.

To make the nightshirts

Seams and hem 1. With right sides together, tack and stitch the back and front shirt pieces at the side and the shoulder seams. Press the seams open. 2. On the lower edge of the nightshirt make a narrow hem by turning over 3 mm ($\frac{1}{8}$ in) and top-stitch. Trim away the excess fabric close to the stitching. Turn up 3 mm ($\frac{1}{8}$ in) and hem as shown. Press the hem flat. **Sleeves** 3. With right sides together, tack and stitch the sleeve seam. Press the seam open. Work two rows

of gathers around the crown of the sleeve between the notches, and the bottom of the sleeve as shown.
4. With right sides together, tack and stitch the short ends of the cuff to form a circle. Press the seam open.
5. With right sides together, matching seams, pin the sleeve to one edge of the cuff, drawing up the gathers to evenly fit. Tack and stitch. Press the seam down towards the cuff.
6. Turn under the seam allowance on

the raw edge of the cuff and stitch it to the stitching line.
7. With right sides together, matching notches, underarm seams and balance mark to shoulder seam, pin the sleeve to the armhole, drawing up the gathers evenly on the crown. Tack and stitch the sleeve to the armhole with the sleeve uppermost. Press seam towards sleeve. Repeat for second sleeve.

Make these nightshirts in cool cotton.

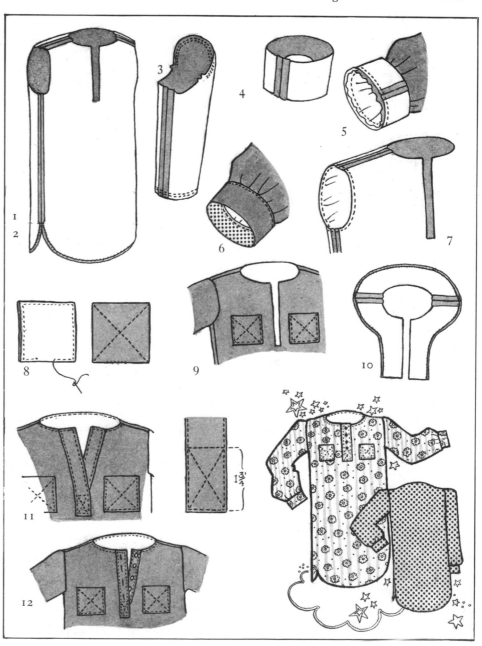

76

Pocket 8. Place the pocket pieces together with right sides facing. Tack and stitch around the three seam edges, leaving an opening to turn the pocket to the right side. Layer the seams and cut across the corners. Turn the pocket right side out and tack around all edges. Slipstitch the opening to close. Press flat. Top-stitch the pocket with diagonal lines as shown. Repeat for second pocket.

9. Tack and stitch the pockets to the nightshirt.

Neck facing and opening 10. With right sides together, tack and stitch the back and front neck facings at the shoulder seams. Press the seams open. Neaten the raw edges of the facing by turning under 3 mm ($\frac{1}{8}$ in) and top-stitch by machine. Press the edges flat. Mark the centre fold on the front facing with tacking stitches.

Tab fastening 11. With right sides together tack and stitch the straight edge of the neck facing to the centre front opening. Layer the seams and press towards the centre front.

With right sides together fold the facing along the tacked fold line. With right sides together, matching shoulder seams, tack and stitch the facing to the nightshirt around the neck edge. Trim and layer the seam allowance, clipping on curves and across corners where necessary.

Turn the facing to the wrong side and tack around the neckline and along the front fold line indicated.

12. On the inside overlap the tab ends, right over left for the woman's shirt and left over right for the man's. Clip 6 mm ($\frac{1}{4}$ in) into inner corners, then with right sides together tack and stitch the lower edges of the tab to the lower end of the opening.

Top-stitch around the neck and all round each tab 1 cm ($\frac{3}{8}$ in) in from the edge. Stitch across the base of both tabs as shown.

Work four buttonholes at equally spaced intervals down the centre of the front tab. Sew buttons centrally in position on the undertab to close.

Note

Short sleeves If short sleeves are required, cut down the sleeve pattern to 12·5 cm (5 in) plus 1·5 cm ($\frac{5}{8}$ in) hem below the underarm.

Finish the sleeve hem as explained in step 2.

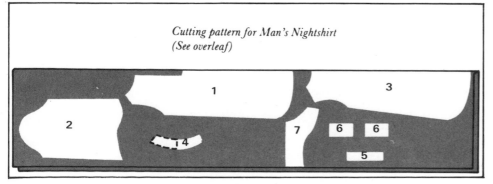

Cutting pattern for Man's Nightshirt (See overleaf)

Graph pattern for men's nightshirt

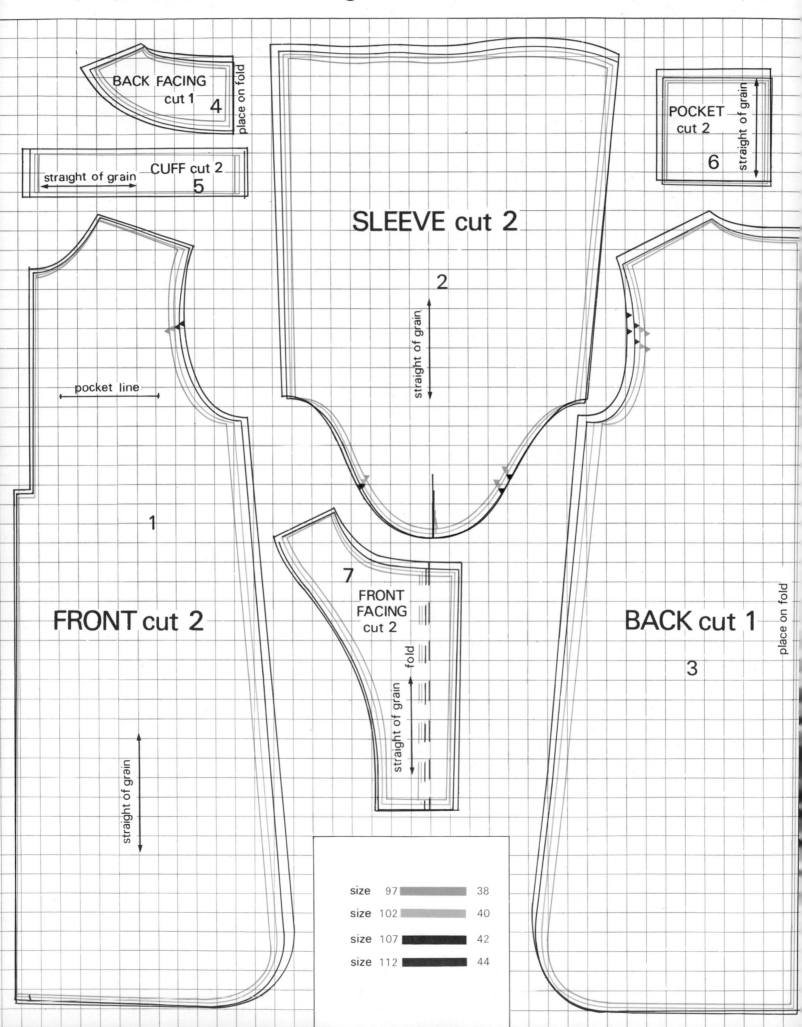

BACK FACING
cut 1
4
place on fold

CUFF cut 2
5
straight of grain

POCKET
cut 2
6
straight of grain

SLEEVE cut 2
2
straight of grain

pocket line

1

FRONT cut 2
straight of grain

7

FRONT
FACING
cut 2
fold
straight of grain

BACK cut 1
3
place on fold

size	97		38
size	102		40
size	107		42
size	112		44

Graph pattern for women's nightshirt

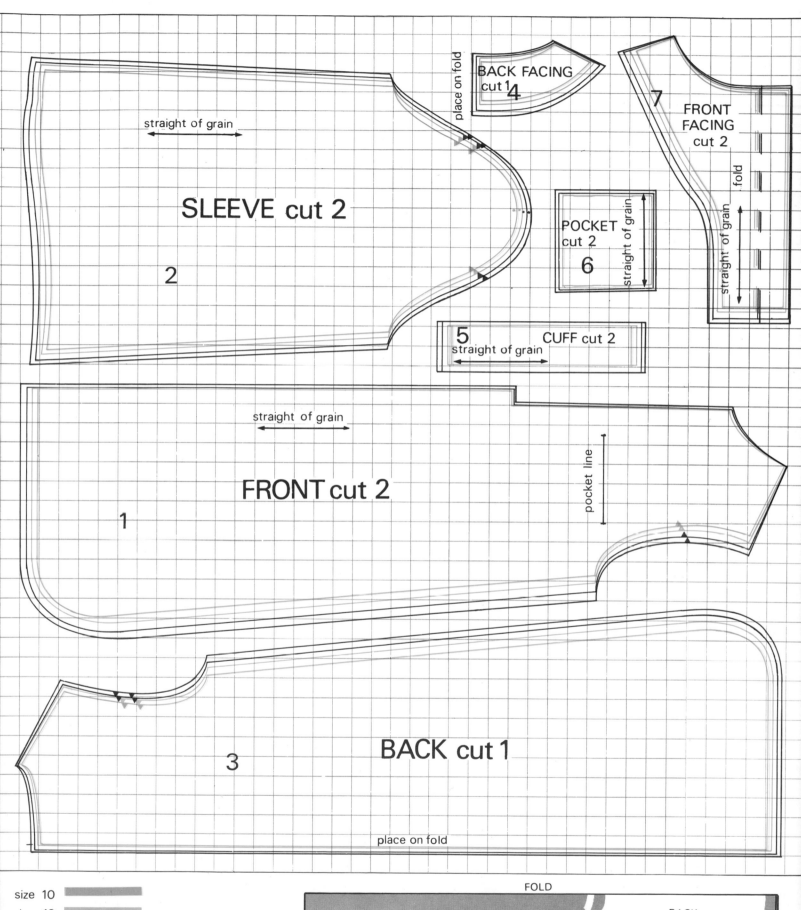

straight of grain

SLEEVE cut 2

2

place on fold

BACK FACING
cut 1 4

7

FRONT
FACING
cut 2

fold

straight of grain

straight of grain

POCKET
cut 2
6

5   CUFF cut 2
straight of grain

straight of grain

FRONT cut 2

1

pocket line

BACK cut 1

3

place on fold

size 10
size 12
size 14
size 16

each square = 1 in (2.5 cm) sq

seam allowance not included

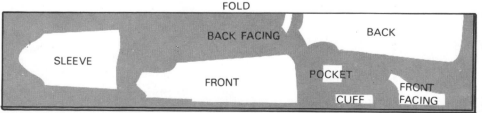

FOLD

BACK FACING

BACK

SLEEVE

FRONT

POCKET

CUFF

FRONT
FACING

SELVEDGES

*115 cm (45 in) wide fabric without
nap. Layout for all sizes.*

Summer Separates

A raglan-sleeved blouse with open-or-closed collar and matching button-through skirt make this an ideal summer outfit which splits into useful separates. Make top and skirt to match or use contrasting or mix and match fabrics.

*Techniques included: raglan sleeves, gathered pockets, tie belt.

Measurements
The pattern is given in women's sizes 10, 12, 14 and 16. Each size is indicated on the graph pattern by a cutting line of a different colour.

Making the pattern
Draw up the pattern to scale from the graph pattern given here. One square represents 2·5 cm (1 in) square.

Suggested fabrics
Cotton mixtures, mix and match cottons, gingham, seersucker.

You will need:
To make the two-piece:
90 cm (36 in) wide fabric, all sizes, 5·20 m (5⅝ yd) or,
115 cm (45 in) wide fabric, all sizes, 4·80 m (5¼ yd).
90 cm (36 in) wide woven interfacing, all sizes, 1 m (1 yd).
Twelve 1 cm (⅜ in) buttons.

To make the blouse:
90 cm (36 in) wide fabric, all sizes,

3 m ($3\frac{1}{4}$ yd) or,
115 cm (45 in) wide fabric, all sizes,
2·30 m ($2\frac{1}{2}$ yd).

To make the skirt:
90 cm (36 in) wide fabric, all sizes,
2·70 m ($2\frac{7}{8}$ yd) or,
115 cm (45 in) wide fabric, all sizes,
2·50 m ($2\frac{3}{4}$ yd).
Two hooks and eyes.
Sewing thread to match fabric.
Squared paper for pattern.

Cutting out

A seam allowance of 1·5 cm ($\frac{5}{8}$ in) has
been allowed on all seam edges and a
hem allowance of 6·5 cm ($2\frac{5}{8}$ in).

To make the blouse
Front and back, *raglan sleeves

1. With right sides together, matching
notches, tack and stitch shoulder darts
of sleeves. Press darts open.

2. With right sides together, matching
notches, tack and stitch centre back
seam. Press seam open.

3. With right sides together, matching
notches and neck edges, tack and
stitch front and back sleeve to front
and back bodices, having the sleeve
uppermost. Ease in fullness between
notches. Press seams towards sleeve.
Repeat for second sleeve.
To neaten outer edge of front facing,
turn under 6 mm ($\frac{1}{4}$ in) and machine
stitch.

4. Tack interfacing to wrong side of
front bodice and neck edge. Catchstitch interfacing to fold line.

5. With right sides together, matching
notches, tack and stitch the side seams
and underarm seams. Clip curves and
press seams open.

Collar
6. Tack interfacing to wrong
side of one collar piece. With right
sides together, matching centre backs
and circles at centre fronts, tack and
stitch collar facing to collar round
outer edge to centre fronts. Trim interfacing close to stitching. Layer
seam and cut across corners. Turn
through to right side, tack close to
stitched edges and press flat.

7. With right sides together, matching
centre backs, circles to shoulder darts,
notches and circles at centre front,
pin and tack undercollar and inter-

*A loose fitting top and button-down
skirt make this outfit the perfect
choice for summer holiday wear.*

facing to back neck edge from shoulder to shoulder and stitch. Pin and tack the under and top collar to the front neck edge from shoulder to centre fronts as shown. With right sides together, matching notches, fold front facing over the collar to shoulder and tack.

Stitch from shoulders to front edges through all thicknesses.

Trim interfacing close to stitching. Layer seam, clip curves and cut across corners. Turn facing to inside and tack along folded edge.

8. On the inside, clip back neck seam allowance to circle at shoulder. Press seam towards collar.

9. Turn under 1·5 cm ($\frac{5}{8}$ in) seam allowance on the top collar and slipstitch to stitching line as shown. Turn under seam allowance of facing and catchstitch to shoulder dart.

Sleeve hems 10. Neaten the lower edge of the sleeve by overcasting by hand or machine. Turn up hem allowance and tack along folded edge. Sew hem to sleeve using invisible hemming stitch.

Repeat for second sleeve hem.

Blouse hem 11. Turn out the front facing at lower edge. Turn 6 mm ($\frac{1}{4}$ in) to inside round lower edge and

90cm (36in) wide fabric with nap. Layout for all sizes.

90cm (36in) wide woven interface for all sizes.

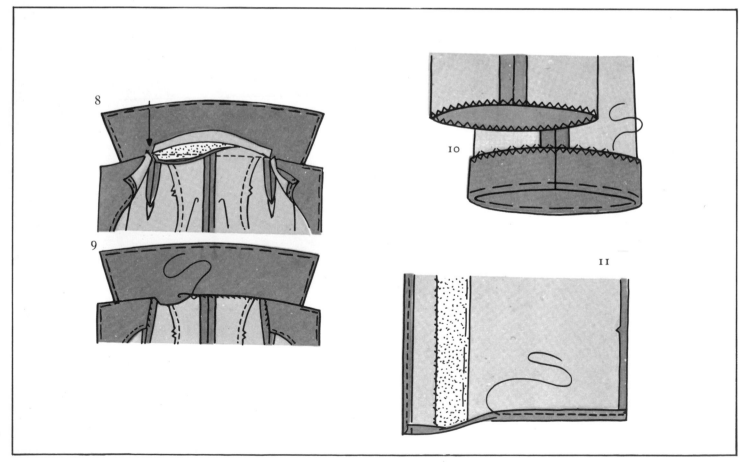

Open fabric
to cut

115cm (44/45in) wide fabric with nap. Layout for all sizes.

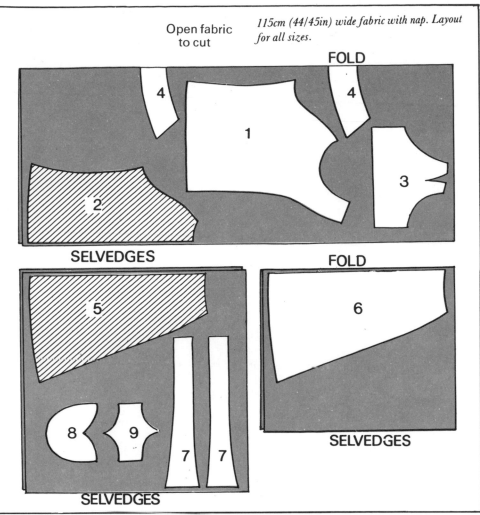

then a further 1 cm ($\frac{3}{8}$ in). Tack and press flat.

Fold facing to inside. Top-stitch 6 mm ($\frac{1}{4}$ in) in from lower edge, front edge and collar as shown.

To finish 12. Make worked or machine buttonholes on right front as indicated on pattern. Sew buttons to left front to correspond with button-holes.

To make the skirt

Front facing and side seams 13. Tack interfacing to wrong side of skirt fronts. Catchstitch to fold line. To neaten raw edge of facing, turn under 6 mm ($\frac{1}{4}$ in) and machine stitch. Turn facing to inside and tack along folded edge.

With right sides together, matching notches, tack and stitch side seams. Press seams open.

*Gathered pockets 14. Stay stitch inner corner of pocket. Work two rows of gathering stitches along top edge of pocket. Draw up gathers until pocket fits welt as shown.

15. With right sides together, tack and stitch pocket welt to pocket. Trim and press seam towards welt.

16. With right sides together, match-

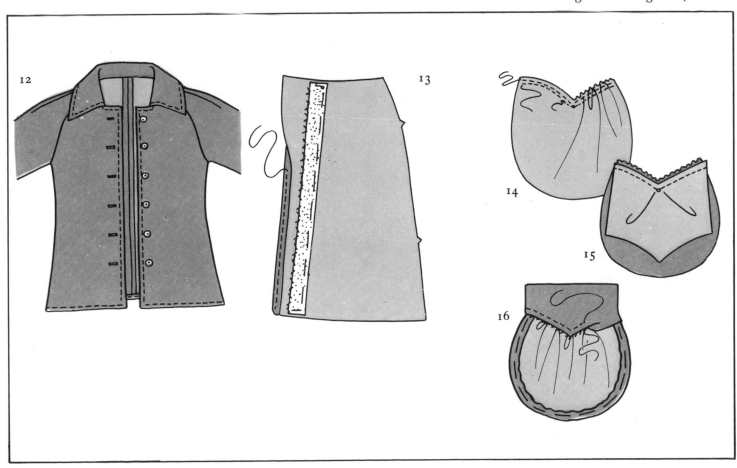

Graph pattern for separates

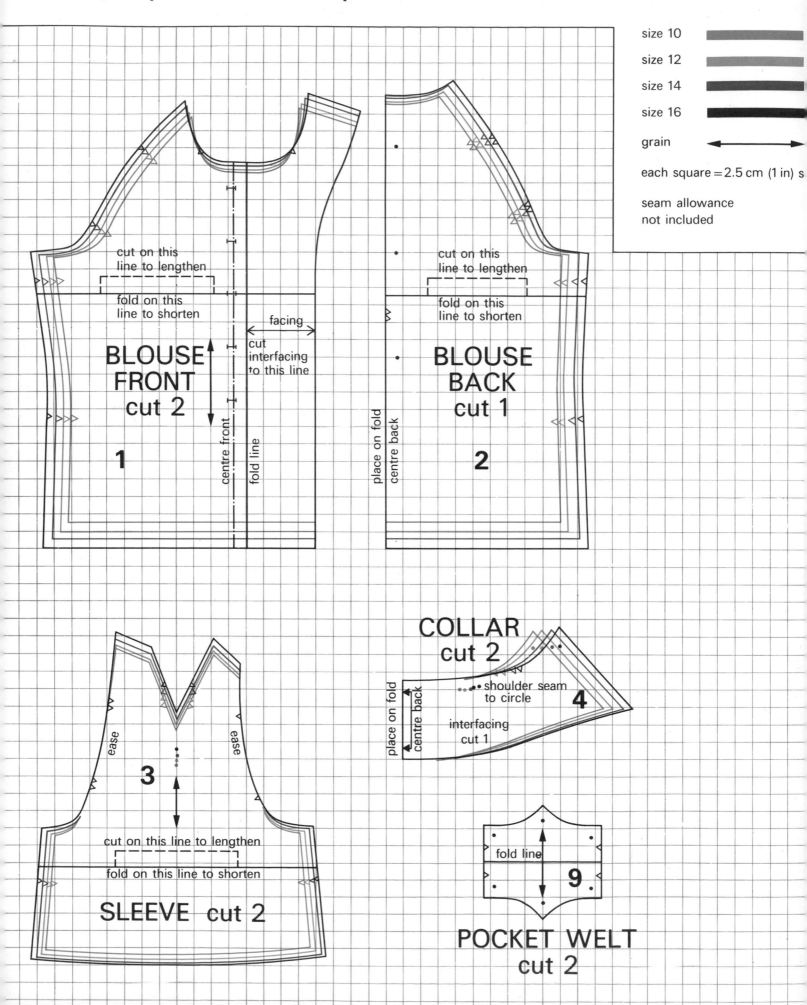

size 10
size 12
size 14
size 16

grain

each square = 2.5 cm (1 in) s

seam allowance
not included

cut on this
line to lengthen

fold on this
line to shorten

facing

cut
interfacing
to this line

BLOUSE
FRONT
cut 2

centre front

fold line

1

cut on this
line to lengthen

fold on this
line to shorten

BLOUSE
BACK
cut 1

place on fold
centre back

2

ease

ease

3

cut on this line to lengthen

fold on this line to shorten

SLEEVE cut 2

COLLAR
cut 2

place on fold
centre back

shoulder seam
to circle

interfacing
cut 1

4

fold line

9

POCKET WELT
cut 2

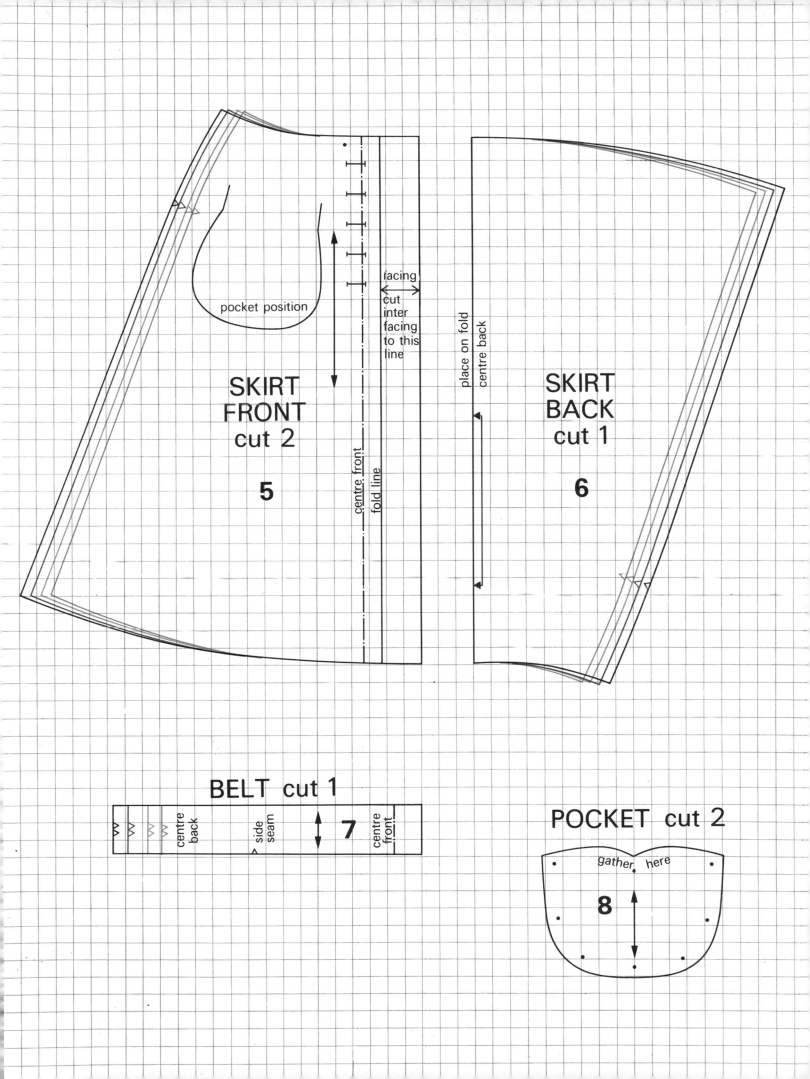

pocket position

SKIRT
FRONT
cut 2

5

facing

cut
inter
facing
to this
line

centre front

fold line

place on fold

centre back

SKIRT
BACK
cut 1

6

BELT cut 1

centre
back

side
seam

7

centre
front

POCKET cut 2

gather here

8

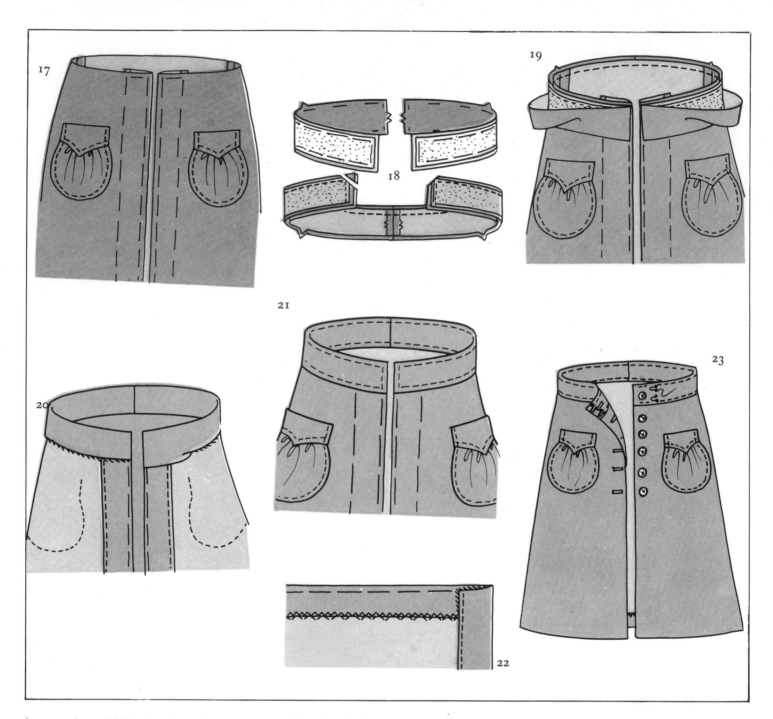

ing notches, fold welt along fold line
Tack and stitch outer edges of welt.
Trim seam and cut across corners.
Turn through to right side. Turn
under seam allowance of welt facing
and slipstitch to stitching line. On
right side, top-stitch 6 mm ($\frac{1}{4}$ in)
away from inner shaped seam of welt
as shown. Turn under seam allowance
round outer edge of pocket and tack.
Repeat for second pocket.

17. Tack pockets in positions indicated on pattern and top-stitch 6 mm
($\frac{1}{4}$ in) in from outer edges of pockets as
shown.

Waistband 18. Tack interfacing to
wrong sides of waistband pieces. With
right sides together, matching notches,

tack and stitch centre back seams of
waistband and waistband facing. Press
seams open. With right sides together,
tack and stitch waistband facing to
waistband along un-notched edge and
ends. Trim interfacing to stitching
line, layer seam and cut across corners.
Turn through to right side. Tack
along stitched edges and press flat.

19. With right sides together, matching centre backs, notches to side seams
and centre fronts, tack and stitch
waistband to skirt. Trim interfacing
close to stitching and layer seam
allowance. Press seam towards waistband.

20. On the inside, turn under seam
allowance and slipstitch to stitching

line, enclosing all thicknesses.

21. On the outside, top-stitch round
all edges of waistband.

Skirt hem 22. Try on skirt and mark
the hem. Turn out front facing at lower
edge. Trim hem allowance to an even
width, turn up hem and tack close to
folded edge. Neaten raw edge by hand
or machine overcasting. Sew the hem
to the skirt using invisible hemming
stitch. Turn facing to inside and slipstitch to hem as shown. Press flat.

To finish 23. Make worked or
machine buttonholes on right front.
Sew buttons to left front to correspond
with buttonholes.

Sew hooks and eyes to waistband as
shown.

Classic Shirt

A fashionable wardrobe is never complete if it lacks a shirt that can be worn for dress or casual occasions. This timeless style changes its look with the way you wear it. This version, in supple Tootal crêpon, would look just as good in fine cotton, silk or wool. To ring the changes you could make it up minus its collar, finishing the neck with the collar band on its own.

*Techniques included: collar and collar band, sleeve opening with wrap extension.

Measurements
The pattern is given in women's sizes 10, 12, 14 and 16. Each size is indicated on the graph pattern by a cutting line of a different colour.

Making the pattern
Draw up the pattern to scale from the graph pattern given here. One square represents 2·5 cm (1 in) square.

Suggested fabrics
Crêpon, seersucker, voile, gingham, silk, wool and cotton mixtures.

You will need:
90 cm (36 in) fabric with nap, all sizes, 3·10 m (3⅜ yd).
90 cm (36 in) woven interfacing, all sizes, 40 cm (⅜ yd).
Eight 1 cm (⅜ in) buttons.
Sewing thread to match fabric.
Squared paper for pattern.

Cutting out
No seam allowance is included on the pattern so add 1·5 cm (⅝ in) for seam and hem allowances.

To make the shirt
Facings 1. Neaten the outer edges of the facings. With right sides together pin, tack and stitch the facings to the front edges. Do not stitch them along the neck and hem edges. Turn the facings to the inside, edge tack and press.

Shoulder and side seams 2. Tack and stitch underarm darts on each front section. Press. Tack and stitch the shoulder seams, making flat fell seams stitched on the outside of the shirt. Tack and stitch the side seams as far as circle on pattern so that the folded edge of the flat fell seam lies towards the front.

Hemming the tails 3. Snip into the front side seam allowance at the bottom of the seams and trim the front seam allowance for flat fell seaming.
Fold the back seam allowance over the trimmed front seam. Pin and tack.
Pin and tack the hem on the front and back to the wrong side. Where the side seam and front hem merge, pin the folded edge of the back hem in line with the side seam. Machine stitch both hems, continuing the stitching into the folded flat fell seam edge so that you stitch the hem and flat fell side seam in one operation.
Stitch across the top of the hem to hold it firmly in place.

*Collar and collar band 4. Pin and tack interfacing to wrong side of one collar piece and to one collar band piece. The interfacing should go on the piece that will be uppermost.
5. Place the top (interfaced) and under collar pieces together, with right sides facing. Pin, tack and stitch along the front edges and the upper curved seam. Trim the seam allowance to 6 mm (¼ in), trim across the corners and turn to the right side. Tack along the stitched edges and press. Top-stitch 6 mm (¼ in) from the edge if you wish.
Matching all markings, place the collar between the inner and outer collar band pieces and stitch with right sides together, leaving the lower edge open.
6. Trim the seam allowance on the stitched edges of the collar band to 6 mm (¼ in) and turn to the right side. Tack along the stitched edges and press.

Stitching on the collar 7. Tack the front facing to the shirt along the neckline. Pin the inner collar band along the inside of the neckline with the raw edges level. Tack, stitch and trim seam allowance.
Turn under the seam allowance on the outer collar band, lay it over the stitching line to cover the machine stitches. Slipstitch in place neatly.

*Sleeve openings with wrap extensions and sleeve seams 8. Cut a straight strip of fabric, 4 by 20 cm (1½ by 8 in). Cut the sleeve opening along the marked line. Pin and tack the fabric strip along the opening with the right side of the strip to the wrong side of the sleeve. Stitch along the opening taking 6 mm (¼ in) seam allowance on the facing but tapering towards the point. At the point pivot the work on the needle, ease the fold to the back of the needle and stitch along the other side. Press the seam towards the strip.
Fold in the long raw edge of the strip, pin and tack it over the seam on the outside of the sleeve and top-stitch. Press the wrap to the inside of the sleeve. Repeat for second sleeve. Pin, tack and stitch the sleeve seams with flat fell seams.
Work two rows of gathering stitches round the lower edge of each sleeve.

Cuffs 9. Pin and tack interfacing to the wrong side of each cuff. Catch-stitch to fold line.
With right sides facing, fold cuff lengthwise and stitch each side up to the seam allowance at the top edge. Trim the seam allowance and turn to the right side. Edge tack and press.
10. With right sides together, pin the cuff to lower end of sleeve, so that interfaced half will be the upper half of the cuff. Pull up the gathers on sleeve until they fit the cuff. Tack, distributing the gathers evenly and stitch. Trim interfacing close to the stitching. Trim seam and press towards cuff.
11. Turn under the remaining raw edge on cuff, pin and slipstitch over the seam on the inside. Attach second cuff in the same way. Top-stitch cuffs 6 mm (¼ in) from the edge if you wish.

Setting in the sleeves 12. Make two rows of running stitches around the top of each sleeve, one on each side of the seam line. Carefully draw up the ease, which is approximately 4 cm (1½ in), and wind the gathering threads on to a pin. Shrink in the fullness, using a sleeve board, steam will help if the fabric does not mark.
13. Pin sleeves into armholes, right sides facing, matching seams and balance marks. Any fullness on the sleeves should be evenly distributed. Tack in the sleeves and stitch. Press seams towards the shirt and trim for flat fell seaming. Complete flat fell seams and press.

To finish 14. Make hand- or machine-worked buttonholes in positions marked on front of shirt, also making one buttonhole on collar band and on each cuff. Sew on buttons to correspond.

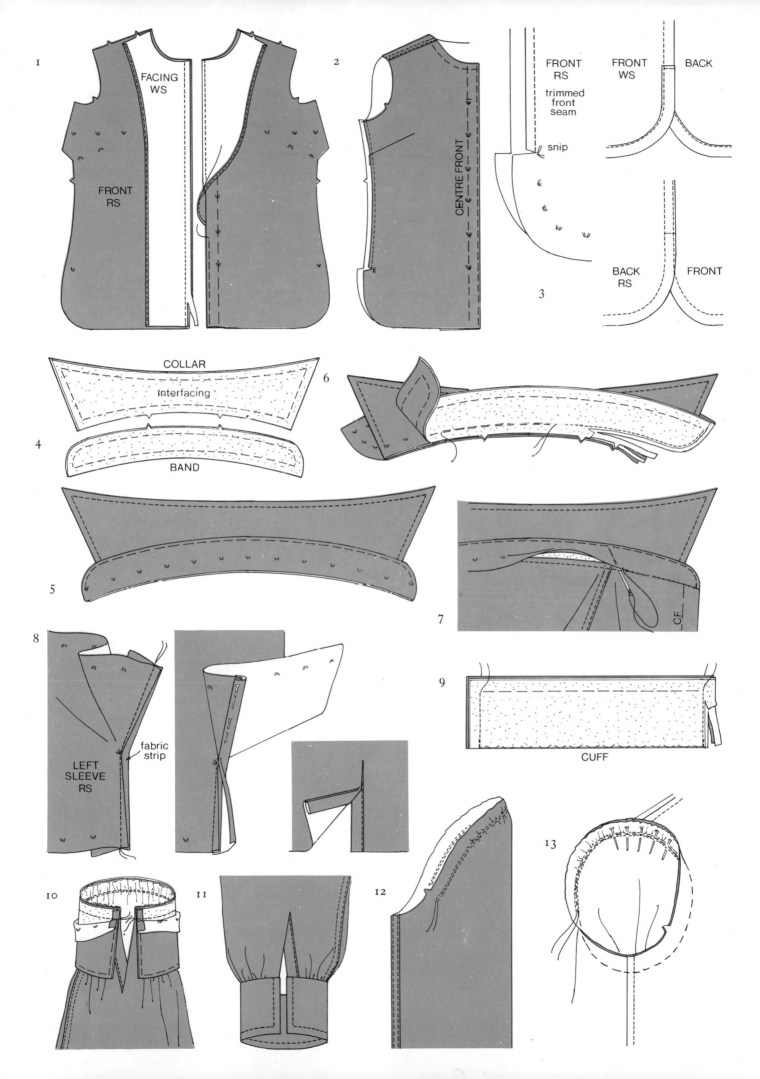

1

FACING
WS

FRONT
RS

2

CENTRE FRONT

3

FRONT
RS

trimmed
front
seam

snip

FRONT
WS

BACK

BACK
RS

FRONT

4

COLLAR

Interfacing

BAND

6

5

7

CF

8

LEFT
SLEEVE
RS

fabric
strip

9

CUFF

10

11

12

13

Graph pattern for shirt

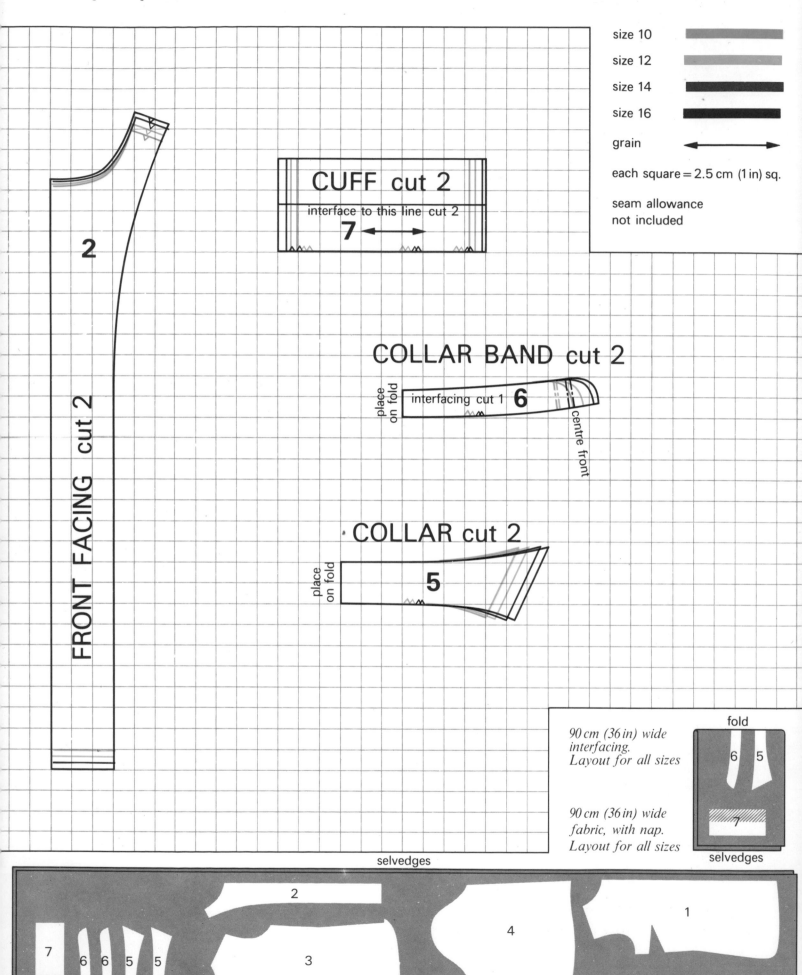

size 10

size 12

size 14

size 16

grain

each square = 2.5 cm (1 in) sq.

seam allowance
not included

CUFF cut 2

interface to this line cut 2

7

2

FRONT FACING cut 2

COLLAR BAND cut 2

place on fold

interfacing cut 1 **6**

centre front

COLLAR cut 2

place on fold

5

90 cm (36 in) wide
interfacing.
Layout for all sizes

90 cm (36 in) wide
fabric, with nap.
Layout for all sizes

fold

6 5

7

selvedges

selvedges

2

1

4

7   6 6 5 5   3

fold

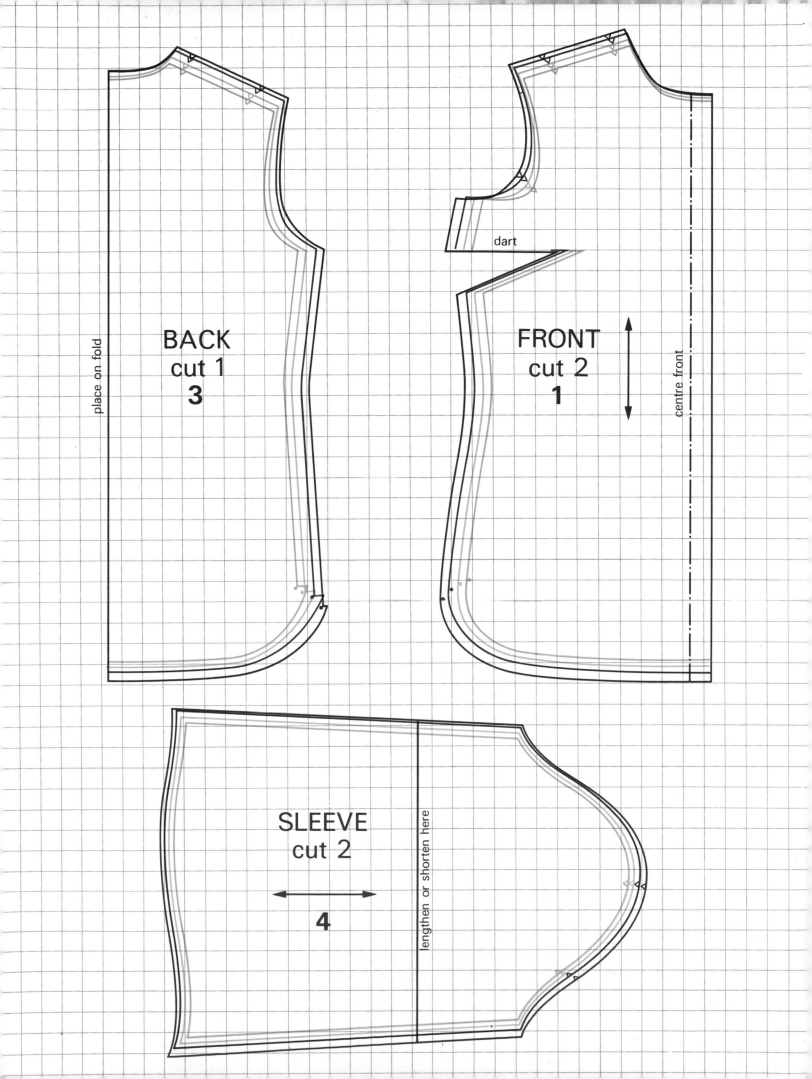

BACK
cut 1
3

place on fold

FRONT
cut 2
1

dart

centre front

SLEEVE
cut 2

4

lengthen or shorten here

Knife-pleated Skirt

More basic know-how
Working with pleats

Pleats are folds of fabric which provide controlled fullness in certain parts of a garment. They can be placed either singly or in a series, and can be pressed flat or left unpressed, as the style of the garment dictates. Pressed pleats give a smooth, slimming line to a garment and unpressed pleats a softer, fuller shape.

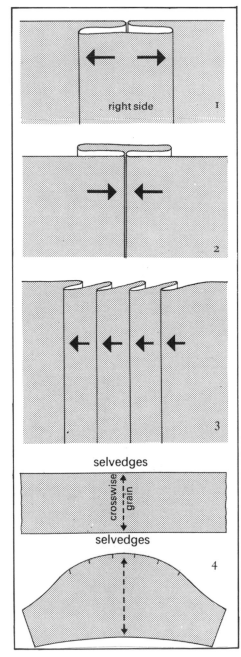

1. *Box pleats.* 2. *Inverted pleats.*
3. *Knife pleats.* 4. *Unpressed pleats (for sleeve crown).* 5. *Making a contrast fabric inverted pleat.*
6. *Top-stitching pleats.*

Fabrics

The type of fabric dictates how the pleats hang, so choose it carefully. Consider the grain and check the layout given with the pattern, remembering that pleats on the lengthwise grain fall well, while those on the crosswise grain tend to bunch out.

Never try to save fabric by cutting one skirt pattern piece on the lengthwise grain and the other on the crosswise grain of the fabric – the effect can be disastrous.

Any firmly woven fabric such as wool, gaberdine or linen will hold a pleat well, but pleats in loosely woven fabrics, knits and silk look better if they are top-stitched.

Patterns for pleated skirts should be bought by the hip measurement and patterns with pleated bodices by the bust measurement. If any alteration in width is required, distribute it evenly throughout all the pleats to keep them uniform. When tapering

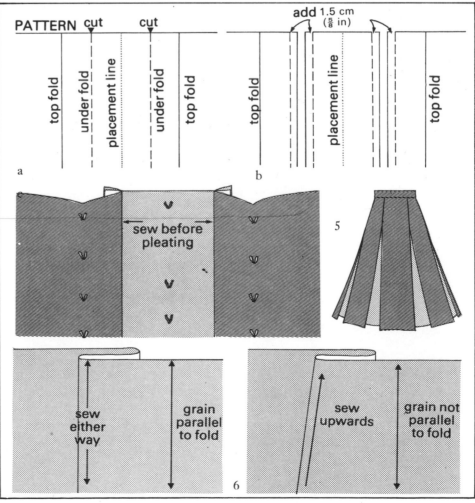

93

pleats to fit the waistline, keep the top fold on the same grain and make any adjustment to the under fold, remembering to distribute alterations evenly.

Types of pleat

Box pleats These are made by making two equal folds and turning them away from each other, the under folds meeting in the centre beneath the pleat (fig. 1).

Inverted pleats Inverted pleats are the reverse of box pleats. Two folds of equal depth are turned towards each other to meet at the centre, the fullness lying underneath (fig. 2).

Knife pleats These are narrow folds all running in the same direction (fig. 3).

Unpressed pleats Unpressed pleats can be folded in the same way as pressed pleats, but are left to hang free and take their own line.

If a bunchy effect is required for a particular design, the fabric should be cut on the crosswise grain. Sometimes a pleated sleeve crown is better cut this way (fig. 4).
A bunchy effect is not generally suitable for unpressed pleats on a skirt, so cut on the lengthwise grain.

Contrast fabric inverted pleat Inverted pleat underlays can look attractive in a contrast fabric. If the pattern does not have a separate piece for the underlay, adjust it as follows.
Cut the pattern on the under fold line and add 1·5 cm ($\frac{5}{8}$ in) turning to all cut edges.
Sew the contrast fabric to the under fold line before making the pleat (fig. 5).

Top-stitching pleats It is possible to make a fashion feature of top-stitched pleats. Tack the pleats before stitching. A bold effect is required, so use a large needle in the sewing

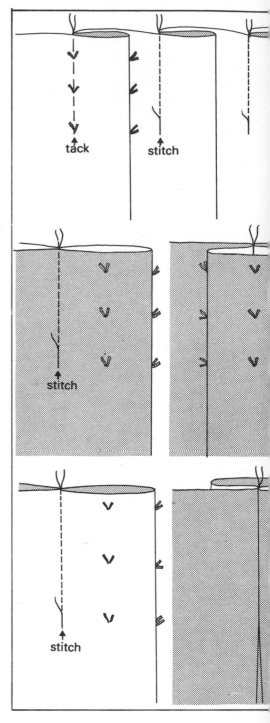

7. *Marking pleats.* 8. *Pinning pleats.* 9. *Tacking pleat folds.* 10. *Stitching knife pleats.* 11. *Stitching box pleats.* 12. *Stitching inverted pleats.* 13. *To reduce bulk on inverted pleats, cut away fabric as shown.* 14. *To hem a pleated skirt, snip the seam as shown and turn up hem to this depth.*

machine, set the machine to the longest stitch and use buttonhole twist for both threads.
Before working the top-stitching on a garment, take a spare piece of the fabric, make some pleats and practise the stitches, adjusting the tension

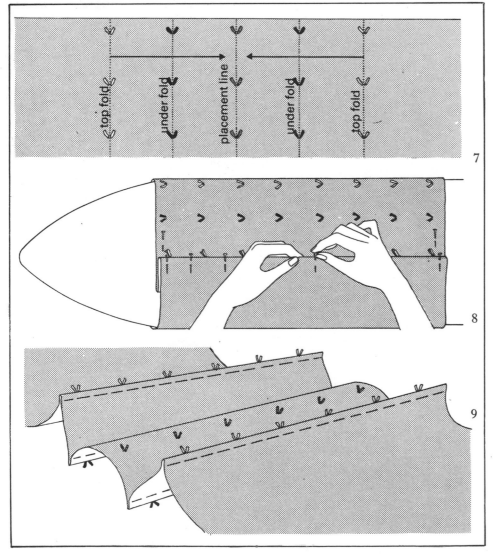

KNIFE
PLEATS

10

BOX
PLEATS

11

INVERTED
PLEAT

12

The best stage at which to work the top-stitching is before the skirt is sewn on to the waistband or the bodice, and after the hemline is finished.

The general construction of pleats
All pleats should be shaped with precision, so always transfer the pattern markings accurately, using different coloured tailor's tacks for the top and under folds and for the placement line (fig. 7). Lay the fabric on a flat surface. An ironing board is ideal, as the fabric can be pinned to the cover when the initial folding takes place. Pin each pleat at the upper and lower ends and then along the length, keeping it free from the under layer (fig. 8).

Beginning at the lower edge, tack the pleat folds on the right side, then turn the fabric over and tack the folds on

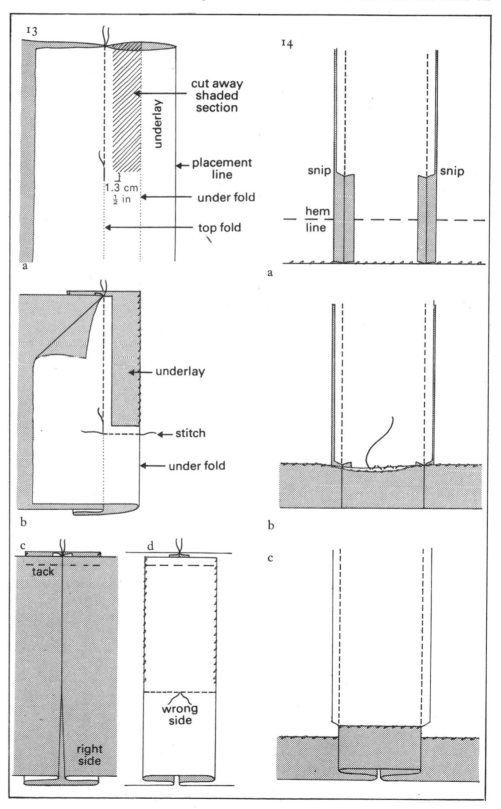

until the desired effect is achieved.
Fine fabrics which do not hold a pleat well are best top-stitched along both top and under folds for the entire length of the pleat.

As long as the pleat is on the straight grain of the fabric. it can be stitched either from the top or the bottom. If the grain is not straight it is better to stitch from the bottom of the pleat upwards to avoid stretching the fabric (fig. 6).

If the fabric is stretched it will create a slight fullness at the hem which means that the pleat will not hang straight.

the wrong side (fig. 9). Tack down any which are to be top-stitched. Tack across pleats at waistline and tack up the garment for fitting.

Fitting When the skirt is tacked up, try it on to make sure that the pleats hang straight. If the skirt is tight over the hips or stomach, adjust each pleat under fold until it hangs correctly. However, the problem should not arise if the pattern has been adjusted correctly before cutting out.
If the pleats spring open at the hem, raise the waistline. Pin the skirt to a length of tape fastened round the waist, and raise the fabric until the pleats hang straight. Re-pin tape to new waistline and adjust the under folds evenly.
If the pleats overlap at the hem, lower the waist slightly in the same way and adjust the pleat under folds evenly.

Finishing the pleats When finishing pleats always work with the front and back of the skirt separated. Mark any fitting alterations before untacking the side seams and starting work on the pleats.
Stitch knife pleats on the wrong side for a smooth effect, making sure to finish them securely at the lower end (fig. 10). Stitch box pleats on the right side for desired length and press pleat flat (fig. 11). Stitch inverted pleats on the wrong side and press flat (fig. 12). If inverted pleats are being made in a heavy fabric, a section of the under fold can be cut away as shown, to reduce bulk (figs. 13a–d).
Machine stitch pleat to the length required and cut away half the under pleat as shown. Neaten the outside raw edge and machine stitch across each side of the pleat, keeping the fold away from the background fabric. Tack across the top of the pleat.

Hemming pleated skirts Run a line of tacking stitches along the hemline. Trim the hem evenly and oversew the raw edge. Measure the hem depth above the hemline and snip seams at this point. Press the seam flat above the snip and open below it (fig. 14). Slipstitch hem, re-tack pleats and press. (also see Hems.)

Knife pleated skirt

A skirt which flatters any figure, it has

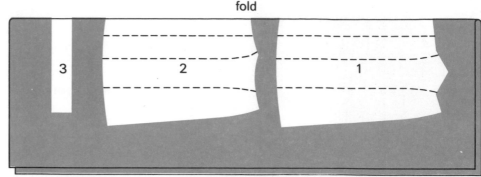

fold

selvedges

slim elegant lines with roomy knife pleats at the back and front to give ease of movement.

Measurements
The pattern is given in women's sizes 10, 12, 14 and 16. Each size is indicated on the graph pattern by a cutting line of a different colour.

Making the pattern
Draw up the pattern to scale from the graph pattern given here. One square represents 2·5 cm (1 in) square.

Suggested fabrics
Wool, worsted, barathea, gaberdine, linen, firmly woven tweed.

You will need:
140 cm (54 in) wide fabric, all sizes, 1·80 m (2 yd)
1 m (1 yd) 2·5 cm (1 in) wide petersham.
18 cm (7 in) zip fastener.
Two hooks and eyes.
Sewing thread to match fabric.
Squared paper for pattern.

Cutting out
No seam allowance is included on the pattern so add 1·5 cm ($\frac{5}{8}$ in) for seams, but add a 2 cm ($\frac{3}{4}$ in) allowance at the waist edge and a 2·5 cm seam allowance for zip fasteners on skirt back. Add 6·5 cm (2½ in) hem allowance.

To make the skirt
Preparing the pleats 1. Mark the pleat lines on the back and front skirt sections with tailor's tacks. Connect the balance marks with horizontal lines of thread tacking.
2. Lay the pleats from right to left on the outside of the skirt. Fold, pin and tack them securely down the edge.

Press lightly.
With the right sides facing, raw edges level pin and tack the side seams.
Try on the skirt to check the fit (see Basic pattern alterations). When you have made any necessary adjustments, fit the skirt again with the tacking at the pleat hems removed. The pleats should hang straight and closed, not jutting forward and pulling open. If you see the pleats spreading, fan-like towards the side seams, lift the skirt and pleats into the waist until the pleats hang straight. If one pleat is hanging badly this will need to be pulled up from the inside.
Top-stitch each pleat 2 mm ($\frac{1}{16}$ in) from the edge as far as the hipline.
Seams and zip fastener 3. Stitch all the seams, starting at the top and working downwards. Leave the left side seam open from the circle to the waist edge for inserting the zip fastener. Insert the zip fastener using the concealed method (see Zip fasteners).
Waistband 4. Pin, tack and sew the waistband to the skirt, making sure that all the pleats are caught flat and firmly into the stitching line. Trim and press the seam upwards. Apply the petersham stiffening and finish the waistband (see Waistbands and belts). Stitch on hooks and eyes.

Hem 5. Try on the skirt to check the length, mark and stitch the hem (see Hems and also Working with pleats). When turning up the hem, make the hem at the inner crease of the pleat about 6 mm (¼ in) shorter, this prevents the inside of the pleat from showing on the right side.
Give pleats a final pressing, carefully press under the pleats on the wrong side to remove any impressions on the fabric.

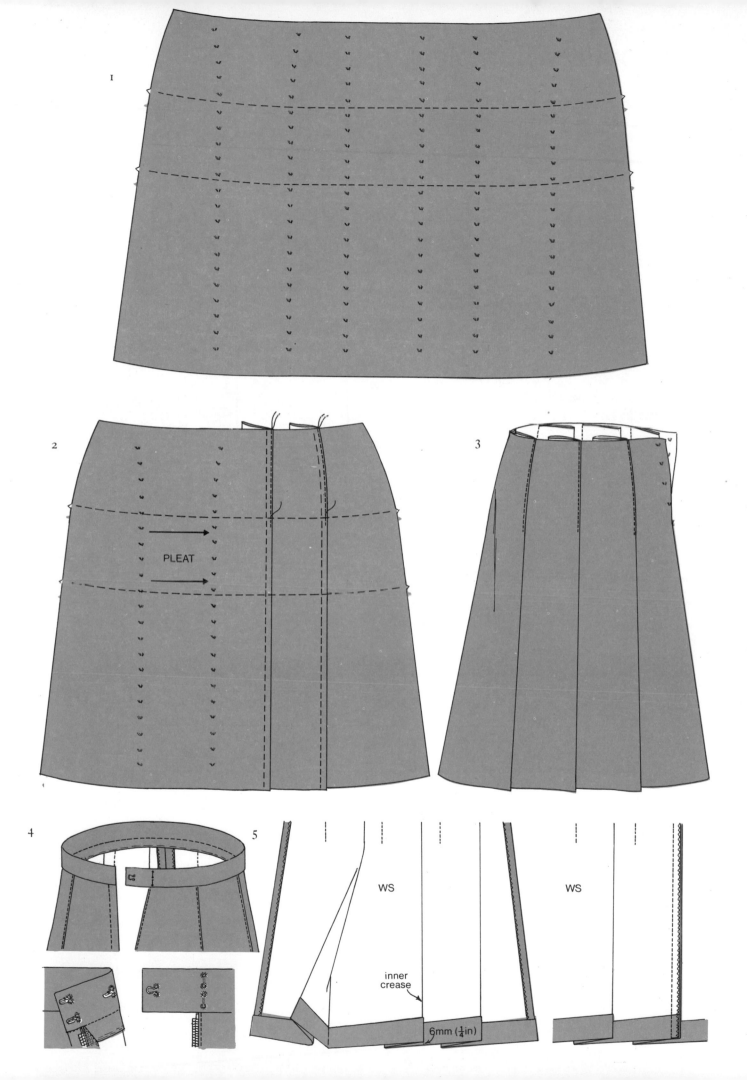

I

2

PLEAT

3

4

5

WS

WS

inner
crease

6mm (¼in)

Graph pattern for pleated skirt

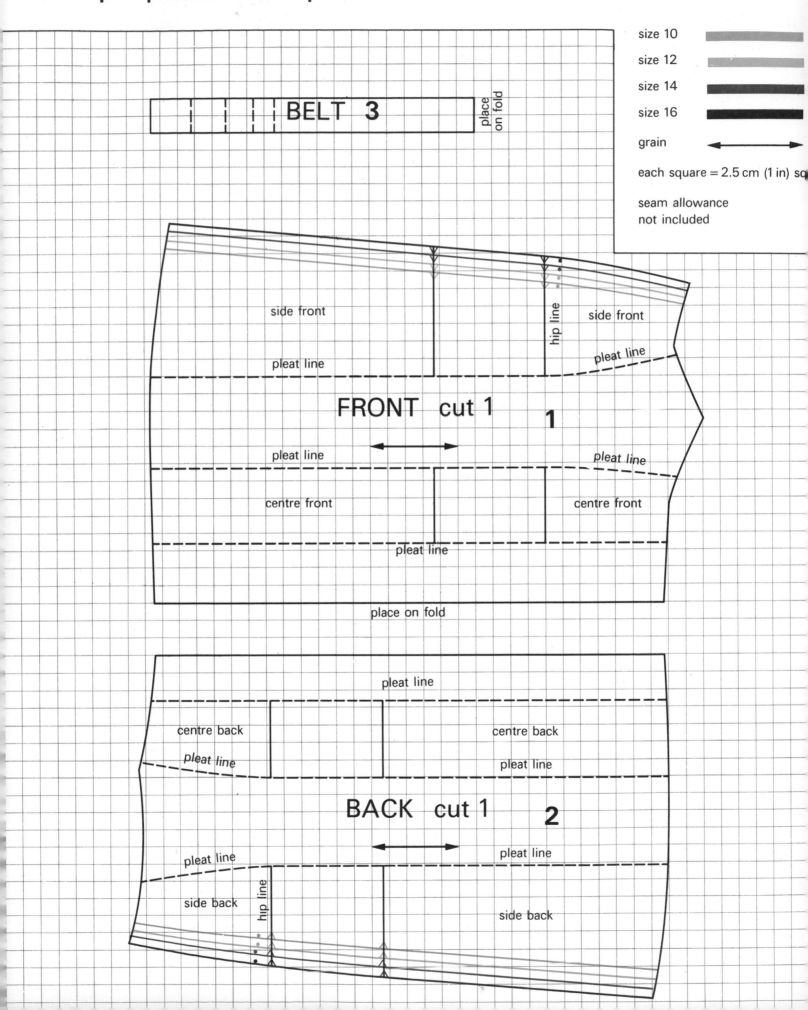

size 10

size 12

size 14

size 16

grain

each square = 2.5 cm (1 in) sq

seam allowance
not included

BELT **3**

place on fold

side front   hip line   side front

pleat line   pleat line

pleat line

FRONT cut 1   **1**

pleat line   pleat line

centre front   centre front

pleat line

place on fold

pleat line

centre back   centre back

pleat line   pleat line

BACK cut 1   **2**

pleat line   pleat line

side back   hip line   side back

Unisex Jackets

More basic know-how
Bound buttonholes
Fabric-bound buttonholes are not difficult to make and give a good-looking finish to lightweight jackets, dresses or suits. Any firmly-woven fabric is suitable as long as it is not too thick.

Size and spacing The buttonhole length is determined by the size of the button used, so buttons should be purchased before making buttonholes. To establish the buttonhole length needed, measure the diameter of the button, then add the thickness. Button positions are marked on the pattern. However, if you have had to lengthen or shorten the pattern or are using a different sized button than the one specified, you must alter the button-hole spacing accordingly. For through buttoning the final buttonhole should be placed about 10 cm (4 in) above the hemline.

Making bound buttonholes Before embarking on your finished work, try out the method using spare scraps of your fabric to perfect the technique.
Each buttonhole requires a piece of fabric cut either on the bias or on the straight grain, 2·5 cm (1 in) longer than the opening and approximately 5 cm (2 in) wide. Mark the buttonhole lines on the garment (fig. 1). Place the square of fabric on the right side of the garment and tack (fig. 2).
From the wrong side, machine stitch the outline of the buttonhole using a small stitch size. Pivot the needle at

the corners to shape a perfect rectangle. Do not start at a corner (fig. 3) and overlap beginning and end of stitching slightly to secure.
With small pointed scissors cut down the centre through both thicknesses to within 6 mm ($\frac{1}{4}$ in) of either end. Cut diagonally into each corner (fig. 4).
On small buttonholes turn strip through to the wrong side (fig. 5) and fold the sides of the facing to meet in the middle so that there is an equal fold on each side (fig. 6). Oversew opening temporarily (fig. 7) and work two or three oversewing stitches at each end to hold the folds in place. Press on wrong side.
Large buttonholes are made similarly but each rolled edge must be worked separately and secured with a small prick stitch along the seam line on the right side (fig. 8).

1. Marking position for buttonhole.
2. Fabric for binding pinned in place.
3. Stitching the buttonhole outline.
4. Clipping the buttonhole.
5. Turning binding to wrong side.
6, 7. Fold binding to meet in the centre and oversew the opening.
8. Secure rolled edge with prick stitch.
9. Slipstitch facing to finished buttonhole. 10. Finished buttonhole.

To finish the buttonhole feel through the facing and mark buttonhole ends with two pins. Cut along the marked buttonhole lines to the width of each buttonhole opening. Fold under the edges and slipstitch on to the wrong side of the buttonhole (fig. 9). Figure 10 shows the finished buttonhole from the right side.

Unisex jackets
These blouson jackets in a classic design are ideal for all seasons. The same pattern will fit both young men and women. The sleeves, made in two pieces, are neatly buttoned at the wrist and the jacket is finished with a lining.

Measurements
The pattern is given in women's sizes 12, 14, 16 and 18 and in men's chest

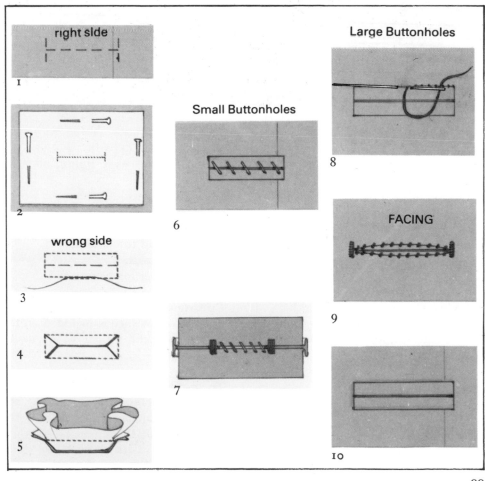

Comfortable unisex jackets.

sizes 81 cm (32 in), 87 cm (34 in) and 92 cm (36 in). Each size is indicated on the graph pattern by a cutting line of a different colour.

Note For young men's garments more ease is required, so use size 12 (87 cm) for an 81 cm (32 in) chest and so on.

Making the pattern
Draw up the pattern to scale from the graph pattern given here. One square represents 2·5 cm (1 in) square.

Suggested fabrics
Plaid wool, corduroy, denim, cotton.

You will need:
140 cm (54 in) fabric without nap, all sizes 2·60 m (2¾ yd) or,

90 cm (36 in) wide fabric, with nap, all sizes 3·50 m (3¾ yd).
90 cm (36 in) wide lining, all sizes 1·90 m (2 yd).
90 cm (36 in) wide lightweight woven interfacing, all sizes 1 m (1 yd).
Eight 2 cm (¾ in) buttons.
Sewing thread to match fabric.
Buttonhole twist.
Squared paper for pattern.

Cutting out
No seam allowance is included on pattern so add 1·5 cm (⅝ in) to all seam edges.

To make the jacket
Front interfacings 1. Tack the interfacing to the wrong side of the jacket fronts.
Pockets 2. Turn under 6 mm (¼ in) on the top edge of the pocket and

neaten by machine. Press flat. With right sides together, fold the pocket on the fold line. Tack and stitch each side of the pocket from the fold line to the lower edge of the facing. Clip the corners of the seam allowance as shown. Turn the pocket to the right side. Turn under the seam allowance on the remainder of the pocket and tack all round. Press flat. Hem the pocket facing edge to the pocket. Tack the pockets in position as indicated on the pattern. Top-stitch in place. Slip-stitch the outer edge of the pocket to the garment to lie flat. Press flat.
Shoulder and side seams 3. With right sides together, tack and stitch the jacket fronts to the jacket back at the shoulder and side seams. Press the seams open. If bound buttonholes are required work the first stage on out-side of garment in positions indicated

on the pattern (right hand side for women, left side for men).

Front facing and lining 4. With right sides together, tack and stitch the front facing to the front lining. Layer the seam and clip on curves where necessary. Press the seam towards the side seam.

5. With right sides together, tack and stitch the front facing and lining to the back lining at the shoulder and side seams. Press the seams open.

Collar 6. Tack the interfacing to the wrong side of the under collar. With right sides together, tack and stitch the upper collar to the under collar around the outer un-notched edge. Trim the interfacing close to the stitching line and layer the seam. Turn the collar to the right side and tack close to the stitched edge, easing into shape. Press flat. Top-stitch around the outer edge of the collar.

7. With the right side of the under collar placed to the right side of the jacket, matching centre backs and notches, tack the collar to the neck edge.

Joining lining and front facing to jacket 8. With right sides together, pin the front facing and lining to the front and neck edges of the jacket, sandwiching the collar between the lining and jacket at the neck edge. Tack and stitch. Layer the seam and clip the curves. Turn the lining to the inside of the jacket and tack round all stitched edges. Complete bound buttonholes. Top-stitch the front and rever edges.

9. Tack the lining to the jacket at the waist seam, matching centre backs, side seams and notches.

10. Work two rows of gathering stitches on the lower edge of the jacket fronts and back between the notches.

Waistband 11. Tack the interfacing to the wrong side of the front and back waistband sections. With right sides together, tack and stitch the front band sections to the back band at the side seams.

Trim the interfacing close to the stitching and press the seams open. On outside work first stage of bound buttonhole if required in position marked (right hand side for women, left for men). With right sides together, tack and stitch the front and back waistband facing sections at the side seams. Press the seams open.

With right sides together, matching centre backs and side seams, tack and stitch the waistband facing to the waistband at un-notched and front edges as shown. Trim the interfacing close to the stitching. Layer the seam allowance and cut across corners. Turn to the right side and tack round the stitched edge. Complete bound buttonhole. Press flat.

Joining waistband to jacket 12. With right sides together, matching

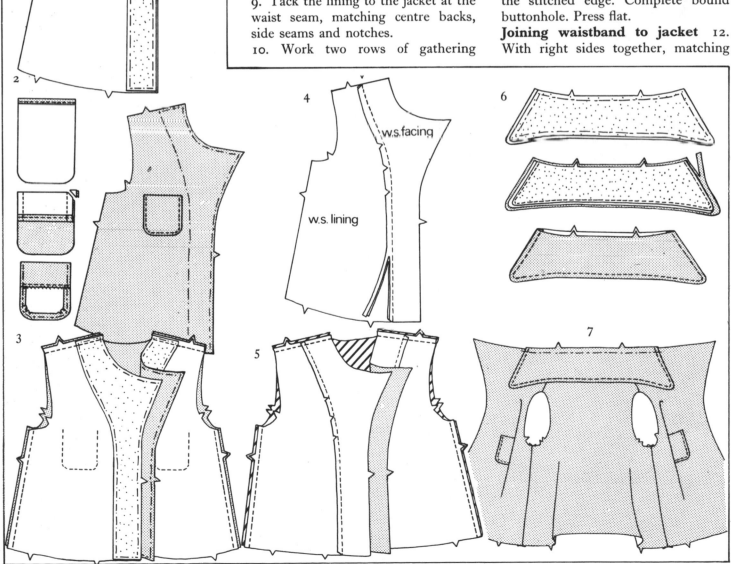

w.s. facing

w.s. lining

W.S.
sleeve

centre backs, side seams and front edges, pin the waistband to the jacket, pulling up the gathers evenly to fit. Tack and stitch the seam. Trim the interfacing close to the stitching and grade the seam allowance. Press the seam towards the waistband.

13. Turn under the seam allowance on the raw edge of the waistband facing and tack. Matching centre backs and seams, hem the facing to the line of stitching. Press flat.

14. Top-stitch round the front and lower edges of the waistband.

Sleeves and sleeve linings 15. With right sides together, matching notches, tack and stitch the under sleeve to the upper sleeve, leaving open below the dot on one seam as indicated on the pattern. Press the seams open. Make up the sleeve lining in the same way. Work two rows of gathering stitches round the sleeve top between the notches.

With wrong sides together, matching seams and opening edges, tack the lining to the sleeve at the lower edge. Slipstitch the lining to the sleeve round the opening. Press flat. Work two rows of gathering stitches at the lower edge of the sleeve through both layers of fabric.

Turn the seam allowance to the wrong side round the lining sleeve top and tack. Work two rows of gathering stitches close to the fold edge between the notches.

Cuffs 16. Tack the interfacing to the wrong side of the cuff. On right side work first part of bound buttonhole in position marked if required. With right sides together, tack and stitch the cuff facing to the cuff round the outer edge to the dot as shown. Trim the interfacing close to the stitching. Layer the seam allowance and trim the corners. Clip to the dot and turn the cuff to the right side. Tack close to the stitched edge, complete bound buttonhole and press flat.

Joining cuff to sleeve 17. With right sides together, matching notches, pin the cuff to the sleeve, pulling up the gathers to fit evenly. Tack and stitch. Trim the interfacing close to the stitching and layer the seam allowance. Press the seam towards the cuff. Turn under the seam allowance on the raw edge of the cuff facing and tack. Hem the cuff facing to the line of stitching. Press flat. Top-stitch round the cuff and sleeve opening edges as

shown. Repeat 15-17 for second sleeve.

Setting in sleeves 18. With wrong sides together, matching shoulder and underarm seam and notches, tack the jacket lining to the jacket round the armhole edge.

With right sides together, matching shoulder seam and notches, pin the sleeve into the armhole, pulling up the gathers evenly to ease in the fullness round the sleeve top. Tack and stitch with the sleeve uppermost. Clip the curves, press seam towards sleeve.

19. With wrong sides together, matching seams and notches, pin the sleeve lining round the armhole covering the raw edges. Using double thread in the needle, hem the sleeve lining firmly to the stitching round the armhole. Repeat steps 18 and 19 for second sleeve.

20. If required make machine- or hand-worked buttonholes on the right hand side of the jacket front and on the cuffs in positions indicated on the pattern. Sew buttons on the left front and on the cuffs to correspond with the buttonholes. Also, sew a button on each pocket as shown.

Note For man's jacket reverse the positioning of the buttons and buttonholes on the front.

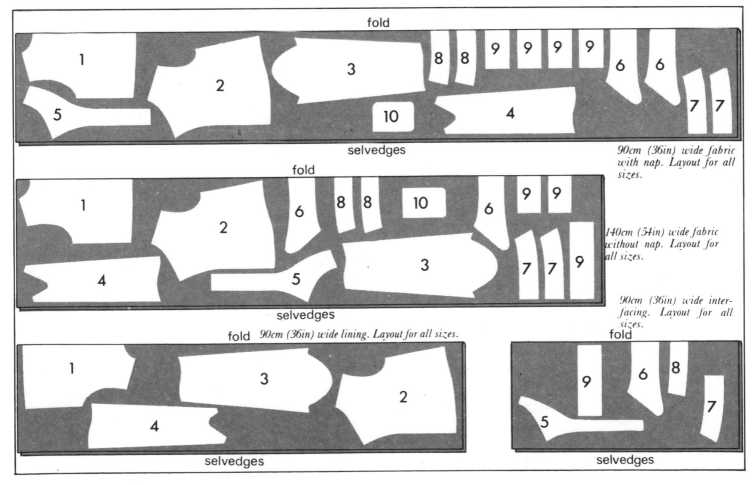

90cm (36in) wide fabric with nap. Layout for all sizes.

140cm (54in) wide fabric without nap. Layout for all sizes.

90cm (36in) wide interfacing. Layout for all sizes.

fold 90cm (36in) wide lining. Layout for all sizes.

Graph pattern for unisex jackets

women's sizes	men's sizes		
12 ————	81 chest		32
14 ————	87 chest		34
16 ————	92 chest		36
18 ————	97 chest		38

grain ⟷

seam allowance not included

each square = 2.5cm (1in) sq

C.B.

place on fold

6

COLLAR cut 1

under collar cut 1

interfacing cut 1

gather
between notches

3

TOP SLEEVE cut 2

lining cut 2

gather

fold line

10

POCKET cut 2

• ← button position

woman's 1.3cm (½in)
less at shoulder

C.B.

1

JACKET BACK cut 2

lining cut 2

place on fold

gather between notches

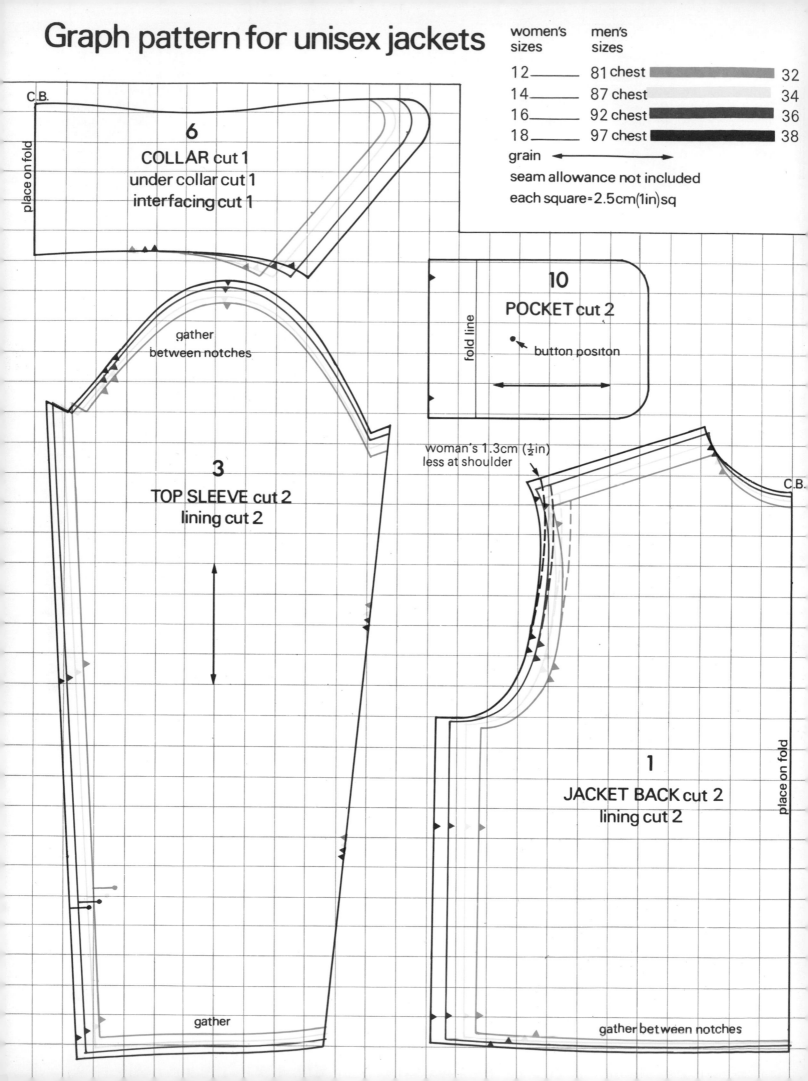

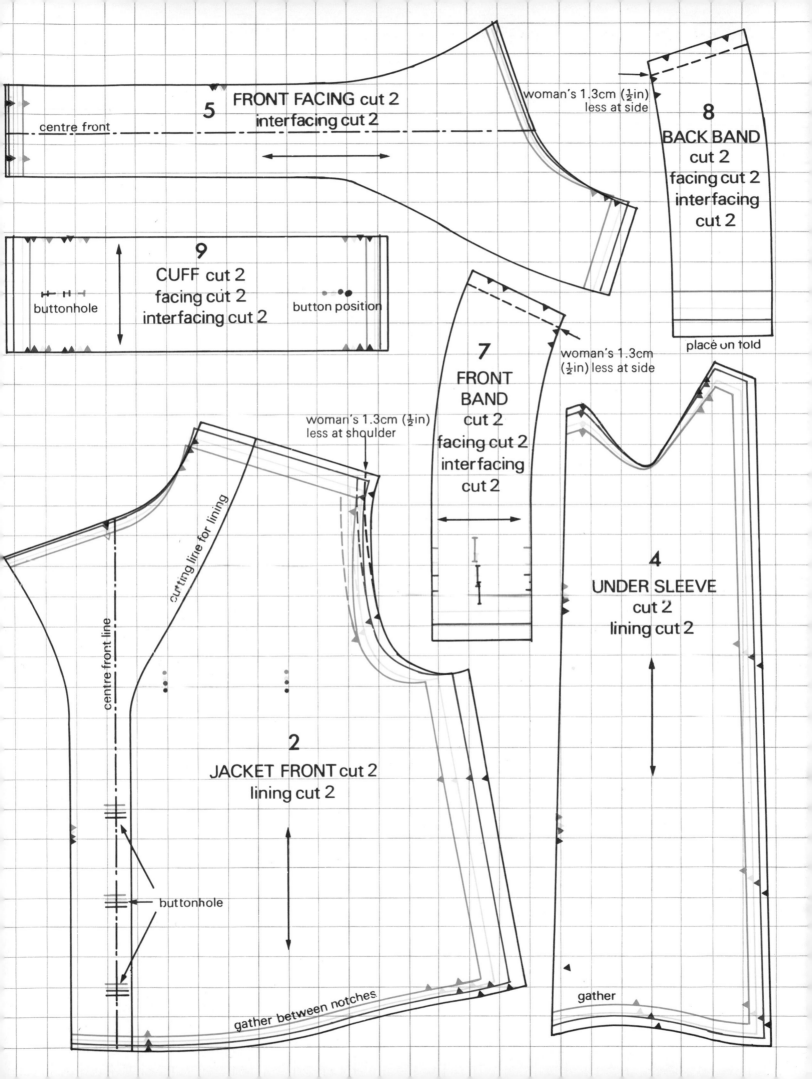

5
FRONT FACING cut 2
interfacing cut 2

centre front

woman's 1.3cm (½in)
less at side

8
BACK BAND
cut 2
facing cut 2
interfacing
cut 2

place on fold

9
CUFF cut 2
facing cut 2
interfacing cut 2

buttonhole

button position

woman's 1.3cm
(½in) less at side

7
**FRONT
BAND
cut 2
facing cut 2
interfacing
cut 2**

woman's 1.3cm (½in)
less at shoulder

cutting line for lining

centre front line

4
UNDER SLEEVE
cut 2
lining cut 2

2
JACKET FRONT cut 2
lining cut 2

buttonhole

gather between notches

gather

Slim-fit Trousers

More basic know-how
Adjusting trouser patterns

Patterns generally conform to the measurements of a standard figure and it is often necessary to alter a pattern to accommodate individual figure proportions. Trousers create special fitting problems because of the complexity of the proportions involved.

It is important for all major alterations to be made on the pattern since little can be done once the garment has been cut out of the fabric. If there are several fitting problems, it would be advisable to test the pattern in calico first. Once a perfect fit has been achieved, use this as a basic pattern which can be adapted for all kinds of trousers.

Trouser patterns should be selected according to the hip measurement. However, there are other measurements which are required to alter the pattern correctly. Before locating the hipline on the pattern, make all the lengthwise adjustments; that is, the crotch length and the trouser length. Before cutting the fabric, check the pattern as described in stages below, and then make the alterations necessary for the figure. Although some further minor adjustments may be necessary in the first fitting, cutting out can be done with the assurance that the pattern has been proportioned to the individual body measurements.

Adjusting the length of the crotch

To determine the crotch length, sit on a hard chair and measure from the waistline to the seat (fig. 1). To this measurement add 1·3 cm (½ in) ease if the hips are less than 89 cm (35 in), 2 cm (¾ in) if the hips are 89 cm to 96·5 cm (35 in to 38 in), and 2·5 cm (1 in) if the hips are more than 96·5 cm (38 in). The body measurement plus ease allowance is the total crotch length.

To adjust the length of the crotch, draw a line across the pattern at right angles to the grain line, from the widest part of the crotch to the side seam. The length of the pattern from the waistline to this line should be the same as the crotch length when taken in the sitting position, plus the ease allowance.

If the pattern is too long, then crease along the shortening line and fold a tuck to take up the desired amount. Tape in place. Re-draw the seams and construction markings to retain the original shape of the side seam and the crotch seam (fig. 2).

If the pattern is too short, cut along the lengthening line and open the pattern to the desired amount. Insert a piece of paper behind this section and tape in place. Re-draw the seams and construction markings to retain the original shape of the side seam and the crotch seam.

Make the same adjustment to the front and back pattern pieces (fig. 3).

Adjusting the trouser length

Measure the length of the pattern from the waistline to the lower edge. This should be the same as the measurement from the waist to the ankle. If the pattern is too short or too long, use the same principle as shown in figs. 2 and 3 to correct this. Make sure that there is adequate length for the hem allowance and for turn-ups if these are required.

Locating the hipline

For the average figure the hipline is measured 20·5 cm (8 in) below the waistline. Measure down 20·5 cm (8 in) from the waist and draw a horizontal line on the pattern. The hip measurement will be taken at this point.

For the disproportionate figure, it is necessary to take three measurements on the body. First, measure 8 cm (3 in) below the waistline. Secondly, measure 18 cm (7 in) below the waistline and then 23 cm (9 in) below the waistline.

Draw three horizontal lines on the pattern at these points. The widest measurement will be showing at or in-between one of these points. The hipline on the pattern will be the larger measurement.

Adjusting the hip

Take the hip measurement on the pattern at the hipline. There should be 5 cm (2 in) ease allowance. If the pattern does not measure 5 cm (2 in) more than the body measurement, the pattern will need adjusting.

To increase the hipline, determine the amount needed, divide this total by four and increase each side seam by this amount. Measure the amount of adjustment out from the hipline edge at the side seam on both front and back pieces, and mark. Tape a piece of tissue underneath each pattern section. Taper from the mark at the hipline into the original cutting line both above the knee and at the waistline, retaining the shape of the leg and the width of the waist (fig. 4).

To decrease the hipline, use the same principle as above but subtract the amount at the side seams (fig. 5).

Adjusting the waistline

The ease allowance at the waistline should be 1·3 cm to 2 cm (½ in to ¾ in). The waistline can be increased or decreased by adjusting the darts. Each dart can be increased or decreased by as much as 6 mm (¼ in) but no more (figs. 6 and 7).

If this adjustment is not sufficient, the side seams can also be altered. Divide the amount of increase or decrease by four, and adjust each side seam edge by this amount. Taper to the hipline, being careful not to change the hip measurement (figs. 8 and 9).

Adjusting width of lower edge

If the lower edge of the pattern is too narrow, determine the amount to be added and divide this by four. Add this amount to the side and inside seam edges at the hemline. Taper from the hemline to the hipline on

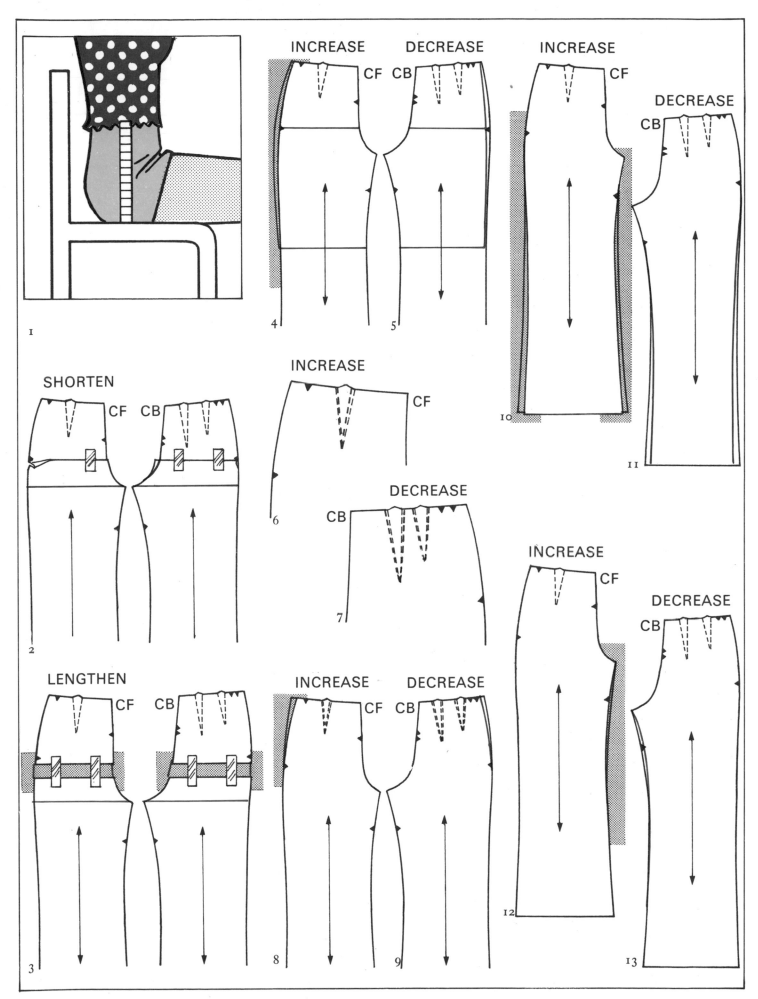

INCREASE   DECREASE

CF CB

INCREASE   CF

DECREASE

CB

1

4   5

10

11

SHORTEN

CF CB

INCREASE

CF

DECREASE

CB

2

6

7

LENGTHEN

CF CB

INCREASE   DECREASE

CF CB

INCREASE

CF

DECREASE

CB

3   8   9

12

13

107

a.

b.

c.

the side seams, also from the hemline to the crotch on the inside seams (fig. 10).

If the pattern is too wide at this point, divide the total amount to be subtracted by four, using the same method as above, but subtracting and not adding (fig. 11).

Adjusting the width of the leg

There is no standard amount of ease required for the width of the leg. This is a matter of personal preference and depends upon the size and shape of the leg.

If a leg is large thighed, then add to the front and back inside leg seams at the crotch point, tapering the line to the lower edge of the pattern. Do not add to the side seams. Tightness in the thigh area means that more width is required in the crotch as well as in the leg, and adding at this point will give both (fig. 12).

Altering a pattern to accommodate thin thighs must never be done by decreasing at the side seams. If the thighs are thin, then decrease both the front and back inside leg seams at the crotch point and taper to the lower edge of the pattern (fig. 13).

Alterations for a sway back If

the figure has a sway back this will cause folds in the trousers below the back waist. These folds can be eliminated by removing the extra fullness at the centre back. Slash straight across the back to the side seam about 9 cm (3½ in) below the waistline.

Overlap the slash line to remove the necessary amount. Re-draw the centre back seam, and also the darts if they have been affected. Consequently the back waistline will have been decreased (figs. 14a and 14b).

If the normal waistline width is re-

quired, add the amount trimmed from the centre back to the side seam and taper from the waistline to the hipline (fig. 15).

Alterations for a large stomach A

person with a large stomach will find this adjustment most useful, especially if wishing to wear fitted trousers, because this style emphasizes the slight-

Illustrations left to right show figure problems to be accommodated:
a. Wide legs, b. Sway back, c. Large stomach, d. Protruding hips and
e. Large and flat seats.

est figure fault.

To make this alteration, draw a line through the centre of the waistline dart to the knee. This line should be

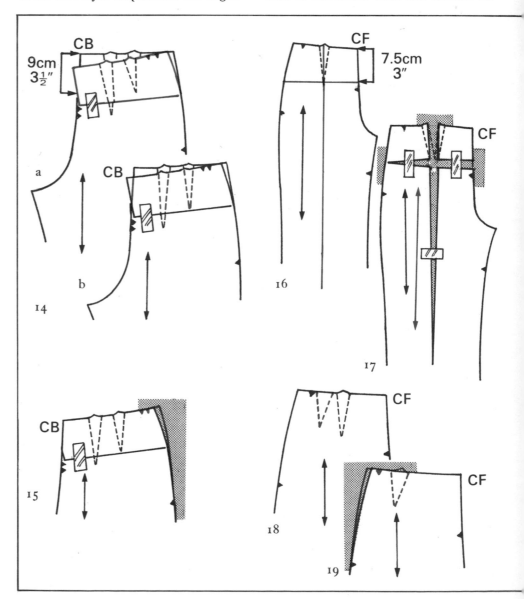

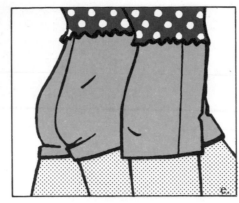

width of the dart so that it is in line with the hip bone – for some figures the dart may need shortening as well (fig. 18). As a result, the waistline becomes smaller, so add the difference to the side seam and taper to the hipline (fig. 19).

Alterations for a large seat To make this alteration, the width and length at the fullest part of the seat must be increased.

Determine the amount of increase necessary for the adjustment. Slash the pattern vertically to the knee, between the centre back and the back dart, parallel to the grain line. Measure 20·5 cm (8 in) below the waistline and slash the pattern horizontally from the centre back to the side seam. Open the vertical and horizontal slashes each to a quarter of the amount required, keeping the centre back straight. Insert a piece of paper and tape in place.

Re-draw the cutting lines. If the waistline becomes too large, divide the adjustment equally between the back darts and increase each one (fig. 20).

Alterations for a flat seat In this case proceed as if making the alteration for a large seat, but instead of opening the vertical and horizontal slashes, overlap them each by a quarter of the amount required. If the waistline becomes too small, divide the vertical adjustment equally between all the back darts and decrease them by this amount (fig. 21).

Alteration for one hip higher than natural hipline Measure down 20·5

parallel to the grain line. Then draw a horizontal line from the centre front to the side seam about 8 cm (3 in) below the waistline (fig. 16).

Slash the horizontal line to the side seam and open the pattern a quarter of the amount required. Slash the vertical line and open the pattern a quarter of the amount required, keeping the centre front straight. Insert a piece of

tissue paper under the slashes and tape in position. Adjust the waistline dart in the middle of the slash, returning it to its original position and size (fig. 17).

Alteration for protruding hips Extra dart fullness released at the point of the hip bones will solve this problem. The larger dart releases more fullness. Re-position and increase the

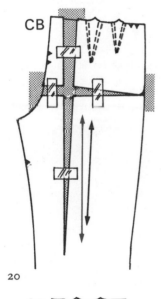

20

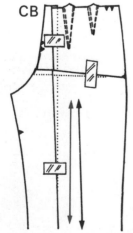

21

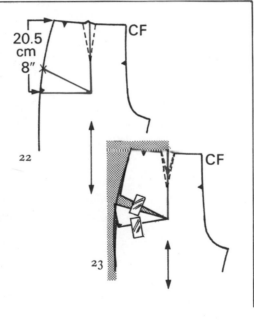

22

23

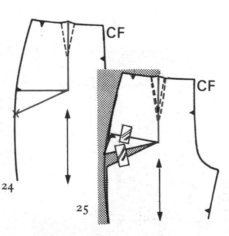

24

25

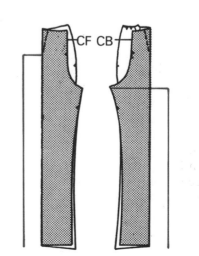

26

cm (8 in) from the waistline and draw a line through the centre of the dart to this position, keeping in line with the straight grain. Square across at the hipline to the vertical line.

At the side seam where the hip is higher, measure down from the waistline to the hip bone and mark. Draw a line from this mark to the point where the vertical and horizontal lines meet (fig. 22).

Slash along this line and the horizontal line and overlap the pattern. This will open the pattern at the new hipline. Adjust the amount overlapping to fit the hip and tape in place. Re-draw the side seam from the waistline, tapering to the new hipline. Make this adjustment to both front and back pattern pieces.

It will be found that after making this adjustment, the dart will need shortening to the level of the new hipline (fig. 23).

Alteration for one hip lower than natural hipline For this alteration, the same method is used as above. Having drawn the vertical and horizontal lines, measure down from the horizontal to the new hipline and mark. Draw a line from this mark to the point where the vertical and horizontal lines meet (fig. 24).

Slash along this line and the horizontal line and overlap the pattern. This will open the pattern at the new hipline. Adjust the amount overlapping to fit the hip and tape in place. Re-draw the side seam from the waistline, tapering to the new hipline (fig. 25).

A final tip on fitting trousers After the pattern pieces have been cut out in the fabric and marked, fold each piece vertically in half with the wrong sides together. Press in the creases firmly. The front crease points to the first dart or pleat, and the back crease stops at the crotch seam (fig. 26).

During the first fitting, ensure that the creases hang straight. If a crease hangs inwards, raise the trousers at the waistline on the appropriate side until the crease hangs correctly. This occurs because the two hips are not exactly the same.

These casual trousers, designed with straight legs, are very easy to fit exactly.

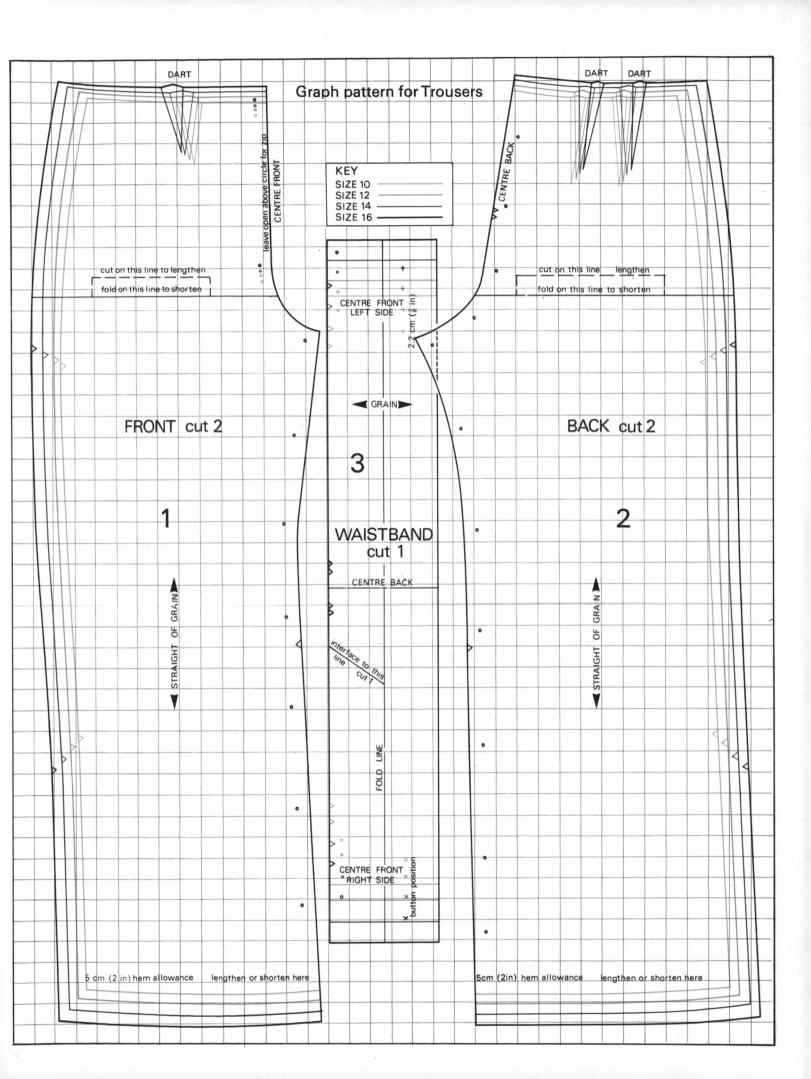

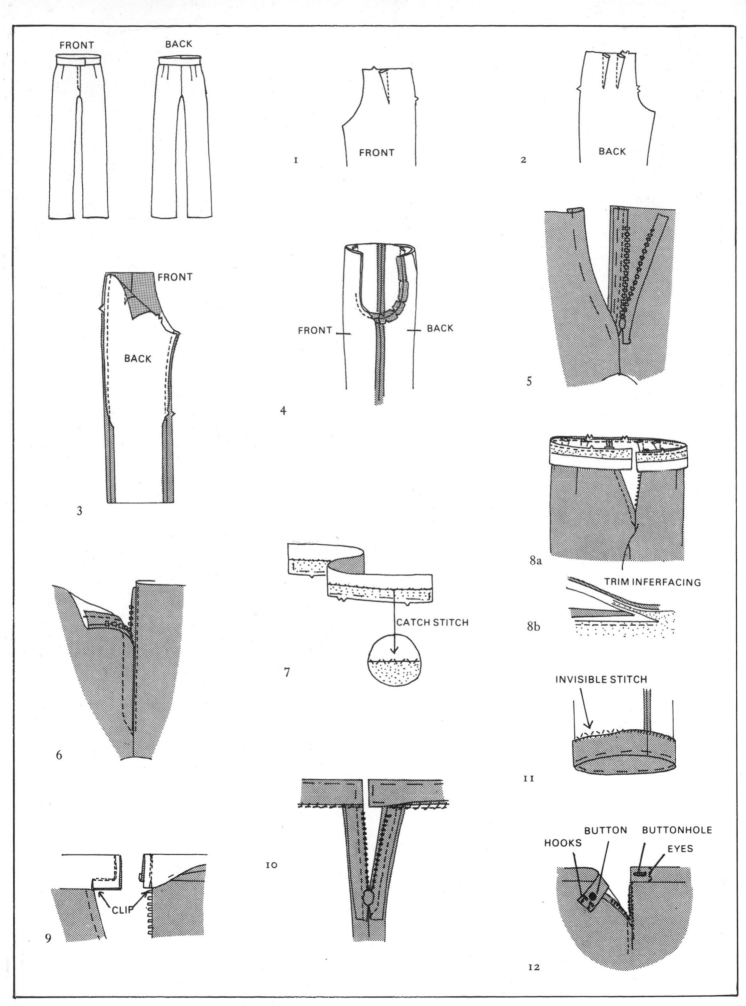

FRONT   BACK

1   FRONT

2   BACK

FRONT

BACK

FRONT — BACK

4

5

3

6

7   CATCH STITCH

8a

8b   TRIM INTERFACING

INVISIBLE STITCH

11

9   CLIP

10

12   HOOKS   BUTTON   BUTTONHOLE   EYES

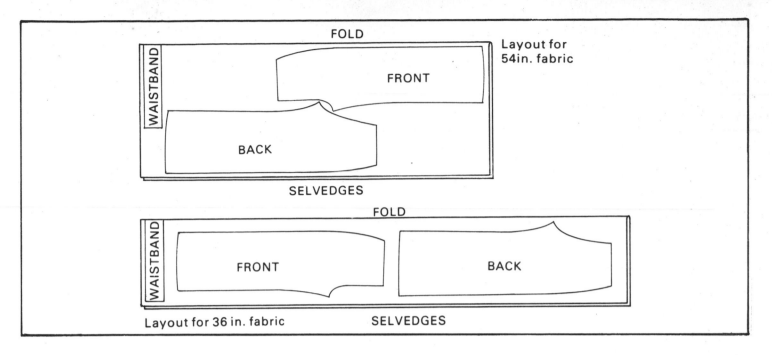

FOLD

WAISTBAND

FRONT

Layout for 54in. fabric

BACK

SELVEDGES

FOLD

WAISTBAND

FRONT

BACK

Layout for 36 in. fabric   SELVEDGES

Slim fit trousers

These trousers are cut on classic lines with straight legs. They look just as good made up in plain fabrics or in bold checks.

Measurements

The pattern is given in sizes 10, 12, 14 and 16. Each size is indicated on the graph pattern by a cutting line of a different colour.

Making the pattern

Draw up the pattern to scale from the graph pattern given here. One square represents 2·5 cm (1 in) square.

Suggested fabrics

Wool, tweed, corduroy, linen, denim.

You will need:

140 cm (54 in) fabric without nap, all sizes 2·40 m (2 yd), or
90 cm (36 in) fabric without nap, all sizes 2·75 m (3 yd).

Note Allow extra fabric for matching design if using checked fabric. (Between 30 to 50 cm ($\frac{1}{4}$ to $\frac{1}{2}$ yd) depending on size of check.)
20 cm ($\frac{1}{8}$ yd) interfacing.
20 cm (8 in) zip fastener.
Two hooks and eyes.
Sewing thread to match fabric.
Squared paper for pattern.

Cutting out

A seam allowance of 1·5 cm ($\frac{5}{8}$ in) has been allowed on all seams and 6 cm ($2\frac{5}{8}$ in) hem allowance.

To make the trousers

Darts 1. With right sides together, tack and stitch the front waist darts. Press the darts towards the centre front.
2. With right sides together, tack and stitch the back waist darts. Press the darts towards the centre back.

Seams 3. With right sides together, matching notches, tack and stitch the inside leg seam and the side seam. Press the seams open.

Crotch 4. With right sides together, matching notches and inside leg seam, tack and stitch the crotch seam to small circle. Clip the curved edges and press the seam open.
5. Turn and tack the seam allowance of the right front to the wrong side and press. Place the zipper face down to the left front opening. Tack and stitch in place using the zipper foot on the machine.
6. Tack and stitch the right front to the zipper as shown. If desired, edge stitch the seam close to the zipper teeth on the left-hand side as shown.

Waistband 7. Cut interfacing for waistband as indicated on pattern. Tack the interfacing to the wrong side of the waistband and catchstitch it down to the fold line.
8. With right sides together, matching notches, tack and stitch the waistband to the trouser waist. Trim the interfacing close to stitching and trim and layer the seam. Press the seam up towards the waistband.
9. With right sides together, fold the waistband on the fold line and stitch

the ends as shown. Clip the seam at centre front to the stitching as shown. Trim and layer the seam and clip across the corners.
10. Turn the waistband to the inside. Tack and press. Turn under the seam allowance and hem to the stitching line.

To finish 11. Try on the trousers and mark the hem. Tack round the folded edge. Trim the hem to an even width all round. Neaten the raw edge of the hem with hand oversewing or machine stitch. Sew the hem with invisible hemming stitch.
12. Work a hand- or machine-made buttonhole in the left front waistband in the position indicated on the pattern. Stitch the button on to the right front waistband on the under band. Stitch on the hooks and eyes at the waistband opening as shown.

Child's dungarees

Measurements

The pattern is given in two sizes to fit a child 4 or 6 years old. Waist sizes, 61 cm (24 in) and 66 cm (26 in).

Making the pattern

Draw up the pattern to scale from the graph pattern given here. One square represents 2·5 cm (1 in) square.

Suggested fabrics

Drill, denim, corduroy.

You will need:

90 cm (36 in) wide fabric, without nap, size 4, 1·90 m (2 yd); size 6,

These tough, practical dungarees are straight-forward and fun to make. For a special effect, choose bright boldly decorative patches and pockets to contrast with the basic dungarees.

2·10 m (2¼ yd).
15 cm (6 in) zip fastener.
Purchased appliqué motif.
Two 2·5 cm (1 in) buttons.
Sewing thread to match fabric.
Buttonhole twist in matching or contrasting colour for top-stitching.
Squared paper for pattern.

Cutting out
There are no seam allowances included on the pattern. When cutting out add 1·5 cm (⅝ in) to all seam edges and 6·5 cm (2½ in) hem allowance.

To make the dungarees
Seams 1. With right sides together, matching the balance marks on the pattern, tack and stitch the centre front and centre back seams, leaving the centre back open where indicated on pattern to allow for inserting the zip fastener.
Insert the zip fastener. Clip curves and press the seams open.
2. With right sides together, tack and stitch the front and back legs together along the side and inside leg seams. Press the seams open.

Bib and facings 3. With right sides together, tack and stitch along three sides of the bib, leaving one long edge open. Layer the seams and turn the bib through to the right side. Tack around the stitched edges and press flat.
4. With right sides together, matching centre fronts, tack and stitch the raw edge of the bib to the trouser front. Layer the seams.
5. With right sides together, tack and stitch the facing pieces together at the side seams and centre front. With right sides together, matching seams, tack and stitch the facing to the waistline. Turn the facing to the inside and tack around the stitched edge. Press flat.
Neaten the seam allowance on the raw edge of the facing and hem it to the tape of the zip.
6. Starting at the centre back, top-stitch along the waistline and bib 1·3 cm (½ in) away from the edge.

Straps 7. With right sides together, stitch around the edges of the straps, leaving an opening of 8 cm (3 in) to turn the strap through. Turn the strap through to the right side. Slipstitch the opening to close. Tack around the stitched edge and press flat. Top-stitch 6 mm (¼ in) away from the edge all round the strap.

Buttonholes and buttons 8. Sew buttons at the positions marked on the pattern. Work hand- or machine-made buttonholes at the positions indicated on the pattern.

To finish 9. Try the dungarees on child, mark the hem and check length of straps. Neaten the raw edges of hem, turn up and stitch. Top-stitch 1·3 cm (½ in) away from the lower edge of the hem if you wish. Stitch shoulder straps firmly into place at back of trousers. Stitch made or purchased appliqué motif to bib or hem a square of fabric for a patch pocket.

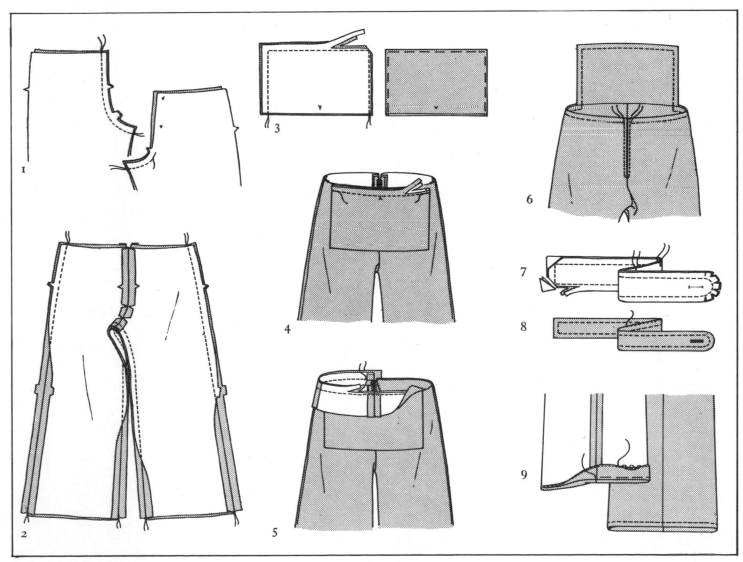

Graph pattern for child's dungarees

Each square = 2.5cm sq (1 in sq)   Seam allowances not included

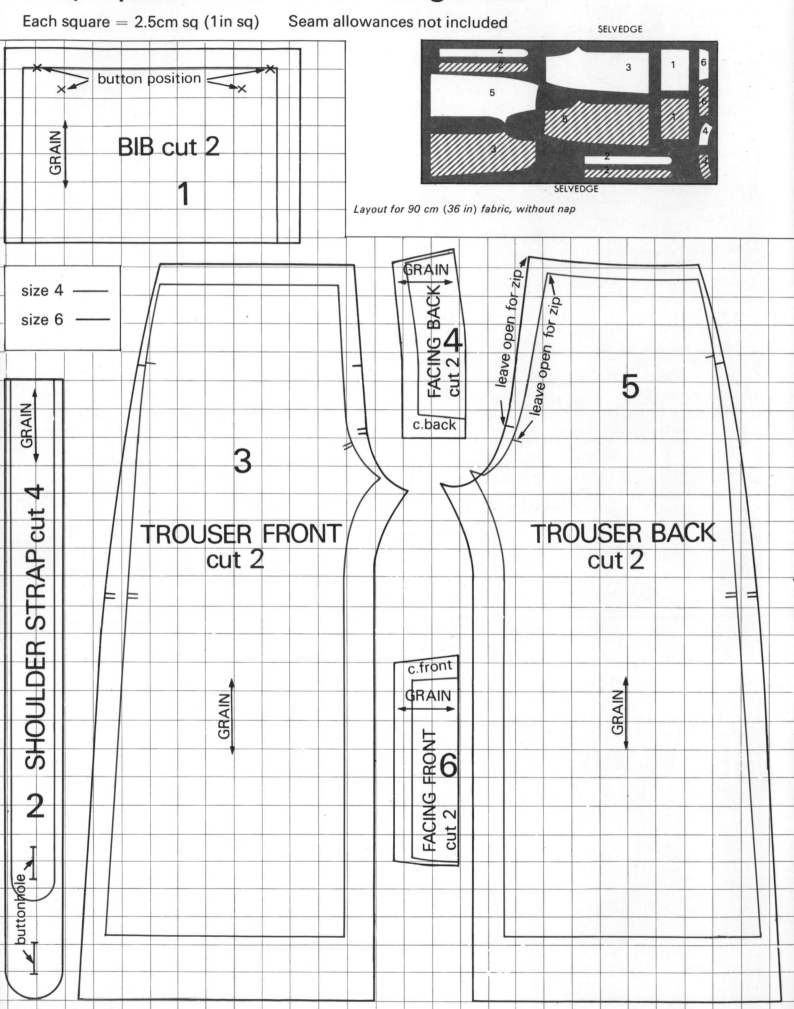

SELVEDGE

Layout for 90 cm (36 in) fabric, without nap

SELVEDGE

button position

GRAIN

BIB cut 2

1

size 4 ———
size 6 ———

GRAIN

SHOULDER STRAP cut 4

2

buttonhole

3

TROUSER FRONT
cut 2

GRAIN

GRAIN

FACING BACK
cut 2

4

c.back

leave open for zip

leave open for zip

5

TROUSER BACK
cut 2

GRAIN

c.front

GRAIN

FACING FRONT
cut 2

6

Home Sewing

Table Linen

Circular tablecloths

Round tables, space saving and fashionable, look attractive in any setting. Here are instructions for making two kinds of elegant circular cloths.

*Techniques included: drawing arcs, pin-and-string method.

A circular tablecloth can be made in one of two ways.

In the method which is more suitable for patterned fabric, the round cloth is produced from a square of fabric, each side of the square being the same length as the required diameter of the finished cloth.

It is possible to buy fabrics suitable for tablecloths in wider than usual widths. In most cases, though, the fabric has to be joined at the sides to produce the full width of the square from which the cloth is to be cut.

The second method of making a circular tablecloth involves cutting a circular piece of cloth to fit the table top, plus seam allowance, and joining two curved pieces to it, for the overhang. This method uses more fabric, but is more suitable than the first for plain fabrics, as a cloth with side seams would be unsightly in a plain fabric.

Choosing fabrics Washable dress or furnishing fabrics, such as cotton, linen, lawn, man-made fibre mixtures and cotton lace are all suitable for tablecloths. Sheeting, available in a variety of patterns and colours, is also suitable, because of its quality and width. For a nursery or kitchen table, PVC is a good choice, although it does not hang as well as cotton fabric.

Deciding the size of a circular tablecloth The cloth should cover the table and should have a generous overhang all round, ranging from about 25 cm (10 in) to floor level. The actual measurement depends upon personal choice.

To determine the depth of the overhang Lay a tape measure across

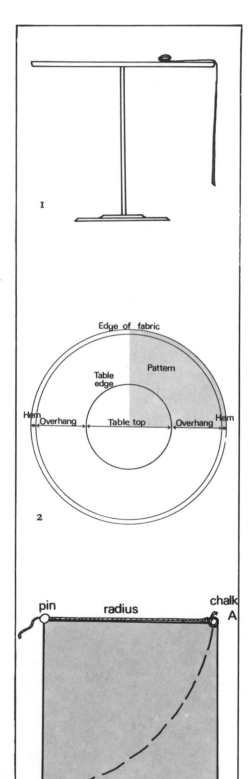

the table top and let one end drop down until it reaches the required depth for the overhang (fig. 1).

To find the diameter of the cloth Measure the diameter of the table top, add this measurement to twice the depth of the overhang, and add 1·5 cm (½ in) all round, for hem (fig. 2).

If the width of the fabric chosen is less than the diameter of the tablecloth, more fabric will have to be joined to the sides of the main piece, so that the width and the length of the fabric when the pieces are joined, are sufficient for the required diameter of the cloth.

Making the tablecloth pattern from a square of fabric
You will need:

A large square of paper, with each side a little longer than the radius (half the diameter) of the proposed tablecloth.

A piece of string 15 cm (6 in) longer than the radius of the cloth.

A stick of chalk.

Several drawing pins.

*Drawing an arc: pin and string method

Work on a flat surface that will not be spoiled if pins are pushed into it.

Tie one end of the string round the chalk. Starting at the chalk end, measure out the radius of the cloth, including 1·5 cm (½ in) hem allowance, along the length of the string. Mark this measurement by pushing a drawing pin through the string at this point. Pin the paper down on the flat working surface and push the drawing pin, retaining the string on the point of the pin, into the top left-hand corner of the paper.

Hold the drawing pin firmly with one

1. Determining the depth of the overhang. 2. Finding the diameter for a circular cloth. 3. Using a pin, string and chalk to make a circular pattern.

hand and draw an arc with the chalk from A, at the top right-hand corner of the paper, to B, at the bottom left-hand corner (fig. 3).

The pattern thus produced is a quarter of the area of the cloth, plus 1·5 cm (½ in) hem allowance.

Making a round tablecloth from a square of fabric
You will need:
Fabric for the cloth.

Trimming, if required, of your own choice (amount required is four times the length of the arc A to B shown in fig. 3, plus 2·5 cm (1 in) for overlap). Fringe, braid or daisy chain edging are all suitable.

Suitable matching thread.

Matching bias binding (the same amount as for the trimming).

Pins.

Tacking thread.

Preparing the fabric If the fabric has to be joined, add pieces to the sides of the main fabric piece; a seam across the middle of the cloth would be very noticeable and could upset the balance of crockery when the table is laid.

Figs. 4 and 5 show how to cut and join 120 cm (48 in) widths to make a round cloth with a diameter of 194 cm (78 in) and a 1·5 cm (½ in) hem. Remember that seam allowances for the joins have to be added.

Join the widths with a machined flat fell seam, stitched with right sides facing (fig. 6). You should now have a square of fabric with each side equal to the diameter of the cloth, plus hem allowance.

Cutting out Matching edges, fold the prepared square of fabric in half, then in half again, and pin the pattern on to the folded fabric, as shown in fig. 7. Cut along the curved pattern edge. Unpin the pattern and unfold the fabric. Snip V-shaped notches into the edge of the cloth 1 cm (⅜ in) deep, at 2·5 cm (1 in) intervals (fig. 8). Turn the edge in 1·5 cm (½ in) to the wrong side, pin and tack it down. The notches will close up, allowing the hem to curve (fig. 9).

Binding the hem Pin and tack the bias binding over the turned hem, to

The trim and the depth of the overhang influences how you use the tablecloth.

119

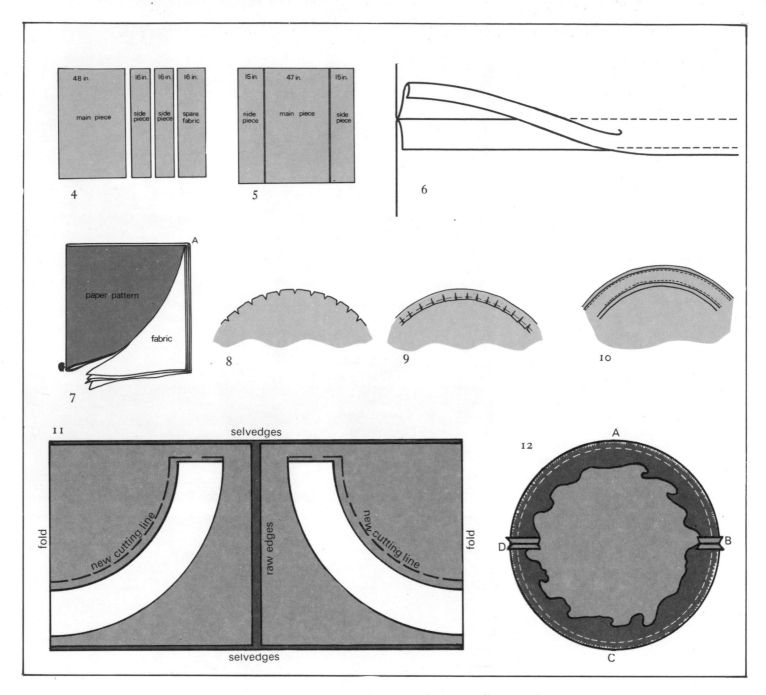

4, 5. *Cutting and joining fabric for a large circular cloth.*

6. *Flat fell seams.*

7. *Pattern pinned to folded fabric.*

8. *Snip the hem edge.* 9. *Turn and tack the hem allowance.* 10. *Stitching on the bias binding.*

11. *Folding the fabric and placing the pattern pieces for cutting the overhang.*

12. *Stitching the overhang on the centre piece of the tablecloth.*

cover the raw edge. Stitch on the bias binding (fig. 10), turning under the raw ends to neaten. Trim if required.

Making a round cloth with curved overhang

This method involves cutting a circular piece of fabric the same size as the table top, plus 1·5 cm (½ in) seam allowance all round, and adding two curved overhang pieces. Thus the fabric to be used should be of a width equal to the diameter of the table top, plus 1·5 cm (½ in) seam allowance all round, and be of sufficient length to allow the top and overlap pieces to be cut.

Measuring for the pattern Double the overhang of the cloth and add to it the diameter of the table top, plus 3 cm (1 in) for seam allowance.

Making the pattern Make a paper pattern of a quarter of the area of the cloth, as for the first method, then draw a smaller arc within the larger arc, the radius the same as the table top radius, plus 1·5 cm (½ in) for turnings. Cut along this inner line, reserving the outer piece of pattern for the overhang.

Cutting out Cut off a square of fabric from the main length with each side equal to the diameter of the table top, plus 1·5 cm (½ in) seam allowance all round. Fold this square in half and in half again, as for the first method, and pin the table top pattern piece to the folded fabric, again as before. Cut out round the curve.

Before unfolding the fabric, mark the straight grain four times at four opposite points on the cloth, by making several tacking stitches in from the edge, along the folds. These stitches will act as guidelines when attaching the overhang, ensuring the grain runs straight on the pieces, so the cloth hangs correctly. Lay the remaining length of fabric flat on the floor and fold over the ends, so they meet in the centre (fig. 11).

Pin the pattern piece for the overhang on the fabric, so that one straight edge is on one of the folds. Using chalk, mark on the fabric the cutting line for the inner edge of the overhang, 3 cm (1 in) from the inner curve of the pattern.

Mark another line 1·5 cm (½ in) from the straight edge of the pattern which is not on the fold of the fabric (fig. 11). Cut along the chalked lines and along the outer edge of the pattern, but do not cut along the fold.

Unpin the pattern and pin the pattern to the fabric at the other fold. Mark the cutting lines as for the first piece. Cut out in the same way.

Clip 1 cm (⅜ in) into the inner edge of both overhang pieces, at 2·5 cm (1 in) intervals. With right sides facing, and overhang on top, match the centre of the inner edge of one overhanging piece to one of the tacking marks on the table top piece (fig. 12). Working outwards from this point, pin the overhang to the table top piece 1·5 cm (½ in) in from the edge. The clips will open out.

Pin the other overhang piece to the table top piece in a similar way, matching the centre to the opposite tacking mark. Where the overhang pieces meet, pin the raw edges together, adjusting the short seam lines so the overhang fits the table top exactly. Tack and machine stitch these seams. Press them open and neaten the raw edges.

Tack and machine stitch the overhang to the table top. Remove the tacking and press the seam allowance down on to the overhang, all round. Overcast the raw edges together. Stitch on the bias binding round the hem, as for the tablecloth made by the first method.

Trimming Trim round tablecloths with bobble braid, fringing, or daisy chain edging. To trim a cloth made by the second method, piping in a contrasting colour could be added to the seam joining the overhang to the centre piece.

Rectangular tablecloths
Ready-made tablecloths tend to come in a few standard sizes which look all wrong if your table is not a standard size too. Try making your own – then you can decide both size and cost.

*Techniques included: fraying, folded mitre, simple stitched mitre, mitring bias binding, mitring corner on tablecloth.

Deciding the size of a rectangular tablecloth Measure the length and width of the table and add on 23 cm to 30 cm (9 in to 12 in) for the overhang on each side (about knee level) or the depth to the floor if you prefer a floor length cloth.

The hem allowance depends on the finish you choose – if the cloth is to have a plain hem, add another 5 cm (2 in) to each side; allow only 1·5 cm (½ in) for a decorative edging or for a floor length cloth. No hem allowance is needed if edges are to be frayed.

If you can buy suitable fabric wide enough – usually from a specialist needlework shop – you will only need one length. If you have to join the fabric to make up the width, you may need twice or three times the length, depending on the width of the fabric and the table, and on where the seams are to fall.

Because a centre seam would look ugly, the best method is to join pieces of fabric of equal width to the long sides of the main piece. Ideally the main piece should, when in position on the table, cover the table top entirely and overhang the sides, as described for a circular tablecloth, so

Small occasional tables often look better with the addition of a simple tablecloth, and cushion covers made to match complete the decorative touch.

than having the joining seams so near the edges that they could upset the balance of the place setting, it might be better to make the centre panel narrower still and make a feature of the seams.

For example, for a table 106 cm (3 ft 6 in) wide the tablecloth – with a 23 cm (9 in) overhang and 5 cm (2 in) hem allowance – would be 157 cm (62 in) wide unfinished. With 120 cm (48 in) fabric, you would need an amount twice the length of the finished cloth plus hems.

The full width of the fabric can be used for the centre panel, which is cut from one 'length', with the side panels cut from the second 'length'.

Work out the width of the panels before buying the fabric. Allow extra fabric for matching a pattern if necessary. You may well find after cutting there will be some fabric left over which can be used for napkins.

Making up the panels   Cut out the panels, including hems, 1·5 cm ($\frac{1}{2}$ in) seam allowance on each side of the centre panel and on the inner edge of the side panels. Join them with a plain seam or – if the cloth is to be washed frequently – a machined flat fell seam in which the edges are enclosed, making the seam flat and easy to press (see Circular tablecloths). If using patterned fabric, make sure that the pattern matches along the seams.

To make a feature of the seams, cover them with braid or ribbon.

Making the hem   For a plain hem on a cloth with 23 to 30 cm (9 to 12 in) overhang, mitre the corners to give a flat, neat appearance. Machine stitch the hem near the edge of the inner fold.

Trimming   There is a wide variety of trimmings available, including braid and lace, which are suitable for trimming the edges of a tablecloth.

When buying trimming allow about 25 cm ($\frac{1}{4}$ yd) extra for mitring corners and neatening the join.

On adjoining sides of the cloth, fold the raw edge 1·5 cm ($\frac{1}{2}$ in) on to the right side and press. With wrong sides together, make a mitred corner on this 1·5 cm ($\frac{1}{2}$ in) raw hem, so that the finished mitre will be on the right side. Pin the trimming round the cloth, over the raw edge, mitring at the corners. Tack and machine stitch along both edges of the trimming.

1. Folds marking the depth of overhang and first rounded corner. 2, 3. Cloth folded to cut remaining corners.
4. Pull threads to fray cloth edges.

that any seams are part of the overhang and do not interrupt the smoothness of the top. If, however, the fabric is narrower than the table top, rather

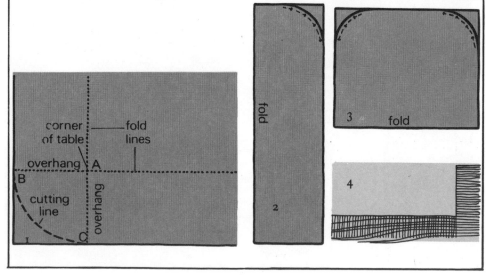

Rounding the corners Before making a hem on a floor length, rectangular cloth it is first necessary to round the corners to stop them trailing on the ground.

On two adjacent sides of the cloth, turn up the depth of the overhang, plus the 1·3 cm (½ in) allowed for the hem. Press and open out the folds (fig. 1). Draw an arc using the pin-and-string method (see Circular tablecloths) from B to C.

Cut along the curved line.

Fold the cloth in half lengthways and pin the arc on the first corner on to the second as a pattern. Cut out second arc and remove pins (fig. 2).

Fold the cloth in half widthways and use the first two corners as a pattern for the third and fourth (fig. 3).

To make a hem on a cloth with rounded corners, snip 1 cm (⅜ in) 'V' notches into the edge at 2·5 cm (1 in) intervals on the curved sections of the edge. Turn in 1·5 cm (½ in) all round the edge (including the straight edges). Finish off the hem with binding as for a circular cloth.

*To fray the edges of a tablecloth or napkins, pull away the threads parallel to the edges to the depth of the fringe required (fig. 4). Overcast the edges to avoid further unwanted fraying.

An alternative to overcasting is to work a line of machine stitching around the cloth or napkin, before fraying the edges, at the depth of fringe required.

Fraying works well on linens and coarse cottons but is not suitable for closely woven cottons.

*Mitring

Folded mitre Used mainly on braids (always on plaited braid which would make a stitched mitre spread). The fullness is simply folded to one side when turning the corner (fig. 1).

Simple stitched mitre Used when applying a bulky braid which will need its turnings trimmed (fig. 2).

Mitring the corner on a tablecloth
On adjoining sides of the cloth, fold over the raw edges 1·5 cm (½ in) to the wrong side and press. Make another fold 3·5 cm (1½ in) from each of the first folded edges and press again. Open out the second folds and turn in the corner on a diagonal line Y-Z going through the point where these fold lines cross, and at an equal distance

from the corner on both sides. Press and then open out the corner fold. Leaving the first 1·5 cm (½ in) folds turned in, trim off the corner 6 mm (¼ in) outside the diagonal crease, cutting firmly through the folded edges (fig. 3).

With right sides together, fold the cloth along A-B and stitch from X-YZ. Press seam open (fig. 4).

Turn the corner right side out, easing out the point gently with a knitting needle. Press (fig. 5).

*Mitring bias binding Unfold one of the creased edges of the binding, and, starting in the middle of one side,

pin it to the cloth, with the raw edges meeting and right sides together. Clip the binding seam allowance at the corners to ease it round. To join the binding, overlap it at the ends, turn-

Napkins to match or contrast with the tablecloth are made from squares of fabric and can be finished with a plain hem, frayed or trimmed with lace as shown here.
1. Making a folded mitre.
2. Making a simple stitch mitre.
3. The corner trimmed away.
4. Corner seam stitched and pressed.
5. The finished mitre.

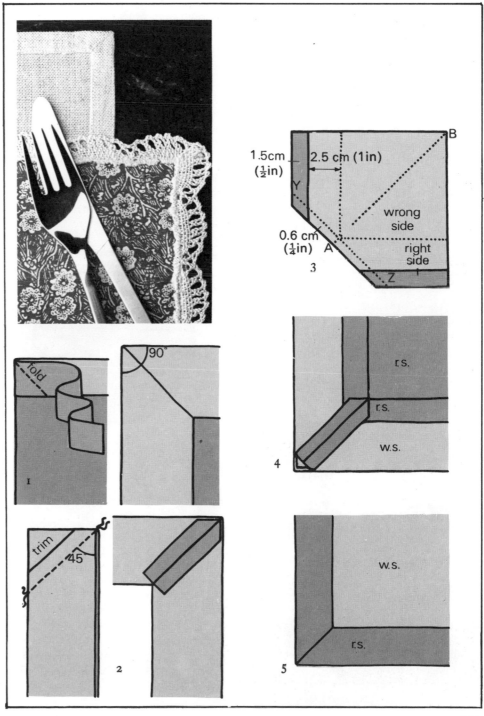

ing under the raw edges to make a neat join. Tack and machine stitch the binding in position, and then press it over completely on to the wrong side of the cloth. Tuck under the excess binding at the four corners, making a diagonal fold. Tack the binding on to the cloth along the inner fold, and machine or hem stitch. Stitch the folds and join with small hem stitching.

Napkins

Dinner napkins traditionally tended to be of a good size, not only to cover laps from possible spills but also because they used to be folded into elaborate shapes. Nowadays, when most people fold napkins simply into four, a practical size – making best use of fabric widths – is 40 cm to 45 cm (16 in to 18 in) square.

Finish napkins with plain hems and mitred corners, as for the tablecloth, but turning over the first fold for 6 mm ($\frac{1}{4}$ in) and the second fold 1·5 cm ($\frac{1}{2}$ in). Stitch by machine, or with small, firm slipstitching.

Place mats

These tend to be more informal than a tablecloth and are ideal for tables with a surface which you want to 'show off' but protect from scratches. If you also want to protect it from heat, use a cork mat under the fabric. A practical size for rectangular place mats is 33 by 45 cm (12 by 16$\frac{1}{2}$ in) finished, but this should be adapted according to the width of the fabric. For plain edges, make hems with mitred corners as for napkins (above). For a frayed edge, remove the threads

parallel to the edges to the depth of the fringe required as described for tablecloths.

Rounded place mats For round tables, mats which are curved at the outer edge and taper towards the centre of the table can make more economical use of the space (fig. 1).

In order to make the curve on the mats 'parallel' to the curve of the table, cut a paper pattern to fit one quarter of the table top using the pin and string method previously described. Then measure an equal amount in from the straight sides – judge the amount by eye to get the size mat you want – and draw straight lines parallel to the sides, and to the required depth. Join the lines at the top and then cut off the excess paper, allowing 6 mm to 1·5 cm ($\frac{1}{4}$ in to $\frac{1}{2}$ in) hem allowance (fig. 2). Cut out the mats so that the grain on the fabric runs parallel to the sides of the mats (otherwise they may stretch and buckle). Finish the edges with bias binding, so that the binding is completely on the wrong side of the fabric when the mats are finished.

The corners can be mitred following the method above.

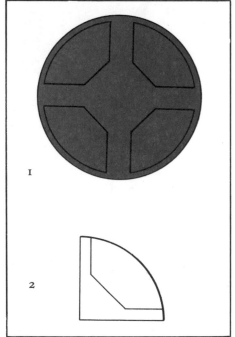

Left. Matching placemats and table napkins are easy to make and enhance the setting for an informal meal.
Right. If you have a circular table and wish to use placemats rather than a cloth, make these mats with a rounded edge. They will make better use of the available space.

Cushions
and Loose Covers

Flat cushion covers

Add an individual character to any room with cushions sewn by you in your own choice of fabric. Make them in a variety of shapes, sizes and textures, in colours to blend with your décor.

*Techniques included: piping, cutting bias strips.

The fabric Most fabrics can be used for flat cushion covers (those without welts), although very fine fabrics usually need backing and can be difficult to work on.

How much fabric? For a plain (unpiped) flat cushion decide on the size of your cushion cover and allow at least twice this amount, plus 1·5 cm (⅝ in) extra all round for turnings. For a well-filled, professional looking cushion make the cover 1·5 cm (⅝ in) smaller all round than its pad. For a cover to fit a 30 cm (12 in) flat square or round cushion you will need a piece of fabric 31·5 by 63 cm (12⅝ by 25¼ in).

To make a plain flat rectangular cushion
You will need:
A cushion pad.
Required amount of fabric.
Sewing thread to match fabric.

Making the cover Keeping the fabric on the straight grain, cut two pieces to the calculated size.
Place the two pieces with right sides together, tack and machine stitch around three sides.
On the fourth side fold down the seam allowances on to the wrong side of each section and press. Trim the stitched corners (fig. 1). Neaten turnings and turn right side out. Press.
Insert the pad and slipstitch the opening neatly by hand. These stitches can be easily removed when the cover is washed.

Making a plain flat round cushion
It is necessary to make a paper pattern to make sure of an accurate curve. Use the pin and string method (see Table linen) to draw a semi-circle on a large sheet of paper. Make the distance between pin and pencil equal to the radius of the finished cover, plus 1·5 cm (⅝ in).

You will need:
Paper for pattern.
A cushion pad.
Required amount of fabric.
Sewing thread to match fabric.

Making the cover Fold the fabric in half lengthways on the straight grain. Place pattern with the straight edge to the fold. Pin into place and cut along curved line only. Mark the grain line along the fold with tacking.

Have fun with fabric and make an array of plain – only in as much as they are easy to sew – cushion covers.

Cut another piece of fabric in the same way.

With right sides together and grain lines matching, place the two sections together. Tack and machine stitch 1·5 cm (⅝ in) from the edge all round the cover, leaving an opening of about one quarter of the circumference to turn through.

Clip small V-shapes to within 3 mm (⅛ in) from the stitching at 3 cm (1 in) intervals all round (fig. 2).

Finish off as for a square cover.

Cushion pads Many large stores sell square and oblong cushion pads in a wide range of sizes. It is, however, quite possible to make your own pads in the size and shape you want.

Filling Down is the most luxurious and most expensive filling and feathers are a good alternative, but many people today prefer to use a synthetic filling such as Terylene wadding which has the advantage of being washable.

Kapok, shredded foam and foam chips are inexpensive alternatives.

Pad covers These can be made from sheeting, calico or any inexpensive, firmly-woven fabric, but if you choose feathers or down for the filling it is essential to buy a down-proof fabric for the pad cover.

Making up Make the cover in the same way as a plain cushion cover with a small opening for filling. Remember that it should be 1·5 cm (⅝ in) larger all round than the outer cushion cover. Turn through to the right side and press.

Stuff the cover with filling so that it is plump but not hard, paying particular attention to the corners.

Pin the folded edges of the opening together. Then tack and machine stitch close to the edge.

*Piping

Piping has several advantages. It gives a stronger seam and a more professional finish to cushions, loose covers or bedspreads. If you are not confident of stitching very straight seams piping will hide minor inaccuracies.

Piping will give a neat, well defined edge and at the same time strengthen the seams of covers to provide greater durability.

It consists of a cord covered with bias-cut strips of fabric and is stitched into a seam.

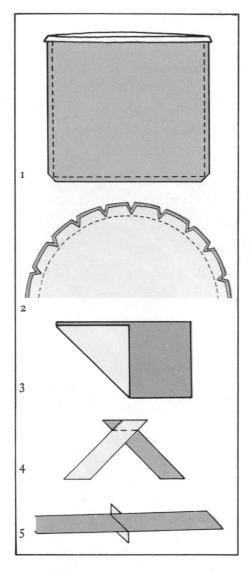

1. Making a plain cushion cover.
2. Clipping seam of a round cover.
3 to 5. Making bias strips.

Piping cord Usually cotton and made up of three strands. It comes in a range of thicknesses. No. 1 is only suitable for fine fabrics such as silk. No. 2 or 3 is most suitable for cushion covers and No. 3 or 4 for loose covers. As the cord is liable to shrink, buy about 25 cm (¼ yd) extra for each cushion. Boil and dry the cord twice before use to ensure that it is fully shrunk.

*Cutting long bias strips

A quick way to cut the long lengths of bias strips needed for piping is as follows:

Take a rectangle of fabric about 23 cm by 46 cm (9 in by 18 in). The length of the fabric should be at least twice the width.

Fold up the bottom left-hand corner to obtain the crossways grain (fig. 3). Press.

Cut off this corner and join to other edge with right sides facing and 6 mm (¼ in) seam (fig. 4).

Press the seam open and trim off any selvedges (fig. 5).

Make a ruler in card to the width of the piping strips. In soft furnishing the width is usually 4·5 cm (1½ in) wide.

Using the ruler and tailor's chalk mark lines on the right side of the fabric, parallel to the ends. Then mark a 6 mm (¼ in) seam allowance along each side. Mark points A and B carefully as shown (fig. 6).

Stick a pin through the wrong side of fabric at point A and bring it across through point B. Pin the two sides together very accurately, right sides facing.

Continue pinning along the marked seam to make a cylindrical shape. Tack, and check that the horizontal lines meet exactly.

Stitch then press seam open using a sleeve board (fig. 7).

Turn to the right side and start cutting along the horizontal lines in a spiral (fig. 8).

Piped square cushion covers

If you intend to pipe the edges of a cushion do not use a loosely woven fabric as the cord will show through. Allow another 50 cm (½ yd) of fabric for making the bias casing strip for the piping cord.

*Techniques include two ways to insert a zip.

You will need:
Paper for pattern.
A cushion pad.
Required amount of fabric.
Matching thread.
Required amount of piping cord.
Zip fastener, 6 cm (2 in) less than cushion width.

Making the cover The piping should be attached before the cover is made up. It is not a good idea to pipe flat round covers as these do not keep a good shape when the pad is inserted.

Cut out cover as previously described.

Cut and join enough 4·5 cm (1½ in) wide bias strips to fit the perimeter of the cover, plus 10 cm (4 in).

Lay the piping cord, slightly longer than the strip, centrally along the wrong side of this strip. Fold the

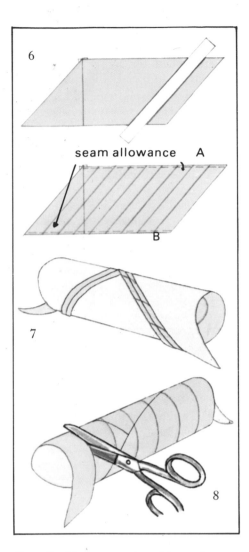

seam allowance A

B

6, 7, 8. How to cut long bias strips.

edges together, with the cord in the middle. Tack or machine stitch casing firmly round cord to within 3 cm (1 in) of each end, keeping the stitching as close as possible to the piping and using the piping foot on the machine (fig. 1).

Starting in the middle of a side, pin the casing all round the edge on the right side of one cover piece. The raw edges of the folded casing must be level with the raw edges of the cover. At each corner, clip into the casing seam allowance to within 3 mm ($\frac{1}{8}$ in) of the tacking stitches of the casing. This will make the piping lie flat (fig. 2).

To make a neat join in the piping, unfold the untacked portion of the casing at each end and overlap ends by 1·5 cm ($\frac{5}{8}$ in). Adjust the overlap to fit the cushion cover exactly. Join the ends as for bias strips, trimming to 6 mm ($\frac{1}{4}$ in).

Overlap the cord for 3 cm (1 in) and trim off the excess. Unravel 3 cm (1 in)

at each end and cut away two strands from one end and one strand from the other. Overlap and twist together the remaining three ends and oversew or bind them firmly (fig. 3).

Fold over the casing and tack round joined cord. Tack the piping to the cushion.

Piping or zipper foot To attach piping successfully by machine it is necessary to use a zipper or piping foot on your sewing machine.

This is made in one piece, instead of split as with the standard foot, enabling the stitching to be worked close to the piping. ·

The cushion cover is usually inserted into the machine with its bulk on the left and the turnings of the seam under the foot.

The needle should be to the left of the foot which is pressed up hard against the piping cord.

Keep the foot in this position throughout the sewing. At the corners, leave the needle down, lift the foot and turn the fabric round to the new position. Lower the foot and continue sewing. Place the second cover piece on top of the piped piece, with right sides together and enclosing the piping. Tack and machine stitch the cover together along three sides, stitching as close as possible to the cord.

Finish as for a plain cover.

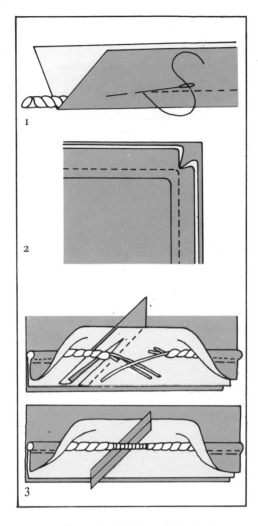

1 to 3. Covering piping cord, fitting to the cover and joining ends. Below. The finished product.

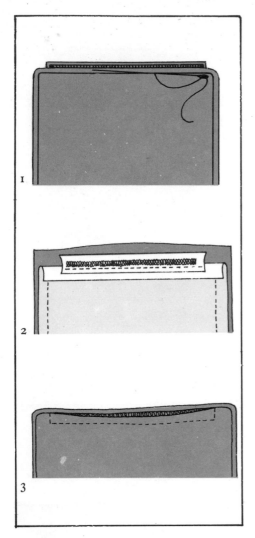

If a cushion cover will have to be removed for laundering, it is a practical idea to make the cover with a zip fastening. Do not use zips on round cushions as they will distort the seams.
1. Zip stitched in by hand. 2, 3. Zip stitched in by machine.

Two ways to insert a zip

When a cover needs to be removed frequently for washing you may prefer to insert a permanent type of fastening, such as a zip fastener.

Zip fasteners are best kept for use on cushions with straight sides as a zip fastener is inclined to distort the shape of a round cushion.

The methods given here are for plain or piped cushions.

Zip fastener stitched by hand

This is a very neat way of putting in a zip.

Make up the cushion in the usual way but stitch along the fourth side for 3 cm (1 in) at each end. Fasten off the stitching securely. Turn the cover right side out.

Press under the turning along the piped edge if piping has been used.

Place the piped edge over the right side of the closed zip so that the folded edge of the turning lies centrally along the teeth of the zip.

On the right side of the cover tack along the gulley between the piping and cover (fig. 1).

Fold under the unpiped edge of the opening and put it on to the zip so that it meets the piped edge. Tack in position close to the edge of the zip teeth, curving the stitching into the fold at the top and bottom.

Using double sewing thread, prick-stitch the zip to the cover along the tacked line.

Zip fastener stitched by machine

With the cover inside out, place the zip face downwards on the piped edge of the opening, with the teeth as close as possible to the piping cord.

Tack and machine stitch the zip to the turning and piping only, close to the teeth, using a zipper foot (fig. 2).

Turn the cover through to the right side and place the other folded edge over the zip to meet the piped edge.

Tack and machine stitch the cover to the zip tape 1 cm ($\frac{3}{8}$ in) from the fold; take the stitching across to the fold at each end (fig. 3).

Turn the cover to the wrong side and snip into the stitched-down turning at each end.

If you prefer, the zip can be inserted before the other three sides are stitched.

Box cushion covers

Box cushions are block-shaped cushions with squared-off edges. They are usually made from foam-rubber pads and are often used on the seats and backs of chairs. They also make good floor cushions. Covers are made with a strip of fabric (the welt) separating the top piece from the bottom. Box cushions are sometimes used with conventional armchairs and sofas. They can be re-covered to match loose covers.

The pad If you are buying your own foam pad to make box cushions, check that it is of the correct quality foam for your purpose. To give the best wear, seat cushions should be of a higher density than back cushions and for comfort they should be 7.5 to 10 cm (3 to 4 in) thick. Back cushions can be slightly thinner.

The fabric If the cushions are to be used regularly, buy the type of fabric recommended for loose covers. It is also advisable to make an inner cover which protects the foam and prevents the main cover from sticking to it. This inner cover can be of calico, curtain lining or any lightweight cotton.

Making a cutting chart The simplest way of estimating the amount of fabric you need is to draw a cutting chart to scale. (Take one small square on the graph paper to represent 2 cm (1 in). To do this, draw a straight line to represent the width of your fabric. Draw two more lines at right angles to each end of this. Then draw on the cover pieces; a top and bottom and four welt pieces (or one long strip to go right round the cushion). The outer cover for a box cushion should be exactly the same size as the pad.

A zip fastener can be inserted into the centre of one of the shorter welt pieces. In this case this section is made in two halves and seam allowances must be added for the zip fastener.

Add 1.5 cm ($\frac{5}{8}$ in) seam allowances for each cover piece. Complete the rectangle after the last piece. Measure the length of the rectangle to give the amount of fabric required. If the cushion is to be piped, add about 50 cm ($\frac{1}{2}$ yd) to pipe the top and bottom of each cushion.

To make a box cusion cover
You will need:

A cushion pad.

Required amount of fabric and matching thread.

Pre-shrunk piping cord (twice perimeter of pad plus 30 cm (12 in)).

Zip fastener, 1.3 cm ($\frac{1}{2}$ in) shorter than width of pad.

Cutting out Pieces should be cut on the straight grain of the fabric. If the fabric has a pile or one-way design this should run from back to front on the top and bottom pieces and from top to bottom on the welt. Cut out one top, one bottom and strips for welt of cushion to sizes marked in cutting chart.

Join the side strips to each side of the front strip along the short edges, taking 1.5 cm ($\frac{5}{8}$ in) turnings. Taper the stitching into the corners 1.3 cm ($\frac{1}{2}$ in) from the beginning and end of each seam (fig. 1).

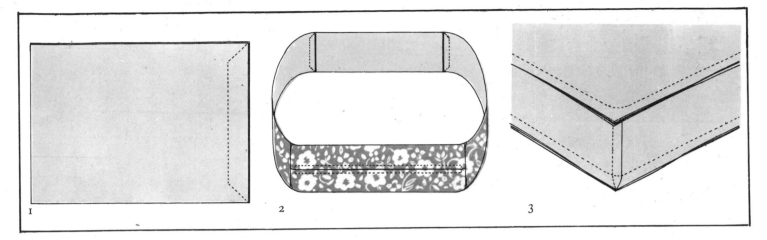

1   2   3

If putting in a zip join the halves of the remaining welt strip for 2 cm (¾ in) at each end, taking 1·5 cm (⅝ in) turnings. Insert zip into the opening. Attach to the ends of the welt strip, taking 1·5 cm (⅝ in) turnings and tapering the stitching as before (fig. 2). Press the turnings to one side.

(If the welt has been cut in one piece, insert the zip fastener centrally on the bottom section.)

Piping A box cushion looks better if it is piped. Make up the piping as previously described and attach it to the top and bottom sections before joining them to the welt.

With right sides together pin top of cover on to welt, matching the seams of the welt to the corners. Tack and machine stitch as close to the piping as possible.

Stitch the bottom section of the cover in the same way (fig. 3). Press and turn the finished cover right side out.

Round cushion with welt

This type of cushion is ideal for bedrooms, bathrooms and kitchens. It can be made up with ties and used to transform a plain wooden stool into

1. Stitching side strips to front piece.
2. Zip fastener stitched into welt strips.
3. Finishing the box cushion.
Below. A day bed is transformed into a settee by matching cushions and cover.

something really attractive.

You will need:
Paper for pattern.
Required amount of fabric and matching thread.
A round welted cushion pad.
Pre-shrunk piping cord, twice the cushion circumference plus 1 m (1 yd).

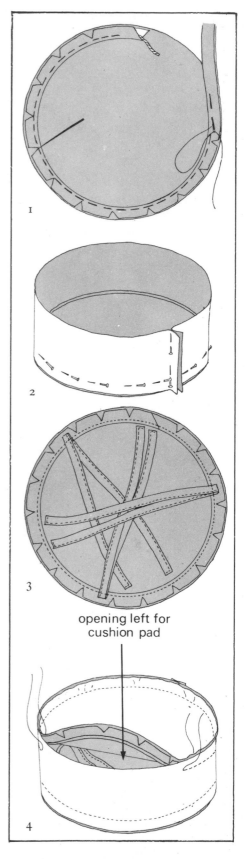

opening left for
cushion pad

*1. Applying piping to the edge of a
round cushion with welt.
2. Pinning the welt to the top cushion
piece.
3. Placing ties on cushion cover.
4. Stitching bottom cushion piece.
A round cushion with welt is ideal for
a kitchen stool.*

Cutting out First make a circular paper pattern to the size of the cushion. For top and bottom cut two circles of fabric, adding 1·5 cm (⅝ in) seam allowances all round. Remember to centre any design when cutting out.

For the welt, cut a piece of fabric on the straight grain of the fabric to the required depth of the welt plus 1·5 cm (⅝ in) seam allowance each side and to the circumference of the circle plus 10 cm (4 in) for seams and easing. Cut 4 cm (1½ in) wide bias strips using the quick spiral method previously described. You will need enough for twice the circumference of the cushion plus 20 cm (8 in) for ease.

Applying the piping Make up and apply the piping as described for piping square cushion covers. Clip into the seam allowance at frequent intervals to enable the piping to mould to the shape (fig. 1).

Piping should be stitched to both top and bottom cushion pieces.

Finishing the cushion Pin the welt to the top cushion piece, wrong sides together, and mark the exact position for the join on the welt (fig. 2).

Tack and machine stitch the welt seam and press seam open.

With right sides together stitch the welt to the cushion top using a piping or zipper foot to stitch as close as possible to the piping.

If you want ties to attach the cushion to a stool, cut three of four 4 cm (1½ in) wide straight strips of fabric each about 60 cm (24 in) long.

Fold in half lengthways, wrong sides together, and press. Turn in all edges for 6 mm (¼ in) and press again. Machine folded edges together.

Mark positions for the ties on the bottom of the cushion. Position them on the right side as shown (fig. 3).

Tack the welt to the bottom of the cushion in the same way as the top, leaving an opening large enough to insert the cushion pad (fig. 4). Stitch. Turn to right side.

Insert the cushion pad and slipstitch opening to close.

Squab cushions
Individually-shaped squab cushions are an easy way to add colour to the

Pretty squab cushions add comfort to dinner table seating arrangements.

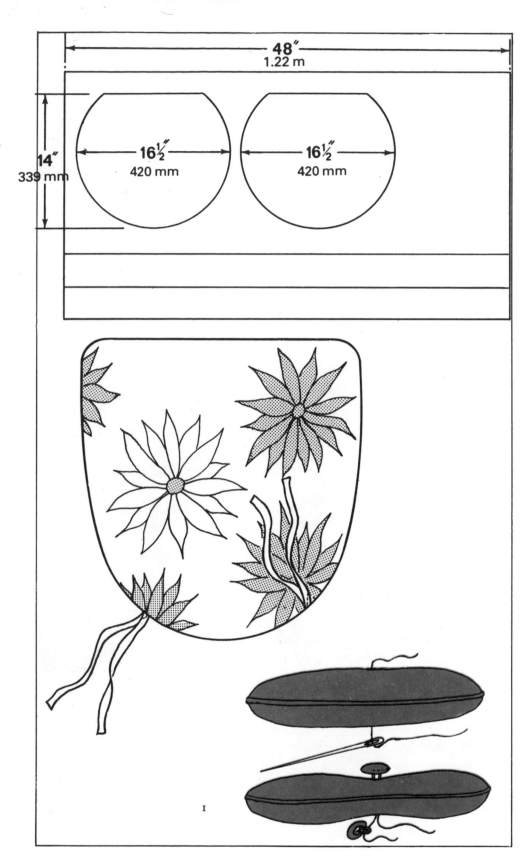

(¾ to 1 in) deep and a little larger than the size of chair seat.

Required number of button moulds and under buttons; also carpet thread for deep buttoning (optional).

Making the pattern Lay a sheet of newspaper across the chair seat and mark round front and side edges of the seat. Mark the shape round any struts at the back of the chair so that the cushion will fit snugly. Check the fit before cutting out a final pattern (fold this in half lengthwise to ensure that sides are uniform). Mark the position of the back chair legs on the pattern.

Cutting out Lay the pattern on to the foam plastic and draw round it with a ballpoint pen. Cut out the shape with scissors. Using the pattern, cut out top and bottom cushion pieces on the straight grain of the fabric, adding 1·5 cm (⅝ in) seam allowances.

To make the squab cushion Cut and make up two fabric ties as described for round cushion with welt. Position the ties to correspond with back legs of chair as marked on pattern. With right sides together tack and machine stitch the two cushion pieces, leaving an opening in the back to insert the cushion pad. Turn to right side. Insert cushion pad and slipstitch opening to close.

*Deep buttoning
To button the cushions, first cover button moulds with cushion cover fabric, following manufacturer's instructions. With long needle and carpet thread, sew through shank of the under button, up through the cushion, through the shank of the top button, down through the cushion and back to the button on the underside. Pull the threads tightly so that the top button sinks into the cushion slightly. Knot the threads firmly (fig. 1).

Loose covers
It is quite simple to make your own loose covers and it is considerably less expensive than having them made. Complicated patterns are not required. The fabric is cut directly on the chair or sofa and 'moulded' to fit the contours of the upholstery by pinning. It

A bedroom chair loose-covered in a brightly coloured fabric, and with the deep skirt box pleated at the corners.

Top. Measuring for squab cushions.
Middle. Position for ties on cushion.
1. Deep-buttoning a cushion.

while more elegant versions could be made in velvet or corduroy.
*Techniques include deep buttoning.

You will need:
Paper for pattern.
Required amount of fabric.
Sewing thread to match fabric.
A piece of foam plastic, 2 to 2·5 cm

plainest kitchen chair.
Fabrics for squab cushions should be firmly woven. Depending on the purpose of the cushion, linen, cotton or repp are all suitable washable fabrics

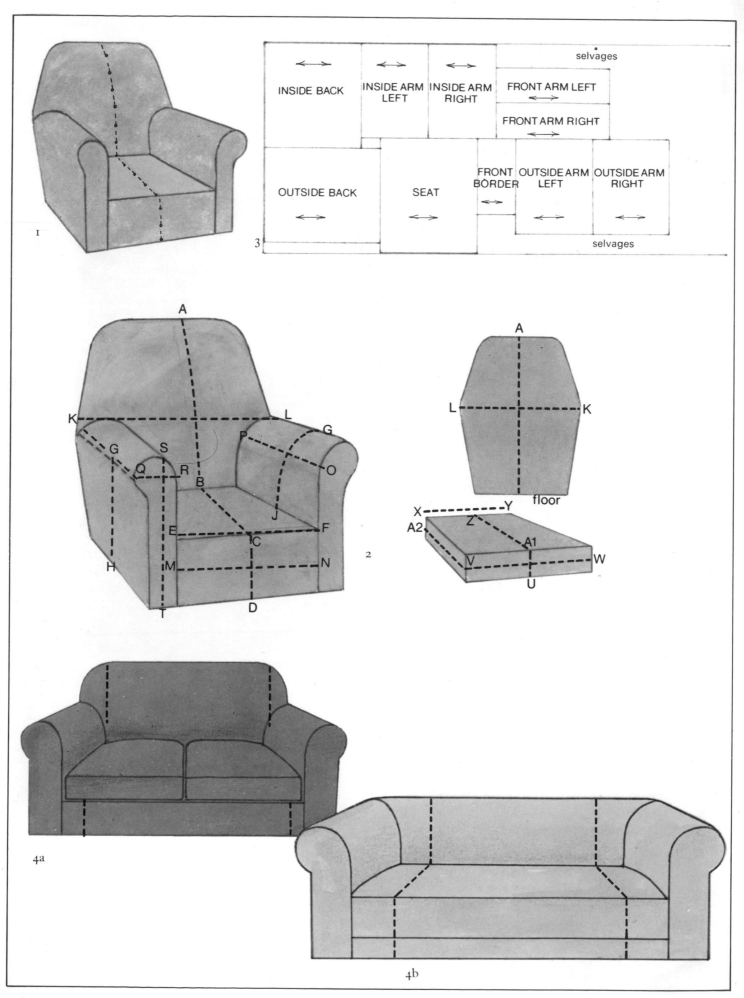

1

3

INSIDE BACK	INSIDE ARM LEFT	INSIDE ARM RIGHT	FRONT ARM LEFT
			FRONT ARM RIGHT

selvages

OUTSIDE BACK	SEAT	FRONT BORDER	OUTSIDE ARM LEFT	OUTSIDE ARM RIGHT

selvages

A

K   L
          G   S   P   G
      G   Q   R   O
                        B
                   E   F
                        C
H   M   N
     T   D

2

A

L   K

floor

X   Y
A2   Z
              A1
    V   W
              U

4a

4b

is a satisfying experience to see the shape emerging as you work.

Although the shapes and sizes of upholstered furniture vary, the same basic techniques are used for all styles both to estimate the fabric required and to cut and fit covers.

One particular chair shape has been used here for the purpose of illustration. Different shapes or additional insets are treated in the same way but it is important to follow the seam lines of the original upholstery as closely as possible.

What can be covered With the exception of velvet and leather almost any upholstered chair or sofa can be fitted with loose covers.

Before you start always clean the chair or sofa with dry upholstery shampoo.

Choosing the fabric Choose furnishing fabrics which are tough and hard wearing, firm in weave, colour fast and pre-shrunk. Avoid very thick fabrics as these will be difficult to work with, especially if you are piping the seams. Medium-weight cottons and linens treated for crease resistance are ideal, but do not attempt to use dress

1. Pins placed down the centre front.
2. Take measurements across the widest and deepest sections of the chair.
3. A sample chart. Use measurements taken to work out your own chart.
4a. Position of seams on a small sofa using 120 cm (48 in) wide fabric.
4b. Position of seams on a large sofa using 120 cm (48 in) wide fabric.
5. Outside back pinned into place.

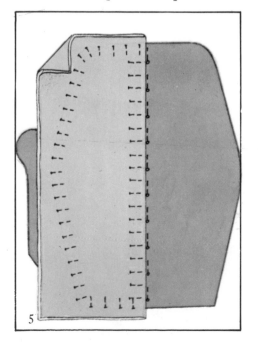

5

fabrics as they are not strong enough.

Taking the measurements
Before buying the fabric and cutting out, the separate sections must be measured.

Write all measurements down as they will be needed for calculating the amount of fabric wanted and again when cutting out the individual sections of fabric.

Remove the cushion or cushions if there are any and mark a line with glass headed pins up the centre of the outside back of the chair, down the inside back and along the seat from the back to the front border (fig. 1).

Using a fabric tape measure, measure each section, including cushions, at its widest point (fig. 2). If your particular chair or sofa sections are not pictured here, these should be measured following the same principle.

Outside back From A to floor; from K to L.

Inside back From A to B plus 15 cm (6 in) for tuck-in; from K to L.

Inside arm From G to J plus 15 cm (6 in) for tuck-in; from P to O plus 15 cm (6 in) for tuck-in.

Outside arm From G to H; from K to Q

Seat From B to C plus 15 cm (6 in) for tuck-in, from E to F plus 30 cm (12 in) for tuck-in.

Border From C to D; from M to N.

Front arm From Q to R; from S to T.

Cushion top From X to Y; from Z to A1.

Cushion front inset V to W; from A1 to U.

Cushion side inset From A2 to V.

Fabric requirements
Most furnishing fabrics are 120 cm (48 in) wide and to cover a chair you will require about five times as much fabric as the height of the back. However, a more precise estimate is needed for each individual piece and this can be accomplished using the measurements just described.

Draw a small chart to scale on a sheet of paper or graph paper. (Large quantities of fabric will be involved.) Draw two parallel lines to scale to represent the width of the fabric. Use a simple scale such as 1 mm for every centimetre ($\frac{1}{10}$ in for every inch).

Using the measurements you have

taken draw out rectangles to scale to represent each section needed for the cover, adding 3 cm (1$\frac{1}{4}$ in) to each measurement for seam allowances (fig. 3). Label each piece and mark the dimensions as you progress. Remember that some sections such as sides, arms and cushion parts have to be cut twice.

Extra allowances Should the fabric you choose have a repeated design this will have to be taken into consideration and extra fabric bought. The quantity depends on the size of the repeat.

Piping Allow an extra 1·40 m (1$\frac{1}{2}$ yd) for cutting bias strips if you intend to pipe a chair. Increase this estimate proportionately for a sofa.

Sofa Special allowances must be made for joins in the fabric if necessary to obtain the correct width (figs. 4a and 4b). A repeated pattern must always match at the seams.

Skirt Extra fabric will also be needed should you want a frill or pleated finish to the bottom.

For a frill, you will need twice the circumference of the bottom of the chair by the depth of frill plus seam and hem allowance.

For a plain tailored skirt with a pleat at each corner you will need the circumference of chair or sofa plus 88 cm (32 in) by the depth of trim plus seam and hem allowance.

Having drawn all the pieces out to scale on paper, measure the total length and convert to full scale to find out the amount of fabric required.

Making loose covers
You will need:
Calculated quantity of fabric.
Sewing thread to match.
Calculated length of No. 3 or 4 piping cord.
Required fastenings.

Cutting the fabric Following the chart you have made, mark out with chalk and cut a rectangle of fabric for each area to be covered. Make sure that the lengthwise grain of each piece runs with the grain of the fabric, and that the pattern, if any, matches. Be sure to add 2·5 cm (1 in) seam allowance round each piece.

Fitting the cover The method of fitting the fabric to the chair is to fold the rectangles of fabric in half with right sides together and, working from the centre marked with pins. fit, pin and trim closely. The fabric is then opened out and the pieces stitched together inserting piping in the appropriate seams.

Starting with the outside back pieces fold in half and place the folded edge level with the pins down the back of the chair, the allowances made for turnings should project at the top, side and bottom. Pin down the fold then smooth the fabric out to the side of the chair and pin it to the padding, placing the pins at right angles to the edge of the fabric. Keep the fabric smooth and taut with the grain of the fabric straight in both directions (fig. 5).

Pin the seat piece to centre of seat in the same way, so that the allowance for the tuck-in lies at the back and side and a seam allowance in the front. Pin the fabric all round and fold back the tuck-in allowance on to the seat for the time being (fig. 6).

Fold the inside back piece, pin it to the centre line, smooth it out and pin it to the padding as before. Then pin to the outside back piece at the top of the chair following the shape of the chair exactly.

With some fabrics you may be able to ease in the fullness. With others, such as linen on a curved back, you may have to make small darts at the corners. Pin the pieces together down the sides working from the top down. As you reach the arm cut into the fabric from the sides so that the inside back can be wrapped round smoothly to join the back. Carefully cut the fabric over the arm to fit the curve and then extend gradually outwards to the full 15 cm (6 in) tuck-in allowance at the bottom of the section (fig. 7). Clip into the seam allowance on the curve.

Fitting the arms Place the two inside arm pieces together with wrong sides facing, then place them on to the inside arm. Pin the front edge to the padding first and the top to the 'sight line'. This is an imaginary line (fig. 8a) where a seam must be made in loose

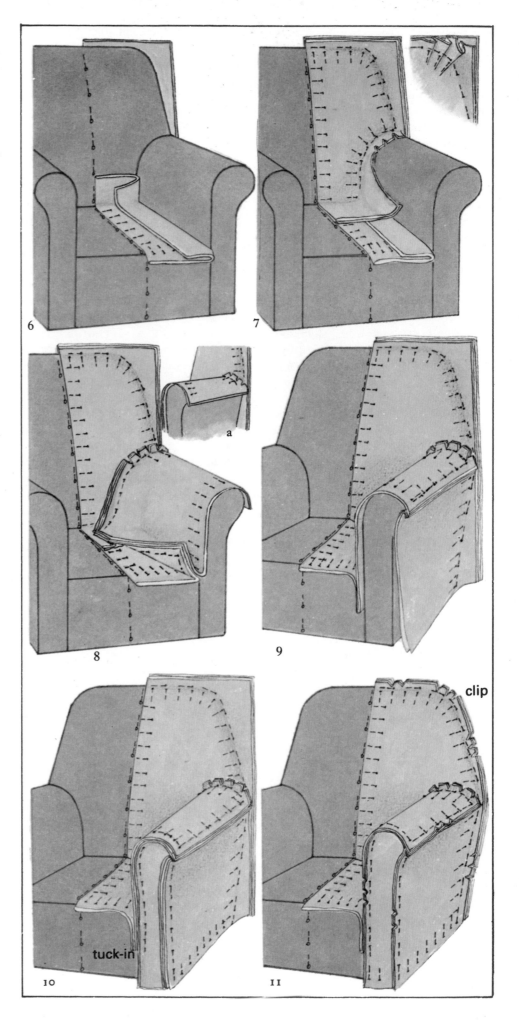

6. Seat piece in position. 7. Inside back pinned to outside back. 8. Inside arm pinned and trimmed. 8a. Dotted line is sight line. 9. Outside arm pinned at top and back. 10. Arm front pinned in place. 11. Seams trimmed and clipped.

covers and does not already exist in the upholstery. The seam allowance should overlap the front and the 'sight line'. Smooth to back of arm, with grain parallel to side of chair. Pin the bottom edge to the tuck-in edge of the seat and cut the back edge of the arm to correspond with the inside back tuck-in. Clip the seam allowance over the top curve of the arm where necessary (fig. 8).

Place the outside arm pieces together with wrong sides facing, keep the straight crosswise grain of the fabric parallel to the floor. Pin the top edge to the inside arm on the 'sight line'. At the very back of the arm where the padding is less rounded, more fabric may have to be pinned into the seam.

12. Piping tacked to outside back, top of outside arm and front arm.
13. Inside back, inside arm, outside arm and seat stitched together.

Pin the back edge of the outside arm piece to the outside back and to padding, leave front edge free (fig. 9).

Fitting the arm fronts Position both front arm pieces together, wrong sides facing, to the widest part of the arm front and pin carefully to the outside arm piece following the shape of the chair as closely as possible. Continue pinning to the inside arm as far as the end of the tuck-in (fig. 10).

The front panel or border This cannot be cut until after the other pieces have been cut and all the main seams have been stitched and tuck-ins positioned correctly.

Trimming the seam allowance If you are satisfied with the fit of the cover so far, trim all the turnings exactly to within 1·5 cm ($\frac{5}{8}$ in) of the pinned fitting lines. Cut notches in the corresponding seams in groups of two and three, so that you will be able to fit the pieces together again (fig. 11). Remove all the pins, take the sections off the chair and open them out.

Make up lengths of piping by enclosing the piping cord in the bias strips as previously described. (see Piped square cushion covers).

Attaching piping Pin and tack the piping on the right side of the fabric sections shown (fig. 12). Make sure raw edges are together. These include the top and sides of the outside back, the front arms and the top edges or 'sight line' of the outside arms. The front border will be cut and piped later.

Box cushions (See Cushions for details of cutting, fitting and making up.)

Stitching and pressing You will find that a neat and crisp finish will be easier to achieve if you press seams as you work.

Remember to take 1·5 cm ($\frac{5}{8}$ in) turnings throughout and before stitching the sections together always pin and tack them first.

Stitch all seams with right sides facing and neaten the raw edges by stitching them together with a zigzag stitch, or oversew by hand. Press all seams away from the front of the chair. Tack and stitch the tuck-in seam at the back of the seat and the bottom of the inside back. This is an unpiped seam.

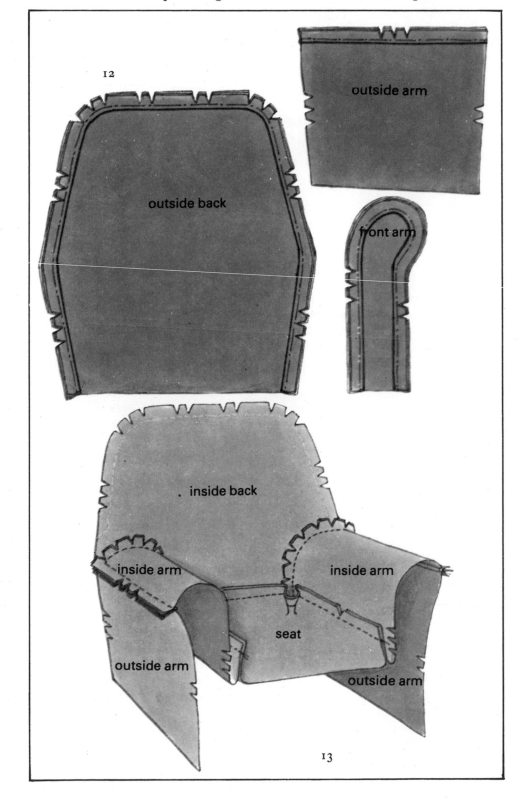

12

outside arm

outside back

front arm

inside back

inside arm

inside arm

seat

outside arm

outside arm

13

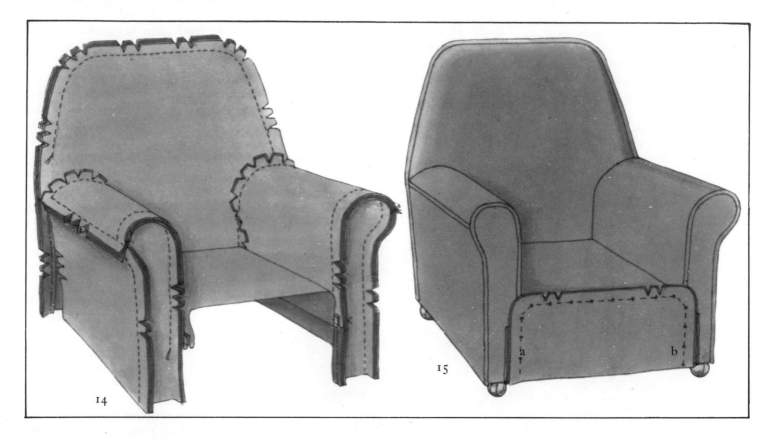

Next stitch the outside arms to the inside arms stitching the piping into the seam.

Stitch the bottom of the inside arms to the sides of the seat tuck-in, then stitch the arm to the inside back. (This seam is not piped). Fig. 13 shows seams stitched together so far.

Stitch the outside and inside back together along the top and down one side continuing down to the bottom of the chair. Then stitch the other side to about 10 cm (4 in) above the top of the arm, leaving an opening so that the cover can be fitted on to the chair. The length of the opening depends on the shape of the chair as you must be able to slip the cover on easily. This is a piped seam.

Stitch the front arm pieces in place. Stitch from the outside arm inwards and finish at the tuck-in on the inside arm (fig. 14).

Fitting the front border Put the cover on to the chair right side out. Tuck in the sides and back tuck-in pieces, and leave the seam allowance protruding at the front edge. It is at this stage that you will be able to decide how long the back opening should be.

Place the front border in position (fig. 15). Pin it to the front of the seat cover and to the seam allowance of the tuck-in at both sides and to the

14. Stitching pieces together.
15. Stitching front border in position.

lower front arms, wrong sides facing. Trim the seam allowance to 1·5 cm ($\frac{5}{8}$ in), mark position with notches and remove the cover from the chair.

Unpin the front border and insert piping along the seam line of the top edge from tuck-in to tuck-in (A to B in fig. 15). Pin together, right sides facing. Tack and stitch the front border into position. The piping will run from A to B along the front of the seat and below A and B on the front arms.

Back opening The opening down the back of the cover can be finished with a zip fastener, hooks and eyes or press studs – they are all equally suitable.

Strong upholstery zips are available and furnishing tape with large press studs or hooks and eyes already inserted can be bought by the metre (yard). If the chair or sofa has a very curved back, separate hooks sewn on by hand with hand-worked bars will give a neater finish. It depends upon the finish at the bottom of the chair how long the zip or tape should be. Take the zip or tape to the planned bottom seam line.

Fitting a zip fastener Measure the length required. The zip should not

come to the bottom corner as the zip pull may protrude.

Clip the front seam allowance at the top of the opening. Press the seam allowance on both edges to the wrong side and tack on the folds.

Place the closed zip to the cover with the right side of the zip to the inside of the cover, and the open end down. From the right side tack the zip into place close to the teeth of the zip. The piping cord will be over the teeth.

Using a zipper or piping foot, machine stitch close to the teeth and again near the outside of the tape to add strength and prevent the zip tape from catchin the zip (fig. 16).

Tape with press studs or hooks Clip the front seam allowance at the top of the opening.

With the two pieces of tape fastened together, pin the tape into the opening making sure there is a stud or hook just above the bottom of the chair cover. One edge of each tape should be on the seam line. Now open the tape and tack and stitch each tape into position. The back tape is stitched on both sides flat against the back but the tape attached to the side bends round to the back of the chair. Stitch side tape close to the seam line. Work another row of stitching on the tape 6 mm ($\frac{1}{4}$ in) from the first (fig. 17 and 18).

With the tape fastened neaten the top raw ends of the tape and stitch together.

Hooks and hand-worked bars Sewn on plain tape. If back of cover is very curved it will be neater to use this method. The tape is attached to the cover in the same way as tape with hooks and eyes or studs. Hooks are then stitched on at about 5 cm (2 in) intervals and bars worked by hand in strong thread to correspond with the hooks. On some curves it will be necessary to place the hooks and bars closer together so that the opening does not gape (fig. 19).

Finishing the bottom There are several ways to finish the bottom of a loose cover depending upon the style of the chair or sofa and your own personal taste.

A plain finish This type of finish can be piped or left plain. It consists of strips of fabric fitted under the chair between the legs, with a narrow hem forming a channel (fig. 20).

If the bottom is to be piped attach the piping to the loose cover with raw edges together and tack into place before proceeding.

Cut four strips of fabric about 10 cm (4 in) wide and the correct length to fit between the legs.

Make a narrow hem at the ends of each piece and a channel 1.5 cm (⅝ in) wide along one long side to hold the tape.

Stitch the raw edges of the strips to the bottom of the cover, sandwiching any piping in between. Neaten the raw edges and press up on to the cover.

Insert a long piece of tape through the channel. Place the cover on the chair and tie the tape in one corner.

Frilled finish (fig. 21) Decide upon depth of frill required and add 1.5 cm (⅝ in) for seam allowances at the top and 2.5 cm (1 in) for a small hem.

Measure around the bottom of the chair and double this measurement. This will be the length of frill required. Cut fabric into strips the required depth and join the strips to obtain the right length taking 1.5 cm (⅝ in) turnings. Clip the selvedges and press the seam open.

Make a small hem along the bottom of the frill by turning up 2.5 cm (1 in). Make a small hem on the short ends for the opening in the same way,

mitring the corners.

Divide the frill into four equal sections and mark with pins. Run a gathering thread between the pins. The open end will go to the back opening.

With the cover on the chair mark the position of the stitching line for the frill with pins, measuring from the floor. Trim the cover to 1.5 cm (⅝ in) below the pins and pipe the bottom of the cover.

Divide the measurement around the piped edge of the cover by four and mark with pins.

Take the cover off the chair. Draw up the gathers on the frill and with right sides and raw edges together, matching the pins, pin and tack the frill to the

cover, distributing the gathers evenly. Stitch and press up, neaten the raw edges together.

Plain tailored finish To make skirting for a plain tailored finish, a border of fabric is placed around the chair or sofa with a pleat at each corner (fig. 22). Measure the bottom front, back and sides of the chair or sofa and add 10 cm (4 in) to each measurement. Cut strips of fabric to these lengths and to the depth of border required

16. Back opening closed with a zip.
17. Using tape fitted with press studs.
18. Alternatively, use tape fitted with hooks and eyes.
19. Closing with hooks and bars.

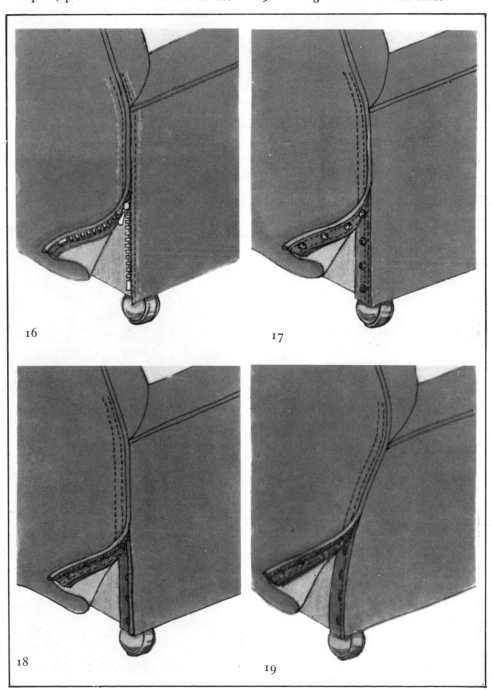

16   17

18   19

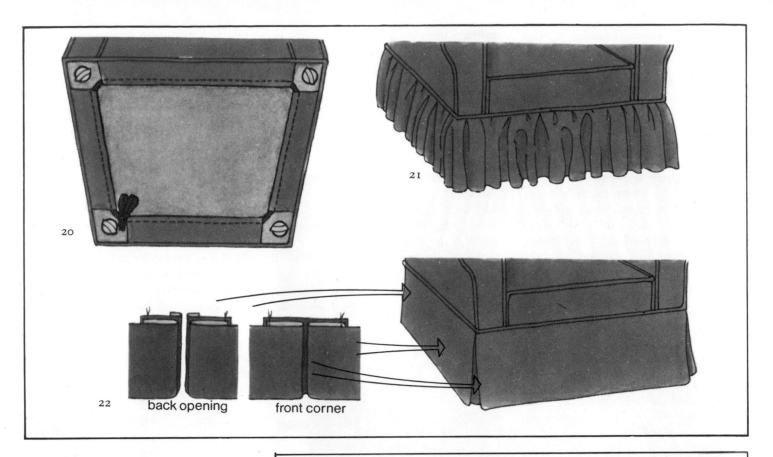

20

21

22   back opening   front corner

20. A piped plain finish, with tape threaded through channel.
21. A frilled finish.
22. Plain tailored finish with box pleats. On a back corner the pleat is left open to extend back opening.

A printed linen loose cover is removable, washable and thus practical.

plus seam and hem allowance; mark each piece. Cut three strips 10 cm (4 in) by the depth of the border and two strips 6·5 cm (2½ in) by the depth of the border. These are for the corners. With the cover on the chair mark the depth of border required with pins and trim the cover to 1·5 cm (⅝ in) below the pin line. Pipe the edge all around the bottom of the cover.

Join the border pieces together placing a short piece to each corner and the two very short pieces to the back opening. Take 1·5 cm (⅝ in) turnings. Make a small hem along the bottom and turn in 1·5 cm (⅝ in) at the ends. Neaten and press.

From the right side make a 4 cm (1½ in) inverted pleat at each corner and tack. The seams will sit inside each pleat.

Tack and stitch the border to the cover with right sides together, sandwiching the piping, neaten and press.

Curtains

This imaginatively done window treatment combines elegant full-length net curtains with prints either side in a bold, modern geometric which matches the slip covers of the sofa. The deep colours of the print create a rich, warm feeling with their earthy tones, while net curtains allow the light to pour in to the room through the French windows, at once counteracting what might have been a heavy, almost rigid, atmosphere.

Unlined curtains

Unlined curtains can work magic in the home, bringing a touch of brilliant colour to rooms which are dull or diffusing harsh light in bright rooms. Problem windows can have their problems solved, or a room given a special character with imaginative use of fabrics and window fittings.

Choosing the fabric Unlined curtains show to best advantage with light filtering through them, and good fabrics for this are the coarsely woven linens and semi-sheers. Some of the beautifully patterned lightweight fabrics, such as lawn, look even better with the light behind them than when lined but it may be necessary to have a thicker roller blind between the curtain and the window for privacy at night.

Furnishing fabrics usually measure about 120 cm (48 in).

Curtain headings There are several types of attractive headings which can be made to give curtains an elegant finish, without using pelmets. The simplest to make is a standard gathered heading, which takes the least amount of fabric and is suitable for all weights of fabric.

Pencil pleated headings take rather more fabric and are particularly suitable for heavier fabrics which need to fall in generous but well regulated folds.

For a really elegant heading, pinch pleats display satins, velvets and large prints to their fullest advantage.

Tapes and hooks Gathering and pleating curtains is made easier by using special gathering tapes which are widely available in the shops. There are several different types: some produce a soft gather and others deep formal pleats.

The tape which produces soft gathers (fig. 1) is designed to gather up one and a half to double the fabric width,

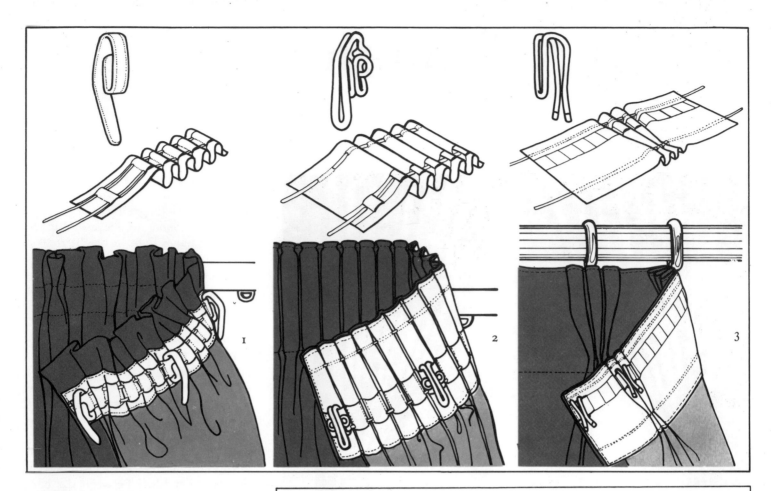

1. Gathered heading: 2.5 cm (1 in) wide tape. Width of curtain required, one and a half to double length of rod. 2. Pencil pleats: 7.5 cm (3 in) wide tape. Width of curtain required, two and a half to three times track length. 3. Pinch pleats: 9 cm (3½ in) wide . tape. Width of curtain required, two and a half to three times track length.

therefore reducing the width of curtain by up to half. The more formal pencil and pinch pleating tapes (figs. 2, 3) gather up to three times the fullness of material reducing the curtain to one third its original width. Also available are tapes designed to produce single, spaced cartridge pleats. If you are using a decorative pole or ceiling track, there are special 'underslung' versions of cartridge or pinch pleating tapes.

Curtain hooks are available in metal or nylon. Make sure the hooks are the correct ones for the tape and track being used. Most curtain tracks have their own range of runners.

Curtain tracks Curtain tracks should extend the width of the window plus 15 cm (6 in) at each end, so that the curtains can be drawn back and away

Widths of fabric required

Width of curtain area	Number of 120 cm (48 in) widths per window (for simple gathered heading)
120 cm (4 ft) and under	2
130 cm to 170 cm (4 ft 6in to 5 ft 6 in)	3
180 cm to 230 cm (6 ft to 7ft 6 in)	4
240 cm to 300 cm (8 ft to 10 ft)	5

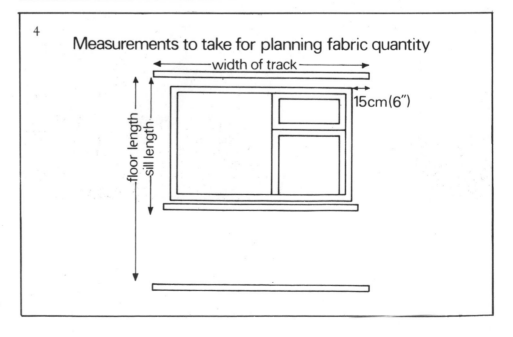

4

Measurements to take for planning fabric quantity

width of track

15cm(6")

floor length

sill length

from the window to give maximum daylight. If the curtains are to overlap in the centre, two sections of track instead of one continuous piece will be required and 10 cm (4 in) extra should be allowed on the length of each track. Each length of track will require two end stops to prevent the curtain hooks from running off.

Fabric requirements
To measure overall width needed
First measure the length of the curtain track and multiply by two for a simple gathered heading. To this add an allowance for side hems, usually 5 cm (2 in) on each side of each curtain. Add a further 15 cm (6 in) to each curtain width if they are to overlap in the centre.

If you have to join widths of fabric to make up the required width it is easiest to base your calculations on full or half widths because any extra width can be incorporated into the curtains. Allow an extra 1·5 cm ($\frac{5}{8}$in) or the width of the selvedge, if this is more, for each width being joined (turning allowance). The chart shows the number of widths you will need for one of a pair of curtains for different sized windows.

Measuring the length needed
Always use a steel tape or long rule to measure from the track to either the window sill or floor (fig. 4). Add to the length 15 cm (6 in) for a double hem at the foot and up to 6·5 cm ($2\frac{1}{2}$ in) for the heading.

The total To calculate how many widths of fabric will be required for each curtain, divide the fabric width into the required width of the curtain and round up the amount to the nearest full width. Multiply this figure by the required length to give the minimum fabric required for each curtain. If the fabric has a repeated pattern, you will have to buy extra for matching the pattern at the seams on each curtain, and to ensure that the pattern falls at the same level on both curtains. To calculate the total fabric required start by checking the length of the pattern repeat, divide this measurement into the calculated length of the curtain to give you the number of pat-

These floor length net curtains have a decorative bordered hem and a neatly finished pencil pleated heading.

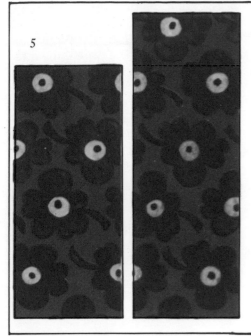

5

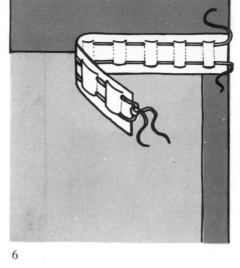

6

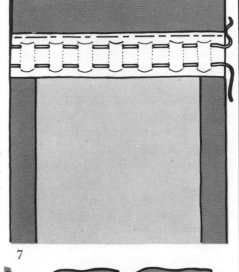

7

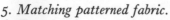

8

9

5. *Matching patterned fabric.*
6. *Tape in place over the raw edge.*
7. *Top of tape tacked to curtain.*
8. *Curtain evenly gathered.*
9. *Inserting hooks in heading tape.*

tern repeats for each curtain. If necessary round up the calculated length of the curtain to be a multiple of the pattern repeat.

If the fabric is not guaranteed preshrunk, allow about 5 cm (2 in) per metre (yard) and wash the fabric before cutting out.

Making the unlined curtains
You will need:

The required length of fabric.
Sewing thread to match fabric.
Curtain tape (same length as curtain top, plus 5 cm (2 in) turnings) and hooks.
Track and runners.
Tape measure and ruler.
Scissors.
Needles and pins.

Lay the fabric on a large flat surface for cutting out – you must be able to see the complete curtain length at once. Use the floor if you haven't a table long or wide enough. Make the top edge absolutely straight by drawing a thread at right-angles to the selvedge, and then cut along the line. Alternatively use a T-square to obtain a straight line. Measure the curtain length from this point, draw another thread and cut along it. Cut the next length in the

same way, matching the pattern if necessary (fig. 5).

For a half width, fold one of the pieces in half lengthwise and cut down the fold.

Plain fabric Use a 1·5 cm ($\frac{5}{8}$ in) plain seam to join the pieces for each curtain placing the right sides of the fabric together, selvedge to selvedge. If using half widths, place them to the outside of each curtain. Machine stitch the pieces together, using a loose tension and a fairly long stitch. Press the seams open and clip into the selvedges if they are tight, or cut off selvedges so that the curtain does not pucker.

Patterned fabric Joining two pieces of fabric so that the pattern matches exactly needs a slightly different technique from that usually used on plain fabric. Begin by finding the same point in the pattern on both pieces of fabric.

With right sides facing, pin the pieces together at this point, with the pin at right angles to the edge (normally the pins are placed on the seam line parallel to the edge). Continue pinning the pieces together at about 5 cm (2 in) intervals, still placing the pins at right angles to the edge. At about 30 cm (12 in) intervals turn the curtain to the right side to check that the pattern still matches. If it has started to slip, take out the pins and re-pin the pieces making sure you are not stretching either of the lengths.

Tack the pieces together along the seam line in the normal way, but leaving the pins in position (if your tacking stitches are usually large, make them smaller for this). Still leaving the pins in, machine stitch, following the tacking line and removing the pins as you are stitching. Remove the tacking and press the seam open.

146

Side hems Use 2·5 cm (1 in) double hems at the sides on unlined curtains as these are heavier than single hems and will prevent the sides from curling back. Trim off the selvedge or snip at intervals.

To make double side hems, fold over edge 2·5 cm (1 in) to the wrong side of the fabric, and then fold this over another 2·5 cm (1 in) so the raw edge is completly enclosed.

Pin and tack the hem down and then slipstitch or machine stitch (if the fabric has a nap like velvet – hand stitch it as machine stitching might spoil the surface).

Attaching the tape For soft gathered curtains turn over the raw edge at the top of the curtains 4 cm (1½ in) to wrong side and tack down. Cut a length of curtain tape the width of each curtain, plus 5 cm (2 in) for turnings.

Pull out about 4 cm (1½ in) of the cords from their slots at both ends of the tape. Knot the cords at one end, but keep the other free for gathering. Place the tape on the curtain so that it covers the raw edge centrally and the top edge of the tape is not more than 2·5 cm (1 in) from the top of the curtain (fig. 6). Make sure that the hook pockets are facing outwards.

Tack along the top edge of the tape turning the ends of the tape under so that the knot is enclosed at one end, but the cords are free at the other (fig. 7).

Tack down the tape along the bottom edge. Machine stitch, outside the cords, along both edges of the tape. (Stitch in the same direction to prevent any drag which would show on the finished curtain.) Stitch down the ends. Remove all the tacking and press.

Gathering the curtains Pull the fabric along the cords until it is all at the knotted end. Pull out again to the right width, distributing the gathers evenly (fig. 8) and knot the cords to secure the width.

Catch the knot to the tape with a few stitches to prevent it from hanging down, but do not cut off the surplus cords. When the curtains need washing or cleaning, the gathers can be released

A wall of curtains with pinch pleated heading can look extremely elegant.

by unpicking the catch stitches and untying the knot.

Insert curtain hooks (fig. 9) into the pockets at each end of the curtains, and at 7·5 cm (3 in) intervals when assembling gathered headings.

To pleat the curtains

Hold the free ends of the cord firmly, and push the first set of pleats into position along the cords. The spaces between the pleats must be kept flat and unpuckered. Push the second set of pleats into position and then push the first set into position again.

Proceed in this way until all the pleats are in position along the heading. Try the curtain on the rail and adjust the pleats if necessary so that they fit exactly.

For pinch pleats and pencil pleats

Turn over the raw edge at the top of the curtain 1·5 cm ($\frac{5}{8}$ in), then make up as for soft gathered curtains but place the top edge of the tape 3 mm ($\frac{1}{8}$ in) from the top of the curtain.

For pencil pleats the hooks are also inserted at 7·5 cm (3 in) intervals but for pinch pleated headings the special hooks are inserted where indicated on the tape.

Making the hem Hang the curtains for a few days before taking up the bottom hems, as some fabrics may stretch during this time.

When you are ready do the hems, mark the line for the length at each side of the curtain while it is still hanging. Full-length curtains should finish 2·5 cm (1 in) above the floor to allow them to hang properly and prevent them dragging and wearing through Sill-length curtains should either just clear the sill, or be about 2·5 cm (1 in) below the sill so that the curtains hang outside it.

Take down the curtains and mark the hemline with pins using a ruler to make sure an accurate measurement is achieved.

Turn the hem up and tack loosely along the edge of the fold through one thickness of fabric.

Turn in the raw edges half the depth of the hem allowance and again to make double hems. Tack them down and machine or hand stitch.

Curtain rings and bars are a less formal way of hanging curtains, suitable both for sheers or unlined curtains.

Remove the tacking and press.

Sheer curtains

Man-made fibres have revolutionized the field of sheer curtains – they are strong, do not shrink or pull out of shape and some, such as Terylene, are resistant to deterioration from light.

The fabric Sheer curtain fabrics fall into two categories: fine nets and semi-sheers.

Fine nets are the traditional type, hung against the window to give privacy to a room which can be seen into, they are usually white and are combined with heavier main curtains which give complete screening at night.

Semi-sheers are heavier than fine nets and have a more open weave. They look particularly attractive with large modern windows where they diffuse the light rather than obscure it. They can also make attractive room dividers. Semi-sheers are made in a variety of colours, weaves and textures, mostly from acrylic fibres which give a warm feel. The curtains are decorative and heavy enough to be hung outside the window recess, and main curtains are often not necessary.

Calculating fabric requirements

Sheer curtains are measured and made up in a similar way to unlined curtains. The main difference is that sheer curtains are fuller – up to three times the width of the area they are to cover.

To save joining several lengths together, which can look ugly as the seams show through to the right side, it is normally better to make several curtains, each of a fabric width, instead of the traditional pair. When these are hung, the edges are hidden by the folds and the effect is one of a complete curtain.

Fortunately sheer and net fabrics are often made in extra wide widths – up to 300 cm (120 in). With fine nets you can often buy the fabric in a set length nearest to the one you require, and the width required is measured off the roll in the same way as the length is measured off for regular fabrics. The hem and heading are already made and you simply have to finish the side hems.

Sewing sheer curtains

Sheer fabrics are not difficult to sew provided you use a fine sharp needle and set your machine with a loose tension to prevent puckering. It is always advisable to tack all folds, hems and seams as the fabric tends to slip while it is being machine stitched. You should also use synthetic thread and specially made gathering tape as these will behave in the same way as the fabric.

If you have difficulty in feeding the fabric through the machine or if it still slips in spite of being tacked, it may help to put strips of tissue paper under the fabric as it is being fed into the machine. This can be torn away afterwards.

Another important point in making sheer curtains of both types is that all the hems – side, bottom and top – must be made double with equal first and second turnings, so you will not get an ugly raw edge showing through to the right side of the curtain and spoiling the effect of much hard work. With semi-sheers, you should also plan the width of the hems and turnings so that any spaces in the weave of the fabric fall on top of each other and the stitching can be worked on a solid section of the weave. In many cases you may not have to make side hems as the selvedges make perfectly good edges.

Deep headings Because of their additional fullness, both types of sheer curtains can be made with a deep heading tape giving either pencil, cartridge, or pinch pleats.

These are stitched on in a similar way to the standard tapes. The essential difference is that the top edge of the curtain should be turned over for the exact depth of the tape and the top edge of the tape should be placed just below the fold.

If you do not like the effect of the curtain tape showing through the mesh of semi-sheers, you can disguise it by inserting a strip of plain fabric in a colour to match the curtains between the curtain and the tape. The strip whould be of a similar fibre to the curtains so that it will react in the same way when washed. Alternatively you could stitch a decorative braid of the same width as the tape on to the front of the curtains.

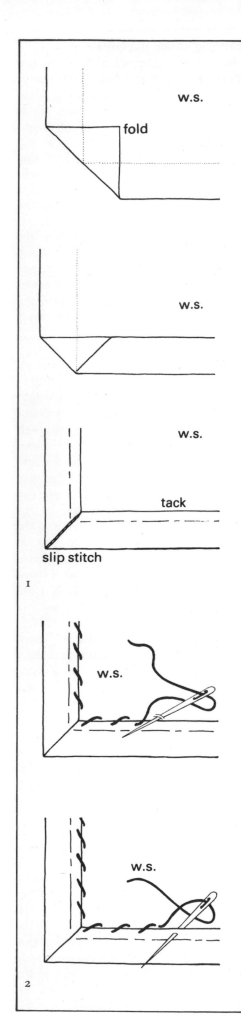

1

2

Lined curtains

*Techniques included: mitred corner, locking, serging.

Well-lined curtains contribute a feeling of warmth and luxury. The curtains will hang well and the lining also helps to insulate the room.

Velvet, brocade, silk, satin and many cottons or fabrics made from man-made fibres should be lined to prevent the fabric from fading and rotting.

Fully-lined curtains have the linings stitched to the curtain round the two sides but hemmed separately. A lining prevents dirt and dust from getting between the curtain and lining fabric, giving more protection to the fabric and making it last longer. There are several methods of making lined curtains, depending on where they are being used, the type of fabric and the size of the curtains. The quickest method is the machine one but this should only be used for short window curtains in a single width lightweight fabric such as cotton and linen-type rayons. For fuller or heavier floor length window curtains (particularly velvet) the hand-stitched method should be used, and for room dividers the reversible method should be followed.

If the fabric is washable the lining can be made detachable so that the curtains can be washed. There is a tape designed especially for this, so that the curtain and lining are attached to the same hooks.

Choosing fabric for lining Traditional linings are made from fine cotton sateen which comes in a wide range of colours. This fabric blends well with most curtain fabrics and although lightweight, is closely woven and firm enough to protect the curtains without being too bulky.

Curtain fabric is usually 120 cm (48 in) wide and must be pre-shrunk. Some curtain fabrics with an open weave or in a light colour will need matching lining, such as white linings for white fabrics.

If you prefer to have lining in a colour to match your curtains and cotton sateen is not available in the colour, choose a fabric that is pre-shrunk,

1. Mitre and slipstitch hems. 2. Work small serge stitches from left to right, pick up raw edges then curtain fabric.

closely woven and light in weight or dye cotton sateen to the colour required before making up.

You will need:

The calculated quantity of curtain fabric (see Unlined curtains).

The same quantity of lining fabric if it is the same width as the curtain fabric or the re-calculated quantity of lining if the width differs.

Sewing thread for fabric and lining.

Heading tape. Measure the width of each ungathered curtain and add 5 cm (2 in).

Special lining tape, if required for detachable linings, to the measured width of each curtain, plus 7·5 cm (3 in).

Curtain track, stops, runners, hooks.

Steel tape and ruler.

Sharp scissors and pins.

Cord tidy, one for each curtain.

Making the curtains Cut out and sew any seams to make the width required.

If the curtains are to hang just below the sill turn in 4 cm (1½ in) at the sides and bottom of the curtain, tack and press.

*Mitre the two bottom corners and, using matching thread, slipstitch by hand (fig. 1).

Using matching thread, *serge stitch by hand round sides and bottom (fig. 2).

For floor length curtains tack the sides and bottom, but only finish the two side seams to about 20 cm (8 in) from the bottom as the curtain should be hung to drop before the hem is finally finished.

Weighting the corners To make the sides of the curtain hang straight, it is a good idea to place a small weight in the hem at the corners. The weights can be bought specially for the purpose from a curtain track department. They should be placed into a little bag made from curtain lining and stitched to the diagonal turning of the mitre before the sides and hem are stitched down, this should come 6 mm (¼ in) above the bottom of the curtain. The weights can also be stitched at the bottom of seams to prevent them from puckering.

As an alternative to individual weights, it is possible to buy lead weighted tape. This is sold in different weights

Beautifully made, fully lined curtains with a pinch pleated heading.

Pale blue lace curtains lined with fabric in a darker tone to accentuate the design of the lace.

to suit different fabrics and is inserted with a bodkin after the hem has been turned up but before it is stitched at the corners.

Preparing the lining Before cutting do not try to draw a thread on lining sateen, square it up on a table or use a set-square. Cut off or snip all selvedges.

Cut the lining the same length as the curtain fabric.

Join widths together to make lining the same width as the curtain; make a plain seam with right sides together taking 1·5 cm ($\frac{5}{8}$ in) seam allowance; press open. Snip any selvedges.

Locking in the lining

*A lining is locked to the fabric to prevent the lining falling away from the top fabric when the curtain is hanging.

Place the curtain on a table with the wrong side facing up.

Lay the lining on top of the curtain, with the wrong sides together – the raw edges of the lining should be flush with the curtain all round, so trim the sides and lower edge by the required amount.

Fold back the lining at the centre of the curtain and lock the lining to the curtain by making long loose stitches. The stitches must be loose to avoid puckering (fig. 3). The locking should start and end 15 to 20 cm (6 to 8 in) from both top and bottom. Secure the

thread to the fold of the lining. Pick up no more than two threads of curtain fabric so that the stitches will not show on the right side.

To help work the stitches in a straight line make a crease mark on the fold of the lining with your thumb.

Locking is usually worked at 30 cm (12 in) intervals across a curtain. So if the curtain is 120 cm (48 in) wide there would be three rows of locking, one down the middle of the curtain and one to each side.

Keep the lining and curtain flat and turn the side edges of the lining under to come 2·5 cm (1 in) from the edge of the curtain (this measurement can be adjusted if necessary so that the lining completely covers the selvedge of the curtain fabric).

Pin in place, placing the pins at right-angles to the edge of the curtains.

Make a line of tacking stitches across the curtain 15 cm (6 in) from the top. This is to keep the lining firmly in place until the heading tape is attached. Slipstitch the fold of the lining loosely to the turning of the curtain. On long curtains, finish the stitching about 7·5 cm (3 in) above the hem of the

3. Lining folded back and locking stitch worked to keep the two layers together. Pick up several threads only.

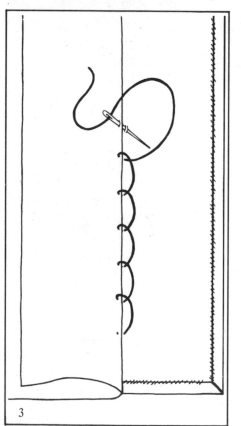

lining. Allow floor length curtains to hang before finishing.

Slipstitch lining to curtain round the two sides and bottom for short curtains.

Attaching the tape Having decided upon the heading preferred, attach the tape as described for unlined curtains, turning in top of curtain and lining together.

To finish Slipstitch remainder of side hems, including lining. Turn up curtain hem, mitring the corners. Slipstitch the remaining part of the lining in position and hang the finished curtains.

Detachable linings

Measure, cut and make the curtains as for unlined curtains.

Making the detachable lining Finished linings should be 2·5 cm (1 in) smaller on either side and 2·5 cm (1 in) shorter than the curtains when the lining is in position.

Carefully measure and cut out the curtain linings.

Join the widths or half widths where necessary, with 1·5 cm ($\frac{5}{8}$ in) plain seams and press open. Snip the selvedges every 10 cm (4 in).

Make side hems by folding over 2·5 cm (1 in) and then another 2·5 cm (1 in). Tack and machine stitch. Do not sew the bottom hems.

Attaching the lining tape To prepare the tape, pull free 4 cm (1½ in) of the draw cords at one end and knot the cords together. Trim off the surplus tape to within 6 mm (¼ in) of the cord (fig. 1).

Fold under 1·5 cm ($\frac{5}{8}$ in) of the knotted raw end and machine stitch across the fold, stitching through the tape to secure the knotted cords (fig. 2).

With the right side of the lining fabric and the corded side of the lining tape facing you, slip the top raw edge of the lining between the two sides of the tape, leaving 2·5 cm (1 in) of tape free at the unprepared end (fig. 3).

Pin and tack the lining in position on the tape. The underside of the tape is slightly wider than the top, so that when stitching from the right side both sides of the tape will be caught in the stitches.

Fold under the surplus tape at the unprepared end, level with the side hem edge of the lining, to give a neat edge. Machine stitch the tape to the lining, finishing the unprepared end in the

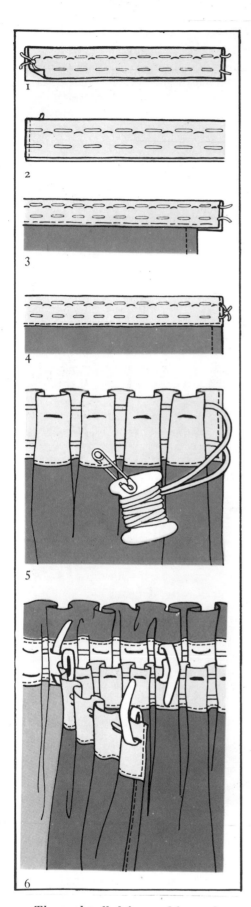

1. *The cord pulled free and knotted.*
2. *End folded under and stitched.*
3. *Raw edges of lining sewn into tape.*
4. *Cord ends knotted.*
5. *Lining gathered, cord put onto tidy.*
6. *Hooks put through curtain.*

same way as before but leaving the cords free for gathering. Knot the loose ends to prevent them disappearing back into the tape (fig. 4).

Gather up the lining to match the gathered or pleated curtains and wind the surplus cord on to the cord tidy. Attach the cord tidy to the lining tape with a safety pin (fig. 5).

Attaching the linings to the curtains With the wrong sides of curtain and lining together, insert the curtain hooks through the 'buttonholes' at the top of the lining tape, then through the pockets in the standard heading tape on the curtain before turning the hooks into their final position. Both the curtains and their linings will hang from the same hooks (fig. 6).

Finishing the lined curtains Note: For a perfectly finished straight hem you must take great care.

On some long curtains it is possible to finish the hem without detaching the lining and taking the gathers out, but unless you are very careful you may find the hem does not hang well.

Hang the lined curtains from the curtain rail and mark the correct length of the linings with a row of pins. The linings should be 2·5 cm (1 in) shorter than the curtains. Take down the curtains and detach the linings.

On each lining, unwind the cord from the cord tidy and pull out the gathers. Lay the lining on a large flat surface and turn up the hem to the line of pins. Slipstitch the hem by hand.

Attach the finished linings to the curtains again and re-hang.

Check linings are the correct length.

Quick machine method

First of all measure and cut out the curtain fabric to the desired size (see Unlined curtains). Work a line of tacking down the centre of each length. Cut out the lining fabric, making it 5 cm (2 in) shorter and 7·5 cm (3 in) narrower than each curtain. Work a line of tacking down the centre of each length.

Make a 7·5 cm (3 in) double hem along the bottom of the lining and machine stitch.

Lay out the curtain fabric right side up and make a tuck of 7·5 cm (3 in) down the middle to make it the same width as the lining (fig. 1).

Place the lining on the curtain with right sides together so that the top and

sides are level. Pin the sides together taking turnings slightly larger than the selvedges on the curtain fabric.

Machine stitch to within 5 cm (2 in) of the foot of the lining. Turn the curtain right side out and match the centre point to the centre of the lining. Lay the curtain out flat with the lining side up and centre the lining on the curtain so there is an equal border of curtain showing along both sides (fig. 2). Press.

Turn down the top edge of the curtain for 4 cm (1½ in) to the wrong side and tack through all thicknesses. Attach gathering tape in the same way as for unlined curtains.

Hang the curtains for a few days to allow the fabric to drop, then mark and stitch the hem.

Reversible curtains

Designed as room dividers and made

1 and 2 below show the main steps in using the quick machine method.

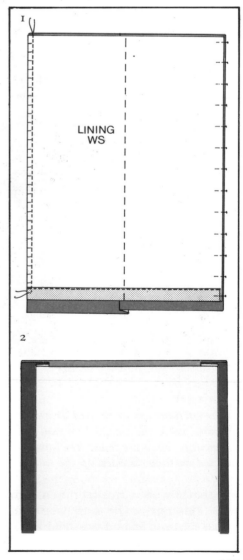

If the curtains are to be used as room dividers, each side should be equally attractive. They are made like long unlined curtains, seamed up the sides.

with equally attractive fabric on each side. This can be the same fabric; in which case you should buy double the amount; or contrasting fabrics of similar weight and type, in which case you should buy the same amount of each fabric. You should also buy double the amount of gathering tape and hooks.

The curtains for room dividers are really made like very wide unlined curtains which are then folded in half and joined down the side.

To make reversible curtains

Cut and join the fabric for the curtains and the 'lining', making them the same length and width.

With right sides together, join the lining to the curtain down one of the side edges, taking 1·3 cm (½ in) turnings or the width of the selvedges if this is greater.

Turn over the top edge of the curtain and lining and attach curtain tape along the entire width (including the lining) (fig. 1).

Pull up the tape to make the curtain and lining double the required width, plus 2·5 cm (1 in). The seam joining the lining should be exactly in the centre.

With the right sides together, join the lining to the curtain down the remaining side edge. Turn right side out and position the seams exactly at the edges. Insert the curtain hooks along the entire width of the curtain and lining and place them into the hooks of the track alternately from the lining and then the curtain and then the lining and so on (fig. 2). Allow to hang for a couple of days before hemming.

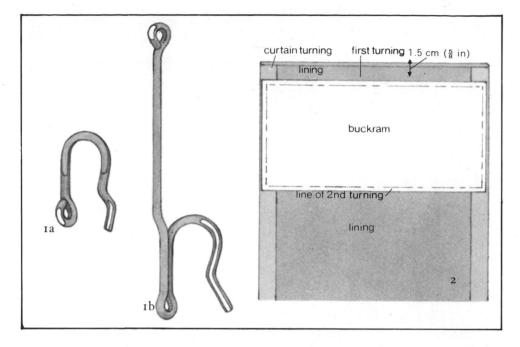

Hand-stitched pinch pleats

When making curtains from expensive fabric it is always worth taking the extra trouble of finishing them by hand and the hallmark of professionally-made curtains is the hand-stitched pinch pleated heading.

Although it is possible to form pinch pleats with a heading tape, hand-stitched pleats are crisper and stay crisp for longer.

Also the hooks used are stronger than those used with heading tapes which is an advantage for heavy fabrics such as velvet.

1. Attaching tape to top of curtain (including the lining).
2. Fixing curtain hooks along entire length of curtain and lining.

Materials you will need

Buckram Used to stiffen the pleats and heading. Buy the sort made specially for curtain headings, which is white, 10 cm (4 in) or 12·5 cm (5 in) wide, and will not lose its stiffness if washed or dry-cleaned. Do not buy the kind of buckram sold for pelmets. This is usually orange (from the stiffening agent used) and cannot be washed or cleaned because the colour runs.

Allow enough buckram to fit the unpleated width of each curtain.

Hooks The types used for this method are always sewn on by hand. Sew-on hooks, as they are called, are brass and have a small hole at the base of the stem for the stitching (fig. 1a).

For curtains intended to cover the curtain track when closed, hooks with long stems and a hole at each end may be used to help stiffen the heading (fig. 1b). Buy one hook per pleat, plus one hook for each side edge of the curtains. For sewing on the hooks and for stitching the headings, buy buttonhole twist in a colour to match the curtain fabric.

Fabric amounts For the length of the curtains use a steel rule to measure from the base of the curtain runner, where the hook will be placed, to the sill or floor as required. Add 15 cm (6 in) for a double hem at the foot and 1·5 cm ($\frac{5}{8}$ in) for the heading or, if the curtain is to cover the track when closed, add 1·5 cm ($\frac{5}{8}$ in) to amount required to cover track. Add a further 11·5 cm ($4\frac{1}{2}$ in) – or the depth of your buckram – for turnings at the top of the curtains.

Make the remaining calculations as described for Unlined curtains.

Calculating the pleats

The spaces The total width of the spaces left at each side edge of the curtain and between each group of pleats must add up to the required finished width of each curtain, plus 2 to 4 cm ($\frac{3}{4}$ to $1\frac{1}{2}$ in) more for ease. Each space may be 10 to 15 cm (4 to 6 in) wide.

Hand-stitched pinch pleats are worth the effort if your fabric is expensive.
1a. Sewn-on hooks for plain curtains.
1b. This hook is for a deep heading.
2. Placing buckram on top edge.

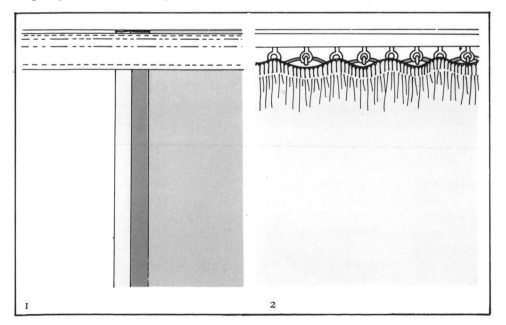

Decide the width you wish the spaces to be and divide this into the required finished width of the curtain to give the number of spaces.

The pleats Because there is a space at each side edge of the curtain, there is always one less group of pleats than the number of spaces.

Start by subtracting the required finished width of the curtain from the unpleated width of fabric (less allowances for turnings and side hems). Into the remaining width divide the number of pleats to give the amount allowed for each pleat.

Making the curtains Make the curtains with sewn-in linings (see Lined curtains), but do not, of course, attach heading tape.

Cut a length of buckram to fit the width of each curtain. Place the buckram on to the wrong side of the curtain to come exactly 1·5 cm ($\frac{5}{8}$ in) from the top edge. Pin and tack all round (fig. 2). Fold over the top edge of the curtain (and lining if this is sewn in) on to the buckram for 1·5 cm ($\frac{5}{8}$ in) and machine stitch through all thicknesses.

Machine stitch through all thicknesses along remaining three sides of the buckram.

Turn the folded edge of the curtain again for the depth of the buckram and tack. Slipstitch the side edges.

Mark the positions of the pleats accurately on the right side of the fabric with pins or tailor's chalk to the depth

3. Depth of pleat marked with pins and then stitched. 4. Pleat folded evenly into three and stitched. 5. Oversew the top edge of each pleat section. 6. Sew hooks in place at top and bottom holes, and then along length of hook.

The stiff heading on these curtains made with hand-stitched pinch pleats holds the top of the curtain neatly along the ceiling, concealing the curtain track and giving a neat finish.

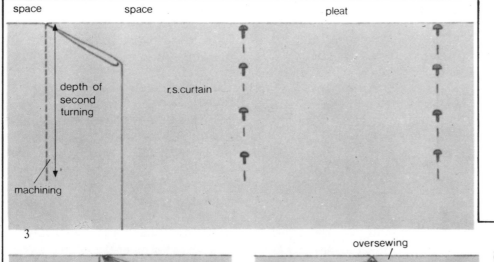

3

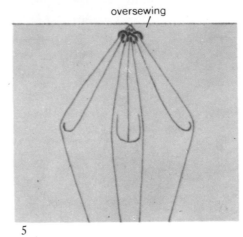

4

5

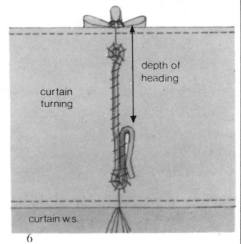

6

of the second turning.

Forming the pleats Working with the right side of the curtain towards you, place the marked edges of each pleat together with wrong sides facing. Pin along the mark to the depth of the second turning. Machine stitch through all thicknesses along this line (fig. 3). Fold the fabric contained in each pleat into three equal pleats as shown in fig. 4 and press the folds firmly with your fingers. Using the buttonhole twist, backstitch by hand through all thicknesses just below the bottom edge of the buckram (you can feel this bottom edge easily).

Oversew the top of each section individually (fig. 5).

Sewing on hooks Place each hook in turn on the wrong side of the curtain in line with the seam line of the pleat. For long stemmed hooks leave the required depth for the heading between the top of the hook and the top of the curtain.

Using buttonhole twist double, oversew the hooks to the curtain through the holes at the bottom and then, on long-stemmed hooks, up the stems and round the holes at the top (fig. 6). Fasten off securely.

Place the hooks for the side edges of the curtain about 6 mm ($\frac{1}{4}$ in) in from sides and the same distance from the

top of the curtain as the other hooks. Sew on as before. The curtains are now ready for hanging.

Café curtains

Most people solve the problem of combining large windows and privacy by hanging net curtains. Café curtains can be a decorative and unusual alternative.

These curtains originated in France in the old coffee houses and are still to be seen in restaurant windows in many parts of Europe. Café curtains

Classic café curtains have a scalloped heading and are suspended from rings.

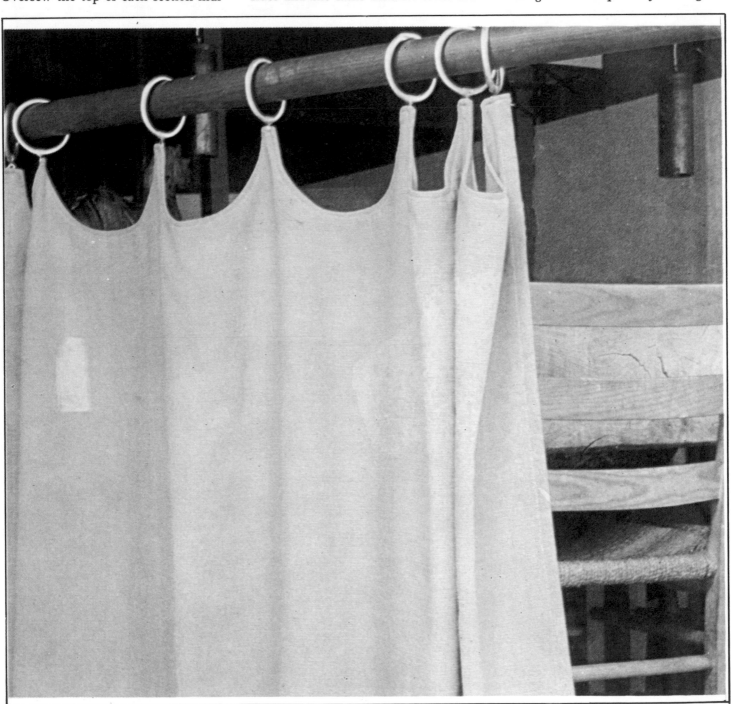

are really short curtains, hung from a rod which is placed halfway down the window, they may be kept permanently closed, thus hiding an unattractive outlook. Café curtains are made and hung in various ways. They can be trimmed with braid or matched to roller blinds or pelmets.

Choosing the heading The simplest type of heading for café curtains where there is a lower tier only is a plain casing, through which a dowel rod or length of expanded wire can be inserted for hanging them in the same way as for net curtains. It is not very easy to draw the curtains with this type of heading so it is suitable only where they will be kept closed.

Alternatively – and this is more attractive but more complicated in the initial calculations and cutting out – the heading can be scalloped. By this method the curtains can be hung from a decorative curtain rod by rings which are stitched to the top of the straps between the scallops, or these straps can be made to loop round the rod. As an extra decoration on curtains to be hung with hooks, the straps can be pinch pleated.

Measuring for café curtains
First decide where the rod or wire should be placed – usually about halfway down the window and preferably in line with a glazing bar. Fix the rod or wire in position.

To measure for café curtains you must determine on the 'drop' required. This is the finished length of the curtain. It will probably be influenced by the amount of privacy needed. Although café curtains conventionally cover half the window sometimes two curtains are used, one for the top half of the window and one for the bottom half. These are called 'tiered cafés' and are both made in exactly the same way.

Café curtains usually hang either to the sill or 5 to 10 cm (2 to 4 in) below the sill.

Measure the track with a metre/yard-stick or steel ruler, not a tape measure as these tend to stretch and an accurate

These doubled-tiered café curtains can be used to cover the window completely.

measurement cannot be obtained. Allow one and a half times the length of the track if a lined curtain is being made. The width needed depends on the weight and texture of the fabric – lighter more delicate fabrics look better with extra fullness. In the case of a scalloped heading less fullness is required to show up the shaped top to advantage.

To the required length add 15 cm (6 in) for both top and bottom hems if using a heading tape or hem casing. For scalloped headings add the depth of the scallop, usually 7·5 cm to 10 cm (3 in to 4 in) plus 12·5 cm (5 in) for turnings. Allow extra length if using a patterned fabric and work out the repeats to see if the curtain lengths will cut economically. Remember when choosing the fabric to ask the size of the pattern repeat as large repeats can be expensive. (See Unlined curtains for table of widths required and making-up methods.)

Suitable fabrics In order to let the maximum amount of daylight filter through, café curtains are best made in cotton and left unlined. However, some fabrics may look more effective used with a light cotton lining and less fullness, particularly where a pattern can be shown to advantage.

To make the café curtain with plain heading

You will need:
Calculated amount of fabric.
Sewing thread to match fabric.
Curtain rod or wire.

Measure and cut out curtains as previously described, joining fabric with plain seams if necessary.

Side hems First cut off the selvedges to avoid pulling, and fold and tack 1·3 cm (½ in) double hems at both sides of the curtain. Stitch by hand or machine (fig. 1).

Turn under 1·5 cm (⅝ in) at the top of the curtain and press down. Turn under the edge of the allowances again for 4 cm (1½ in) and tack and stitch down. Press.

Insert the rod or wire through the hem at the top of the curtain, arranging the gathers evenly along its length, and try the curtain in position. Leave it for a couple of days in case the fabric stretches and then. mark the exact position of the lower edge of the hemline with pins while it is still hanging. Take down the curtain, mark hemline with tacking.

Bottom hem Turn up 5 cm (2 in) along marked hemline, trimming if necessary and make a 2·5 cm (1 in) double hem. Hand-stitched hems look better and hang well, and really are worth the extra trouble (fig. 1). Press the finished curtain completely and re-hang it.

Frilled heading As a variation to the plain top casing, you could make a casing with a frill above it. Add an extra 5 cm (2 in) to the allowance at the top of the curtain and turn over 2·5 cm (1 in) of this with the main allowance. Stitch as before and make a second line of stitching 2·5 cm (1 in) below the top fold. Insert the rod or wire in the casing between the rows of stitching. By gathering the curtain up to fit the rod, the fabric above it will form a frill (fig. 2).

Strap heading If you are using straps to hang the curtains, add on an amount equal to the circumference of the rod plus about 2·5 cm (1 in) for ease. If you are making curtains in two tiers, the top tier should be long enough to cover the scallops of the lower tier when closed, so add the depth of the scallops plus 10 cm (4 in) for the hem to the bottom of the curtain.

Scalloped café curtains
*Working out scallops To make a paper pattern for the scallops, cut a piece of paper as wide as the curtain fabric and about 30 cm (12 in) deep. A piece of wallpaper or lining paper is ideal for this.
Draw a line across the paper about 7·5 cm (3 in) down from the upper

1. Sewing side and bottom hems.
2. A frilled heading is made by stitching along the centre of the top hem edge.
3. Working out pattern for scallops.
4. Stitching scalloped heading.
5. Hemming the scalloped edge.
6. Sew a ring to each strap.

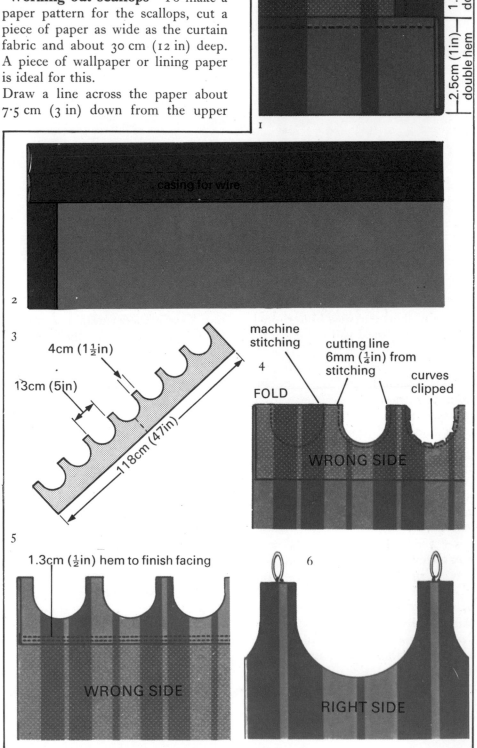

Allowance is made for pinch pleats in the width of each scallop.

edge. Decide at this point how deep you want the scallops to be. Draw another line the depth of the scallop below the first line. Now mark the paper vertically down the middle because it is easier to plan scallops on a narrower width. Plan one half of the width first and then trace off another half for accurate placing.

Use a pair of compasses and a pencil for drawing the first scallop. You may have to try several times until you can fit a complete row of scallops into your planned width of fabric.

Make a cardboard template when you have finalized the size and shape of the scallops. If you draw round the template the scallops will be of uni-

form size. Leave no less than 4 cm (1½ in) between each scallop and approximately 4 cm (1½ in) each end of the curtain. When all the scallops have been drawn in, cut the scallops out for a pattern (fig. 3).

To make the scalloped café curtain

You will need:
Prepared paper pattern.
Calculated amount of fabric.
Sewing thread to match fabric.
Button thread.
Iron-on interfacing.
Curtain rings.

Measure and cut out curtains. Make side hems as for the café curtain with a plain heading.

With right side of fabric up, fold over top of the curtain to the depth of the scallops plus 7·5 cm (3 in) (fig. 4). Tack. If the fabric is flimsy, cut a piece of iron-on interfacing to fit the width of the curtain and slightly deeper than the scallops. Iron it inside the heading allowance so that its edge comes level with the fold.

Place and pin the prepared paper pattern to the fold and mark round the scallops with tailor's chalk. Remove the pattern and machine stitch on the marked line. Cut out scallops 6 mm (¼ in) outside the stitching line. Clip into curves and trim corners diagonally.

Turn the heading to the right side. Poke out the corners of the straps carefully, then tack along the seam line so that none of the facing shows

on the right side of the curtain. Press. Turn under the lower edge of the facing for 1·3 cm ($\frac{1}{2}$ in) and machine or slipstitch to the curtain (fig. 5).

If you are making the straps into pinch pleats form these by hand or stitch on tape (see Curtain headings and Hand-stitched pinch pleats).

Sew brass or plastic curtain rings to the top of the straps using button thread (fig. 6). Stitch fairly loosely, to allow the ring to twist round when it is fitted on the rod.

If you are using the straps to hang the curtains, turn over the amount allowed for fitting it round the pole and stitch firmly in position.

Hang the curtains and turn up the

hems as for café curtain with plain heading.

Tie backs

Tie backs were very common in Regency and Victorian times when windows were tall and narrow, and the curtains would simply be looped back to the sides without actually being drawn back along the track. It is still a good style for these windows because it relieves their bare outline. Tie backs are also good where curtains may blow through open windows and where they reduce the amount of daylight entering a room.

Tie backs may be made from fabric to match curtains in which case they

Shaped tie-backs can add a touch of glamour to floor length curtains.

can be shaped, or from a commercial braid when they normally have to be straight. Rings are sewn to each end of the tie back and these are slotted on to a hook on the wall at the side of the window.

To calculate the length of the tie back Loop a tape measure round the curtain, adjusting it so that the curtain is not crushed, 5 to 6·5 cm (2 to 2$\frac{1}{2}$ in) is usually the best width. Decide on the position of the tie back and height of the hooks and attach a hook firmly to the wall on the window frame on each side. If you are using braid, cut a piece of the right length and turn under the ends to make a V-shaped point. Hem in position and sew on a curtain ring to each end.

If you are making a shaped fabric tie back, cut a paper pattern first and hold it in position to see the effect. You may want to try out several different shapes, such as curves or scallops, before you finally choose.

To calculate the amount of fabric
For a curved tie back cut a piece of paper just wider than the length required, fold in half and draw the shape from the centre fold to one side. Cut round the shape, open it out and you will have a pattern (fig. 1). Add 7.5 cm (3 in) all round, measure the width and depth to give you the amount of fabric needed. Double this for two tie backs.

To make a pair of shaped fabric tie backs
You will need:
The calculated quantity of fabric.
The same quantity of interlining, buckram and lining fabric.

Prepare a pattern for the tie-backs, and place centre front on fabric fold.

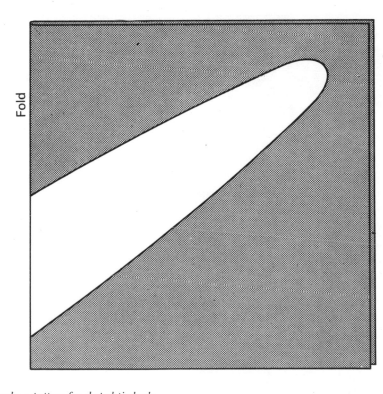
To make a pattern for shaped tie-backs

Sewing thread to match fabric and strong button thread.
Four 2.5 cm (1 in) diameter brass curtain rings.
Two cup hooks or decorative hooks.
Prepared paper pattern. Fabric adhesive.

Preparing the tie backs Fold the tie back fabric in half lengthways along the grain and place the paper pattern on it with the centre line to the fold. Cut out, adding 1.3 cm ($\frac{1}{2}$ in) seam allowance all round. Cut out the lining in the same way. Cut the interlining and buckram without seam allowances. Repeat for second tie back.

Lay fabric flat with its right side facing down. Place the interlining on top, then the buckram leaving an equal seam allowance all round. Tack through all layers. Turn the edges of the fabric over on to the buckram and press down with your fingers, keeping the fold of the fabric exactly level with the edge of the buckram. Snip the fabric where necessary round the shaping. Carefully stick down the edges of the fabric over the buckram, using a little fabric adhesive. Do not pull the fabric too tightly as it should

'give' a little when the tie back is bent into its final shape.

Turn under 1.5 cm ($\frac{5}{8}$ in) all round the edge of the lining, snipping where necessary, and press down. Place the lining centrally to the back of the tie back and pin it to the turnings only (so that the pins do not go through to the right side). Slipstitch the lining to the turnings all round.

To finish off, sew a brass curtain ring to each end of tie back using strong thread and buttonhole stitch. Make second tie back in the same way.

Quick and easy roller blinds
By making your own blinds in a fabric that matches or contrasts with your curtains and covers, or to match the wallpaper, you will achieve a co-ordinated look to your room.

Roller blinds are very easy to make using a roller blind kit, available in roller lengths from 61 cm (2 ft) to 2.75 m (9 ft).

The blind can be hung either inside or outside the window recess. If the recess is deep, hang the blind inside it, if the recess is shallow or the window narrow, hang the blind outside. Make the blind as wide as the window frame will allow – because if it is only fractionally wider, it will be sucked in and out by the breeze when the window is ajar and the edges of the blind will be spoiled. Before buying your kit check that the brackets are suitable for hanging from the position required.

Fixing a blind is simple. The only tools needed are those normally needed for domestic repairs.

To make a roller blind
You will need:
A roller blind kit containing wooden roller the required length or longer, and fitted at one end with a spring; metal cap and special lipped nail which fits on to the other end; two metal wall brackets, one slotted and one with a round hole; wooden lath for bottom of blind; plastic cord holder and cord; acorn with cap and several tiny screws and tacks.
Fabric and matching thread.
Blind stiffening spray.
Saw, hammer, small tacks.
Screws, wall-plugs, screwdriver.
Scissors and tape measure.
Bias binding if required.
Pins.

Calculating fabric requirements

For a blind inside the recess (fig. 1)
Measure the width of the recess. Use a wooden metre/yard stick or steel rule, rather than a fabric tape measure, so that the measurements are absolutely accurate. The roller should be cut 2·5 cm (1 in) smaller than this measurement to allow for the pins and brackets to be fitted at each end of the roller.

The width of the fabric should be the same as the roller before the pins are attached plus 5 cm (2 in) if turnings are required at the sides.

For the length of fabric required measure the height of the recess from the window sill to the top. Add 30·5 cm (12 in) to allow for the fabric to be attached to the roller at the top and for the lath casing at the bottom; this also allows the fabric to cover the wooden roller when the blind is down.

For a blind outside the recess (fig. 2) Measure the width of the recess and add 15 cm (6 in). Cut the roller to this length. The roller will extend beyond the recess at either side by 7·5 cm (3 in). The width of the fabric should be the same as the roller plus 5 cm (2 in) for side hems if required. The finished blind should be placed 7·5 cm (3 in) above the recess and have 7·5 cm (3 in) below the recess.

For the length of fabric required, measure the length of the blind required and add 30·5 cm (12 in). This allows for the fabric to be attached to the roller at the top and for the lath casing at the bottom; it also allows the fabric to cover the wooden roller when the blind is down.

Choosing the fabric Fabric for a roller blind should be firm and closely woven. Holland (a stiff linen) is widely used and available in many widths and colours. The main advantage of using holland is that it can be trimmed to the correct width and does not fray, so you need not hem. Closely woven fabrics such as cotton and canvas can also be used although you will need to make side hems. Fabrics with large pictorial scenes or very large designs are often best as blinds. If you use a special blind stiffening spray hems may not be necessary. PVC fabric in strong colours and patterns is ideal for the kitchen or bathroom.

Cutting the fabric The fabric must be cut accurately and the grain of the fabric must be straight so that the blind hangs well and rolls up smoothly without puckering. To straighten fabric pull out a thread and cut along this line or measure accurately from the selvedge, mark with pins and cut out.

If you have to use more than one width of fabric, to get the size required, add extra fabric to each side of the full width so that a centre seam is avoided. Should the pattern go into the selvedges join each half section to the sides of the main piece by overlapping the selvedges for 1·3 cm (½ in) and machine once down each edge (fig. 3).

If the pattern does not extend across the selvedge or the selvedges do not match each other, trim them and then join the pieces with a flat fell seam (fig. 4). Press well on both sides.

Making the blind

Cut out the fabric to the correct size. If the edges need finishing either bind them with bias binding or hem the sides. To bind the edges place the edge of the blind to the centre of the binding and then fold over the sides of the

This original way of using a roller blind gives privacy during the day, and the matching lined curtains can be pulled over the door in the evening for extra warmth and luxury.

1. A roller blind fitted inside the window recess.
2. A roller blind fitted outside the window recess.

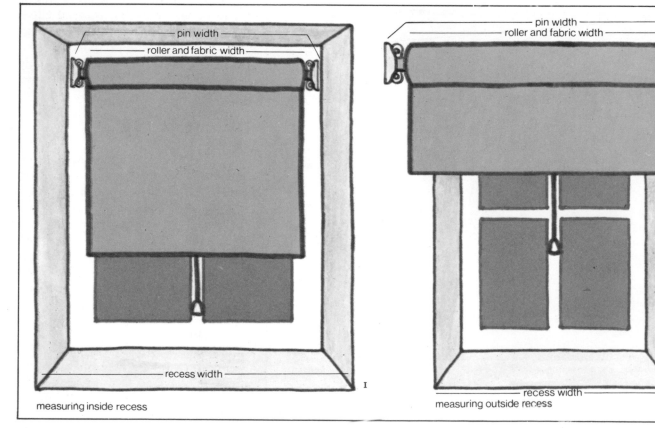

pin width — roller and fabric width — recess width — measuring inside recess

pin width — roller and fabric width — recess width — measuring outside recess

binding equally, tack and machine stitch through all thicknesses (fig. 5). To hem the sides fold over 2·5 cm (1 in) on to the wrong side along both edges, press and tack. (For PVC fabric crease the fold and hold in place with adhesive tape, as the holes made by the needle when tacking will not close up when the tacking is removed). Machine stitch using a large zig-zag stitch and positioning the raw edges in the centre of the stitch (fig. 6). Altern- atively, raw edges can be neatened by hand and then straight-stitched by machine.

To make the lath casing along the bottom edge turn under 1·3 cm (½ in) on to the wrong side. Turn under another 4 cm (1½ in) and machine stitch close to the first fold.

Cut the lath 1·3 cm (½ in) shorter than the fabric width and insert it into the hem. Stitch up the openings at the sides (fig. 7).

Thread the cord through the holder, knot to secure and screw the holder to the centre of the lath so that the cord hangs down (fig. 8).

Stiffening Before attaching the fabric to the roller, iron and then spray with the blind stiffening spray. Spray fabric on both sides working in a well ventilated room. Hang fabric up to dry.

Assembly Following the manufacturer's instructions assemble the roller

3

5

7

wrong side of fabric

8

4

6

9

3. Overlap and stitch the selvedges.
4. On raw edges stitch a flat fell seam.
5. The side edges can be fiinished with a binding.
6. To hem the sides, fold over the raw edge and zig-zag stitch.
7. Insert the lath into the bottom hem.
8. Fix cord holder on the wrong side.
9. Tack the fabric to the roller with the spring on the left.
10. The right way (top) and wrong way (bottom) of hanging the blind.

right

wrong

10

and the end pins. Screw the brackets into place. If the blind is to go inside the recess allow enough room above the brackets to give clearance for the fabric when it is rolled up.

Place the prepared fabric right side up on the floor. Lay the roller across the top with the spring mechanism on the left.

Attach the fabric to the roller with small tacks, working from the centre towards the edges (fig. 9).

Roll up the blind by hand and place into the brackets. Pull the blind down and make sure it hangs properly and rolls up smoothly, if not, take it down and roll it up again by hand. Be careful not to overtension the spring because

A dormer window can be a problem to cover. A fabric blind, such as this tie-dyed one, is the perfect solution.

if it snaps up too quickly the mechanism may be damaged. The blind should hang with the fabric nearer to the window and the roller towards the room (fig. 10).

Thread the loose end of the cord into the acorn.

Note: If your window is wider than 2·75 m (9 ft) it would be possible and effective to divide the window into two, three or even four and place the blinds side by side. The brackets should then be placed close together on to the window frame.

*Roller blinds are an inexpensive way
to insure privacy and can be used
successfully to cover both windows and
doors as shown.*

Bed Linen

Throwover bedspreads

The focal point of a bedroom should be the bed – and the bedspread is the finishing touch. A throwover bedspread is one of the quickest and easiest pieces of soft furnishing to make and, if you team the fabric with your wall covering and curtains, it will give the room an immediate co-ordinated effect.

*Techniques included: fitting around bedposts.

Calculating fabric requirements

Measure the bed with its bedclothes and pillows as shown in fig. 1. For the width measure from the floor on one side up and across the bed to the floor on the other side. For the length measure from the top of the pillow to the floor at the foot of the bed (fig. 1). If you wish to tuck the bedspread around the pillows, add an extra 30 cm (12 in) to the length.

As furnishing fabrics are usually 120 cm (48 in) wide, you will need to join two fabric widths for either a single or a small double bed, so double the length measurement to calculate how many metres (yards) you should buy. Very large beds may need three lengths. 5·50 to 7·50 m (6 to 8 yd) is usually ample for an average single or double bed.

If your fabric has a large design or motif, add extra to the overall length in order to match it at the seams or to position it to best advantage on the bed – the additional amount could vary from an extra half pattern to as much as two pattern repeats. Ask your retailer for advice if in doubt, because so much will depend on where the first measurement is taken on the fabric roll. Choose a time for buying the fabric when the store is quiet and take a note of the bed measurements with

The centrepiece of a bedroom is the bed. Throwover spreads accentuate this, especially if they are made to measure, and for twin beds, in matching fabric.

you. Ask to have the fabric unrolled so you can examine the design fully and decide how you would like it positioned on the bed.

Making the bedspread

If you are using two lengths to avoid having an ugly seam down the centre of the bedspread, cut the fabric across into two equal lengths and then cut one of these pieces in half lengthwise, thus making one full width of fabric for the centre panel and two half widths for the sides. Allowing a total of 11 cm (4½ in) for seams and side hems, with 120 cm (48 in) wide fabric, the bedspread will have a maximum finished width of 229 cm (7ft 7½ in).

For a single bed however, this would mean that the seams run along the side of the bed, rather than the top, and the panelled effect is lost. To avoid this, cut off the excess from the full width,

rather than the halves (the leftover piece could be used for cushion covers).

Joining the panels To join the side pieces to each side of the centre panel pin and tack with right sides together, raw edges level, taking 1·5 cm (⅝ in) seams. Make sure the pattern is matched and the fabric runs the same way on each panel. Place the bedspread on the bed and check the size. Cut off any excess fabric at top and bottom leaving 2·5 cm (1 in) for hems. Measure and cut the sides in the same way.

Machine stitch the seams using a medium length stitch, following the tacking line. Remove the tacking. Clip the selvedges at intervals if they are tight (this helps the seam to lie flat), and press the seams open. Neaten the raw edges by oversewing by hand or by machine.

Square corners To make 2 cm (¾ in) double hems down the long sides of the bedspread, fold over the raw edge 6 mm (¼ in) to the wrong side of the fabric. Make a second fold 2 cm (¾ in) deep, so the raw edge is now enclosed. Tack and machine stitch through the three thicknesses, along the first fold. Remove the tacking and press the hems. Turn under 2 cm (¾ in) hems at the top and bottom, making the corners square (alternatively the corners can be mitred). Tack, machine stitch and press (fig. 2). Trim with braid or fringing if you wish.

Rounded corners Join the panels as above. Position the bedspread carefully on the bed. Place a row of pins along the top edges on one side and along the foot to mark the depth of the overhang, plus 2·5 cm (1 in) for hems.

Remove the bedspread, place flat and continue the line of pins to the edges. Draw an arc on this corner, using the pin and string method (see Table linen). Cut along the curved line, including the seam allowance (fig. 3).

Fold the bedspread in half lengthways, pin and cut the other corner to match. Turn under the hem at the foot and along the sides of the bedspread, easing the fabric at the corners. Tack and machine stitch the hem, remove the tacking and press the hem. Make a hem the same depth at the top of the bedspread, leaving the corners square. Press. Trim with braid or fringing if you wish.

*Fitting around bedposts

Join the panels as above. Place the bedspread on the bed and fold back the side panels from the edge of the bed with the fold lying just inside the posts (fig. 4). Pin a line along the fold from the corner of the bed (point A) down to the floor. Unfold the sides

Left. This double bedspread has the bottom corners rounded.

Top right. Joining seams can be concealed with decorative braid.

1. Measure the bed with the covers and pillow in place.
2. Finishing square corners.
3. Making rounded corners.
4, 5. Fitting around bedposts.

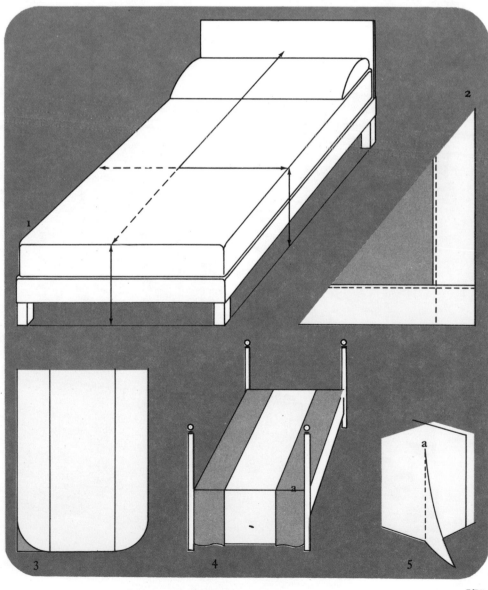

and fold up the foot of the bedspread in a similar way. Pin along this fold from point A to the floor (the pin lines should meet at point A).

Remove the bedspread and, using the pin lines as a guide, pin the corner as shown in fig. 5. Check fit, then cut off the corner 1·5 cm ($\frac{5}{8}$ in) from the line of pins. Using this as a guide, cut out a similar corner from the other side of the bedspread. Clip into the angle and make a narrow hem, press. Make 2 cm ($\frac{3}{4}$ in) hems all round the bedspread, leaving the corners square. Press.

Flounced bedspreads
*Techniques included: drawing a cutting plan, making a flounce.

A bedspread with a gathered flounce gives a softer look to a room. A throwover flap is attached to keep your pillows neatly covered.

Suitable fabrics Light or medium-weight fabrics, including dress and lacy fabrics can be used but do not use a heavy fabric for this type of bedspread, as it will not gather easily. Avoid very large patterns, because you will have wastage in matching it at seams, particularly on the flounce.

Calculating fabric requirements
Measure the bed with its bedclothes but without the pillows. For the width, measure from edge to edge across the bed and add 3 cm ($1\frac{1}{4}$ in) for the seam allowances. For the length, measure from the top of the bed to the foot and add 3 cm ($1\frac{1}{4}$ in) seam allowances. If the bed has a footboard, add 45 cm (18 in) to the length measurement so that the bedspread can be tucked in at the bottom. For the depth of the flounce, measure from the edge of the bed to the floor and add 4 cm ($1\frac{5}{8}$ in) hem and seam allowance. To determine the length of the flounce, multiply the bed's length by three – (i.e. a length and a half for each side, excluding any extra length allowed for the tuck-in extension).

For divans, the flounce should also go round the foot, so add on one and a half times the bed's width.

Next, put the pillows on to the bed and measure for the throwover flap

The addition of flounced skirt to a bedspread gives a softer, more decorative look to a bed.

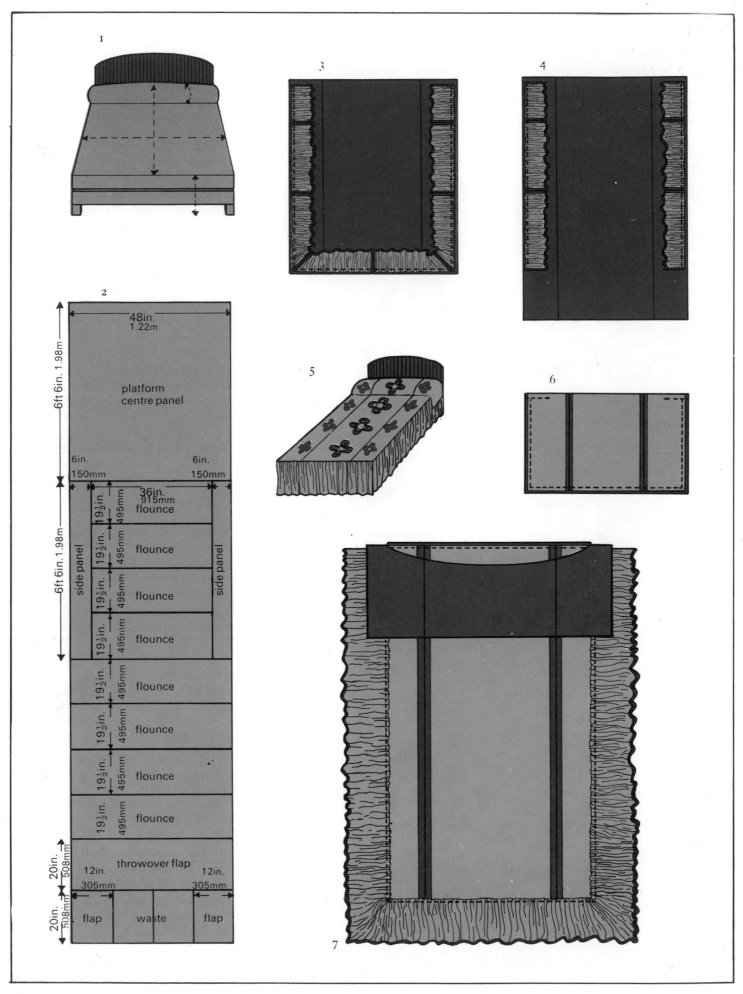

1

2

48in.
1.22m

6ft 6in. 1.98m

platform
centre panel

6in. | 6in.
150mm | 150mm

36in.
915mm
flounce

6ft 6in. 1.98m

side panel

19½in. 495mm flounce
19½in. 495mm flounce
19½in. 495mm flounce
19½in. 495mm flounce

side panel

19½in. 495mm flounce
19½in. 495mm flounce
19½in. 495mm flounce
19½in. 495mm flounce

20in. 508mm

throwover flap

12in. | 12in.
305mm | 305mm

20in. 508mm

flap | waste | flap

3

4

5

6

7

from the bottom of the pile of pillows at the top of the bed, up and over the pillows to the other side (fig. 1). Add 15 cm (6 in) for seam allowances and so that the flap can be tucked in. For the width of the flap, add 30 cm (12 in) to the width of the bed, so that the flap will cover the pillows easily. To calculate the quantity of fabric required, draw a cutting plan. Fig. 2 shows a layout for an average double bed. The simplest scale to use is 1 cm to 10 cm (1 in to 10 in). Draw the main section first. If the bed is wider than the fabric, measure the remaining section on either side, adding 3 cm (1¼ in) to the width of each section for turnings.

Draw these panels along the selvedges so that the pattern can be more easily matched with the main piece.

For the flounce, cut strips across the width of the fabric, so that the pattern will run down towards the floor.

To calculate the number of strips needed for the flounce, draw the strips to the required depth. Work out how many strips would be needed to make up the required length. Allow 3 cm (1¼ in) on each width for turnings.

Draw the pieces for the throwover flap, working out the width as for the main section.

Cutting out and making up

Cut out the centre and side panels (if any) as calculated above, matching the pattern. Join the pieces with a 1·5 cm (⅝ in) plain seam, clip the selvedges or neaten raw edges, and press the seams open.

*Making a flounce Cut out and join all the strips for the flounce with 1·5 cm (⅝ in) plain seams. Clip the selvedges or neaten any raw edges and press the seams open. Make 1·5 cm (⅝ in) hems on the short sides of the flounce, and press. Make a 2·5 cm (1 in) hem along the foot of the flounce, stitch and press.

Divide the flounce into eight sections for the sides and foot of the bed, marking the divisions with pins. Then divide the side sections and foot of the main section into eight similarly. Gather the flounce, using a long machine stitch or running stitches, 6 mm (¼ in) down from the top edge and again 1 cm (⅜ in) from the edge (it is advisable to stitch each division separately, as such a long length of

gathering is liable to break when the thread is pulled up).

Match the divisions on the flounce to those on the top. With the right sides of the fabric facing, pin the pieces together at the division marks with the pins at right-angles to the edge. Pin the ends of the flounce to the top section 1·5 cm (⅝ in) in from the edge.

Lay the top section out flat (use the floor if necessary), with the flounce on top of it. Secure one end of each gathering thread, and, leaving the divisional pins in position, draw up the other end until the flounce fits the top. Secure the threads by winding them round the divisional pins.

Space out the gathers evenly, pin the flounce to the top (putting the pins at right-angles to the edge at 2·5 cm (1 in) intervals), and tack, using small stitches (fig. 3). Remove the pins and taking 1·5 cm (⅝ in) seams, machine stitch the pieces together, with the flounce uppermost (this helps to keep the gathers from puckering as you stitch). Remove the tacking and gathering threads, and press the seam towards the top section. Neaten the raw edges with bias binding, or by oversewing them together.

Footboard beds Make the flounce for each side separately, and attach them to the top section, leaving the 45 cm (18 in) extension free (fig. 4). Make a narrow hem on the sides and foot of the extension.

Throwover flap Join the pieces of the flap as for the main section. With right sides facing, stitch the lining to the flap with a 1·5 cm (⅝ in) seam, leaving an opening the width of the main section along the top edge (fig. 5). With the right side of the flap facing the wrong side of the main section, fit the top edge of the main section into the opening, and pin it to the flap only, leaving the lining free. Stitch the pieces with a 1·5 cm (⅝ in) seam (fig. 6). Press the seam towards the flap. Fold the lining over the seam and hem, enclosing the raw edges. Press. Fig. 7 shows finished bedspread.

Duvet set

A light, snug duvet ensures a good night's sleep and a duvet cover is simple to make as it is simply two rectangles of fabric stitched together

and fastened at one end with a zip or touch and close tape. Complete the set with pillowcases, a fitted sheet and a frilled valance to disguise the base of the bed. Make them to match or in complementary fabrics.

The quantities and instructions are for either single or small double beds. The set can be made in polyester and cotton sheeting or plain cotton sheeting which is made in especially wide widths for the purpose.

Note Individual quantities have been given for each piece of the set. If you are making the set for a single bed it is worth while making a cutting layout before buying your fabric (see Flounced bedspreads) as you will be able to cut either pillowcases or valance frills from the extra width of fabric.

Duvet cover

Measurements The average size of a duvet is 137 by 198 cm (54 by 78 in) for a single bed and 198 cm (78 in) square for a small double bed. The duvet cover should be about 5 cm (2 in) larger all round than the duvet. This enables the duvet to move freely inside the cover.

You will need: (for either size of bed)

228 cm (90 in) wide fabric: 4·30 m (4⅝ yd).

1 m (40 in) touch and close fastening.

75 cm (30 in) zip fastener.

Sewing thread to match fabric.

Cutting out For a single cover: cut two rectangles each 150 by 211 cm (59 by 83 in). For a double cover: cut two rectangles each 211 cm (83 in) square.

To make the duvet cover

Neaten the raw edges at one end of each piece of fabric with zig-zag stitch. Turn 2·5 cm (1 in) to the wrong side and press.

With right sides together, stitch the edges along creased line, leaving an opening in the centre of the seam for inserting touch and close fastening or a zip fastener.

Insert the zip fastener or stitch fastening tape to both sides of the opening. Stitch the remaining three sides together with french seams. Turn cover to right side and press lightly.

Fitted sheet

A fitted bottom sheet with elastic corners to fit neatly over the mattress.

You will need: (for either size of bed)

228 cm (90 in) wide fabric: 2·70 m (3 yd).

1 m (40 in) narrow elastic.

Sewing thread to match fabric.

Cutting out   Cut a rectangle of fabric to cover the top and sides of the mattress plus 38 cm (15 in) all round.

To make the fitted sheet

Position the sheet centrally on the bed and mark the position of each corner with a pin. Mark two lines from the corner point to the two edges thus forming a square (fig. 1). These two lines then form the seam line for the corner. With right sides facing stitch the seam at each corner, trim, oversew and press (fig. 1).

Measure 25·5 cm (10 in) along each side of each corner and mark these points. Work a small hem around the outside edge of the sheet, first turn under 6 mm ($\frac{1}{4}$ in) and then 2 cm ($\frac{3}{4}$ in). Machine stitch close to the fold. The hems between points marked at corners will be channels for the elastic. Unpick a few stitches at each end, thread a 25 cm (10 in) length of elastic through channel. Secure ends by top-stitching firmly by machine (fig. 2). Repeat with the remaining corners.

If you do not look forward to the daily chore of making up the bed – tucking in sheets, folding blankets, straightening bedspreads – why not use a duvet and a bottom sheet? A duvet cover, fitted sheets and pillowcases, are easy to make.
1. Preparing the corners for a fitted sheet. 2. Inserting elastic in corners.
3. Folding the fabric for a pillowcase.
4. Pin the layers together. 5. Stitch down each long side.

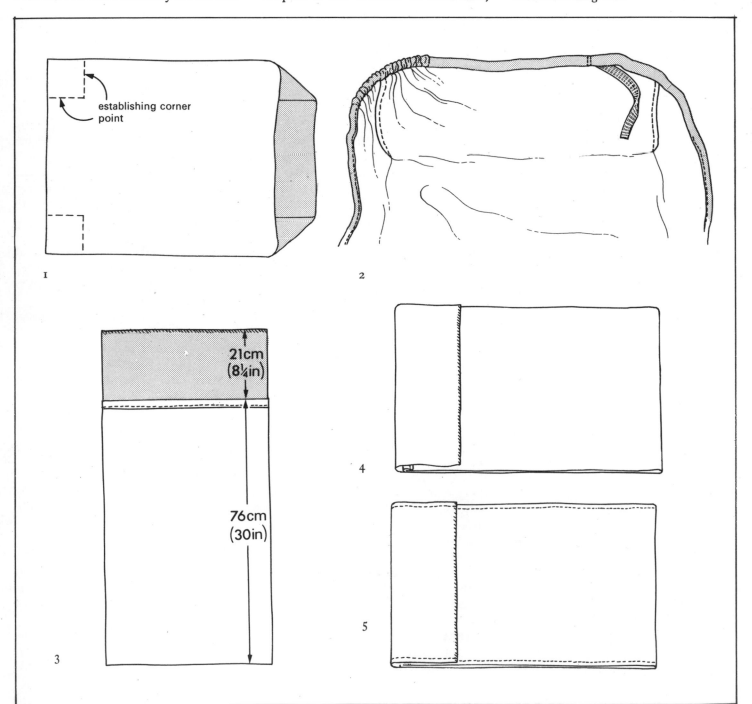

establishing corner point

1

2

21cm (8¼in)

76cm (30in)

3

4

5

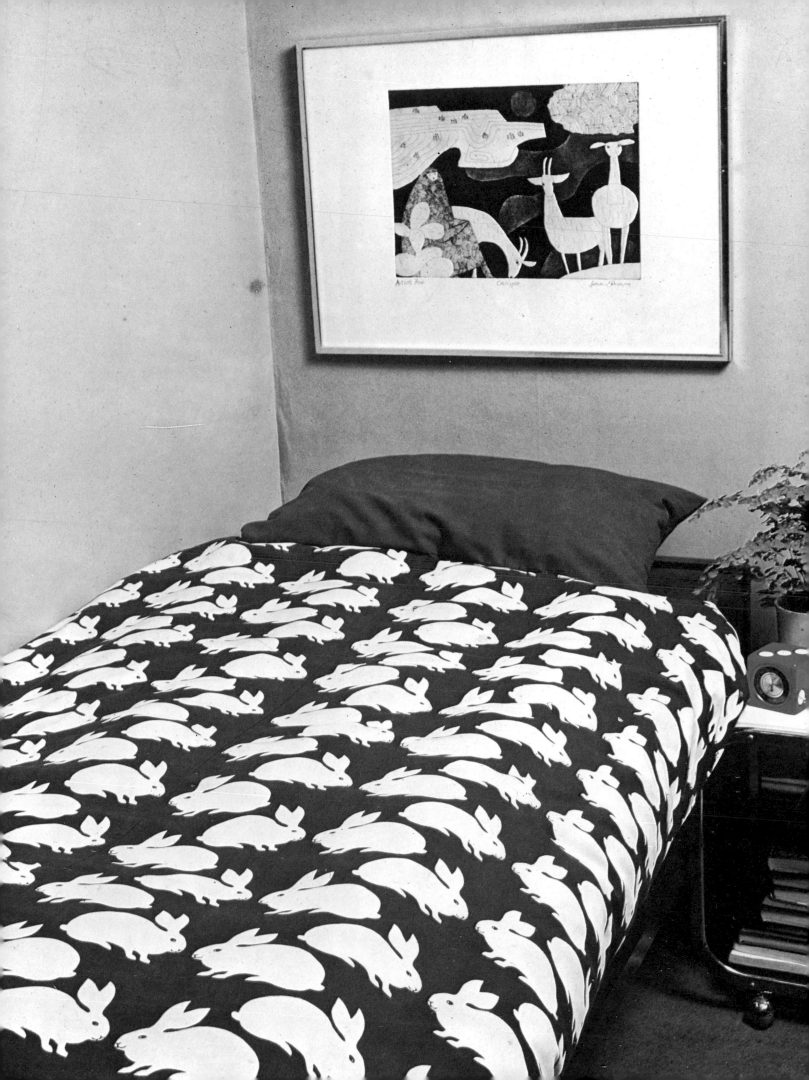

Valance

A valance is a frill of fabric attached to a rectangle of matching fabric or calico and placed under the mattress so that the frill hangs to the floor, covering the base of the bed.

You will need: (for either size of bed)

228 cm (90 in) wide fabric: 4·10 m (4½ yd).

5 m (7½ yd) tape for ties.

Sewing thread to match fabric.

Cutting out Cut a rectangle of fabric to fit the top of the bed, plus 1·5 cm (⅝ in) turnings all round.

For the frill, cut four strips of fabric each from the full width of the fabric, 33·5 cm (13½ in) deep.

To make the valance

Stitch the frill pieces into one long strip, make a 1·5 cm (⅝ in) double hem along one long edge and across short ends. Attach to the top section (see Flounced bedspreads).

Cut the tape into four equal lengths and stitch the centre of each piece to a corner of the valance on the wrong side. Press.

Place the completed valance on the base under the mattress and tie the tapes around the legs of the bed under the frill.

Pillowcase

Measurements The finished pillowcase measures 47 by 76 cm (18½ by 30 in).

You will need:

For two pillowcases:

228 cm (90 in) wide fabric: 1 m (1 yd).

Sewing thread to match fabric.

Cutting out For each pillowcase, cut a rectangle of fabric 50 by 175·5 cm (19½ by 69 in).

To make the pillowcase

At one short end turn 5 mm (¼ in), then 1·5 cm (⅝ in) to make a 1·5 cm (⅝ in) double hem.

Oversew the other short edge of the panel to neaten, or make a small double hem.

Fold the fabric 76 cm (30 in) from the hemmed end with the hem on the outside. The neatened end then extends 21·5 cm (8⅛ in) beyond the hemmed end (fig. 3). Fold this flap over the top of the hemmed end and pin the three layers together (fig. 4).

Pin and stitch down each side of the pillowcase, taking 1·5 cm (⅝ in) turnings (fig. 5). Neaten the seams. Turn the pillowcase the right way out and press.

A beautifully made bed with matching pillowcases, duvet cover and valance which conceals the box spring. The fitted bottom sheet is in a contrasting colour.

Lampshades

All about frames and fabrics
Preparing the frame and covering methods

Fabric shades in traditional or modern designs are undoubtedly the most popular – and among the most expensive to buy. However, they can be made economically and the techniques are not difficult to master. Some basic facts are given here to introduce you to this craft.

Fabric lampshades can be made in many shapes and sizes but in most cases the basic techniques involved are the same and once you have learned how to make one shape you can easily go on to make the others.

The frame This is the basis of every type of lampshade. Frames are available in several different styles and sizes with various fittings for attaching them to the lamp. They are made from tinned or copper wire and joined by spot welding or – on better made frames – by soldering.

Each frame consists of two rings, one of which contains the fitting for attaching the lampshade to the base. The rings are joined by struts or staves, which may be curved or straight. The relative diameters of the rings and the length of the struts determine the size of the lampshade and the shape of the rings and the struts governs its shape. The most common shapes available are shown here. When you buy your frame, check that the struts are evenly spaced and firmly fixed to the rings and their shape has not become distorted by storage. If you cannot find the shape and size of frame you want ready made, some lampshade-frame suppliers will make a frame.

The fitting Shades have a variety of fittings and you should choose the correct one for your purpose.

Pendant fitting (fig. 1) Used for hanging shades. It consists of a small ring held by two or three arms which are joined to opposite sides of the top ring. The small ring fits on to the lampholder (this is the fitting which holds the bulb and has a small ring which is unscrewed so that the lampshade can be put on). Some frames are fitted with a dropped pendant (fig. 2) which ensures that the lampholder is hidden. Some straight drum frames have this type of fitting so that the frame can be used with the pendant at the bottom for a table lamp.

Duplex fitting (fig. 3) Designed for standard lamps or big table lamps. It consists of an inner ring of about 10 cm (4 in) diameter which is attached to the top ring by four arms and positioned 7·5 cm (3 in) below the top ring. The inner ring sits on a separate shade carrier (fig. 3a) which is screwed to the lampholder. Shade carriers are available in different heights and you should choose one which will position the shade so that the bulb is in the middle of it.

Gimbal fitting (fig. 4) Used for table lamps. It consists of a small ring attached to the top ring by hinged arms so that the shade can be tilted to direct the light in any direction.

Butterfly clip fitting (fig. 5) Used on small shades for wall fittings or multiple ceiling fittings as well as small table lamps. The clip fits over the bulb.

The fabric Medium to light natural fibre fabrics can be used to make lampshades, although for those styles which are fitted on the bias or cross of the fabric some printed fabrics with a definite design – such as flowers with stems – may not be suitable.

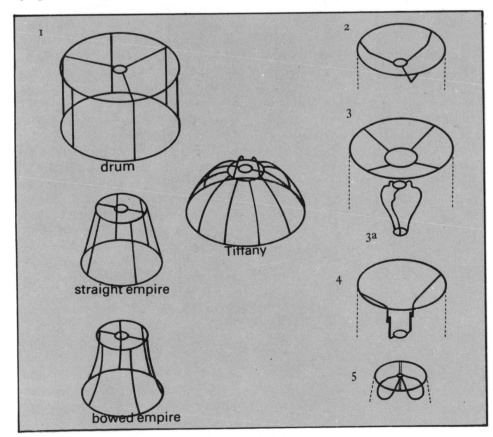

1. These classic shade shapes have a pendent fitting.
2. Shade with a dropped pendent.
3. Duplex fitting. 3a. Shade carrier.
4. Gimbal fitting.
5. Butterfly clip fitting.

179

Choose the fabric initially to suit the decorative scheme of your room but bear in mind the fact that some colours change when seen under artificial light or they may vary the type of light which the shade will give. Dark colours, for example, tend to absorb the light whereas pale colours reflect it and allow the light to pass through. Lining a dark colour with a white, pink or beige fabric will help to give more light. If possible hold your chosen fabric with the lining over a lighted bulb to get an idea of the effect before you buy it.

Silk This is the traditional fabric for lampshades and although it is the most expensive of the fabrics you might choose, it is worth the extra cost because it is pliable and easy to fit, it does not sag or split easily, it cleans well and does not shrink. Most kinds of pure silk can be used and there are some imitation silks which are also suitable.

Most lampshade frame suppliers have a selection of suitable silks but you may find a wider selection among dress fabrics. Beware of using furnishing fabrics which are stiff and do not have much give.

Cottons All kinds can be used for most styles of lampshade, although you may be restricted to frames with straight struts if you choose a design which cannot be used on the bias.

Linens These are too firmly woven to be good for lampshades and they are difficult to fit smoothly and may not allow much light to pass through. Some of the finer embroidery linens, however, may be used for drum or panelled shades, particularly where a lace effect has been worked, perhaps by drawn or pulled thread work.

Man-made fabrics Avoid nylon or polyester, these are unsuitable because they tend to sag and some weights split.

Fabric requirements

For a tailored cover On frames with straight struts, such as the drum or the straight empire, the fabric is fitted on the straight of the grain. Measure half the circumference of the bottom ring of the frame (or its widest measurement) between two struts on opposite sides and then measure the height of the frame (fig. 6). Allow enough fabric to cut two rectangles to

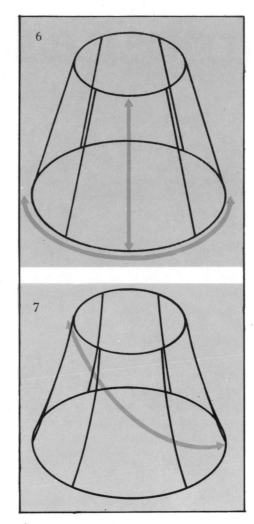

6. *Measuring for a tailored cover.*
7. *Measuring for bias-cut cover.*

these measurements plus about 7·5 cm (3 in) all round for fitting.

For frames with curved or bowed struts On a bowed empire frame, the fabric is fitted on the bias. Measure the frame diagonally over struts on opposite sides of the frame from the top ring to the bottom ring (fig. 7). Allow enough fabric to cut two squares of the fabric along the grain to this measurement plus about 7·5 cm (3 in) for fitting.

Covering methods

There are two main methods of making the cover for a fabric shade.

Semi-fitted This is the simplest fitted cover and also the quickest. The cover is made to fit the widest part of the frame and is gathered or pleated to reduce the fullness on either or both rings if they are narrower than the widest part.

Use this method for Tiffanys, balloon shades (like a Tiffany, but spherical) and any type of frame with straight

struts.

Fully fitted or tailored This is the method requiring most skill and time. The cover is made to fit the frame tightly all over so that the finished lampshade is smooth and taut. With the exception of the drum shape, this is normally achieved by using the fabric on the bias although some pliable fabrics can be used on the straight grain. The cover is usually made in two halves, one for each side of the frame. The seams joining the halves should be placed exactly over the struts of the frame. This method can be used for all styles of shade with circular rings.

The trimming

The trimming is the finishing touch and is fitted round the rings to hide the stitching and raw edges of the fabrics.

You can fit braid to both rings or you could fit the braid to the top ring only and use a co-ordinating fringe for the bottom ring.

Suppliers of lampshade materials have large selections of trimmings and it is preferable to use these rather than furnishing trimmings.

For a more tailored finish you could use velvet ribbon in a colour to match your fabric or you could make your own trimming from spare pieces of bias fabric to match your cover.

To calculate how much trimming to buy, measure the circumference of the rings and add on 2·5 cm (1 in).

Tools you will need

You do not need any specialized tools for lampshade-making and those you do need you will probably have already.

Scissors with sharp blades, for cutting the fabric and trimming the edges.

Pins – use rustless steel dressmaker's pins or the glass-headed type for fitting the cover. Lills pins (short fine pins) are useful when stitching the fabric to the frame as they are less likely to scratch you.

Sewing thread to match your cover fabric.

Needles. 'Betweens' needles are ideal because they are short and stiff and

Bowed empire lampshades such as these are usually lined and finished with a simple binding around the rings.

unlikely to bend or break when they touch the frame.

Clear, non-staining contact adhesive for finishing seams and for attaching the trimming.

Preparing the frames

If the frame is not a plastic-coated one, paint it first, using a metal primer and a fast-drying enamel or cellulose paint to match the colour of the cover. This will prevent the frame from rusting and also looks better if the shade is unlined. Stand the frame on newspaper and paint it. You may have to do this in two or more stages so that you can reach all sides of the rings without smudging. The paint is usually touch dry quite quickly but leave the frame for 24 hours so that it can harden before you bind it. Next, when the paint is completely dry, bind those rings and struts of the frame to which the fabric is to be fitted and stitched. ('The traditional method whereby all

the struts and rings were bound is considered unnecessary these days because it can spoil the smooth finish of the shade.)

Use 1·3 cm ($\frac{1}{2}$ in) cotton tape sold for the purpose. Allow twice the circumference for the rings and one and a half times the length for each strut.

The binding is the most important stage of the preparation. It must be very tight or it will slip and the fabric will not be tautly stretched over the frame however much time you spend on the fitting. For most styles of lampshade the rings and two struts, on opposite sides of the frame, are bound so that the fabric can be pinned and fitted on to them.

The binding on the struts is then removed because it is no longer needed but it is kept on the rings so that the cover can be stitched in place.

To bind the top ring, place the end of the tape under the ring at the top of a strut (fig. 1a). Bring the tape over the

A detachable shade is a quick way of covering a Tiffany frame, and best suited to an informal setting.

joint of the ring and strut and bind over the end of the tape (fig. 1b). Continue binding as tightly as possible, keeping the tape at an acute angle and overlapping it slightly. At each strut, wrap the binding round the ring an extra time and then go on to the next section (fig. 1c, d, e, f). To finish, stitch down the end of the tape on the outside of the ring. Turn the frame upside down and bind the bottom ring as above.

To bind the struts, start at the top of one strut and loop the end of the tape round the T-joint (fig. 2a). Bind over the end and continue tightly down the strut (fig. 2b, c). Finish by winding round the ring on both sides of the strut (fig. 2d). Pull the end through a previous loop. Bind opposite strut in the same way.

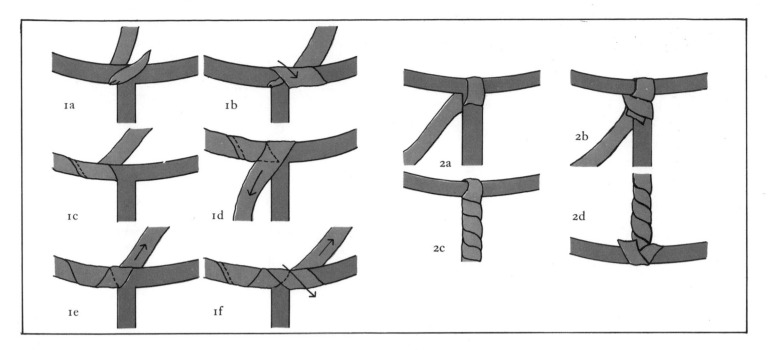

Detachable Tiffany cover

One of the easiest and quickest ways of covering a Tiffany frame is to make a detachable cover. This method has the extra advantage in that the cover can easily be removed for washing, and you do not need to bind the frame because the cover is not fitted or stitched directly to it. It is, however, advisable to paint the frame.

You will need:

Fabric (see below).
Painted frame.
Matching thread.
Elastic, 6 mm (¼ in) wide by the circumference of the bottom ring.
Cotton tape, 6 mm (¼ in) wide by the circumference of the top ring, plus about 10 cm (4 in).
Bodkin, needle, sewing thread, pins.
Washable trimming (optional) to widest circumference of fabric plus 2·5 cm (1 in) for joining.

Making the cover Measure the frame at its widest part (this is not necessarily the bottom ring). If the measurement is less than the width of the fabric, the cover can be made in one piece. If it is more, the cover should be made in two halves.
Measure the length of the struts and add 9 cm (3½ in). If you are making the cover from one piece of fabric, allow enough to cut one piece along the grain to the length of the struts plus 9 cm (3½ in) by the measurement of the circumference of the widest part plus 2·5 cm (1 in). If you are

making it in two halves, allow enough to cut two pieces along the grain to the length of the struts plus 9 cm (3½ in) by the measurement of half the circumference plus 2·5 cm (1 in).
First join the fabric so that it fits the widest part of the frame. Use a plain seam and trim the turnings to 3 mm (⅛ in). Finish the edge by overcasting or with a machine zig-zag stitch; or you could use a French seam.
Fold over 6 mm (¼ in) on to the wrong side along both long edges of the fabric and press. Fold over 1·3 cm (½ in) again to make casings, tack and machine stitch, leaving openings in the stitching of about 1·3 cm (½ in).
Pin and machine stitch the trimming (if used) 2·5 cm (1 in) above the lower edge of the cover.
Thread the elastic through the casing along the lower edge of the cover, draw up the elastic and pin the ends together.
Thread the tape through the casing along the upper edge of the cover.
Place the cover on the frame so that the trimming is positioned on the lower ring. Draw up the elastic tightly to draw the margin of fabric under the frame. Pin and stitch the elastic at the required place and trim off the excess. Arrange the gathers of fabric neatly.
Arrange the fabric neatly on the frame at the top and draw up the tape so that the cover is firmly held over the frame making sure the trimming is still correctly positioned. Tie the tape neatly and trim off the excess length. Stitch up the openings in the casings.

1a-1f. Binding top ring.
2a-2d. Binding the struts.

Semi-fitted Tiffany shade

The cover fits the bottom tightly but is gathered to fit the much narrower top, and it looks prettiest in a light cotton or broderie anglaise fabric. A scalloped or lace trimming can be added.

You will need:

Prepared frame (painted, with top and bottom rings bound).
Fabric as for detachable Tiffany cover.
Sewing thread.
Trimming (If using fringe or braid you will need the measurement of the circumference of the bottom ring plus 1·5 cm (⅝ in) for turnings.)
For co-ordinating braid, you will need the measurement of the circumference of the top ring, plus 1·5 cm (½ in) for turnings.
Clear adhesive.

Fitting the cover

Cut out the fabric to the required measurements. If you are using one piece, fold it in half with the shorter edges together and mark the fold with tacking. If you are using two pieces, join them down one side as for detachable Tiffany shade.
Place the fabric with the right side facing out on to the frame so that the seam or line of tacking is level with one of the bound struts. Centre the fabric on the length of the strut so

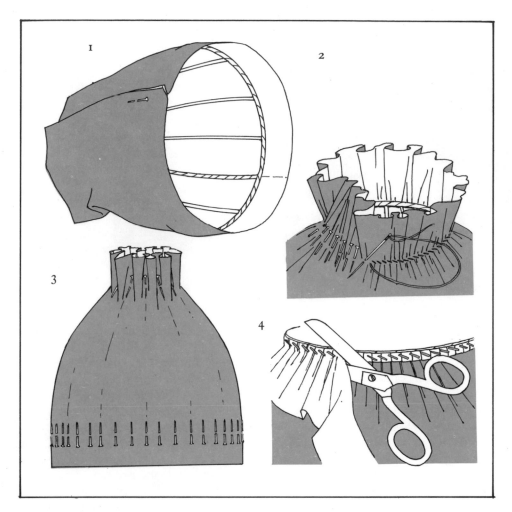

For a semi-fitted Tiffany shade:
1. Fit fabric round frame to fit snugly at widest part.
2. Pin fullness into tiny pleats between the struts.
3. Stitch fabric to ring bindings working in a clockwise direction.
4. Trim away surplus fabric.

Keep checking that the braid is level with the rings as you progress. When you reach the other end, fold it under to meet the first fold exactly and stick down. Secure with a pin.

The braid is attached to the top ring in a similar way but the outer edge should be pinched up slightly with your fingers so that the inner edge will lie flat.

Trimming can also be stitched in position.

Lined lampshades

The cover for tailored, lined lampshades is made in two sections, one for each half of the frame. One of the sections is fitted and shaped on the frame itself and then used as a template for the other section. The pieces are then seamed together and the whole cover replaced on the frame and stitched to the rings.

Usually you have a choice of whether to fit the cover on the straight or bias grain. Of the two methods, fitting on the bias grain is easier because the fabric is more pliable, but it is more wasteful and some patterns do not look right when used this way.

Straight drum shapes should always be fitted on the straight grain because it helps to maintain the correct shape. Very waisted shapes – where the circumference is less in the middle of the frame than at the top – must be fitted on the bias grain so that the fabric will be stretched at the top ring when it is replaced on the frame.

The fabric for the lining can be cut on the bias grain but if you use a pliable fabric, such as crêpe-backed satin, it can easily be fitted on the straight grain which is less wasteful.

Instructions in this section are for a bias-grain cover with a straight-grain lining. To fit a straight-grain cover, follow the instructions for fitting the lining but mark and stitch the two sections as for the bias-grain cover. The instructions for a drum shape are given at the end of the section.

that 4·5 cm (1¾ in) extends at the top and bottom. Pin the seam or tacking line to the bound strut in one or two places in the middle.

Wrap the fabric round the frame and pin the edges together in line with the opposite bound strut so that the cover fits tightly at the widest part of the frame but does not distort the fabric (fig. 1). Remove the fabric from the frame and tack along the straight grain level with the pin.

Join the fabric as described for the detachable Tiffany shade.

Stitching the fabric to the frame

Place the cover on the frame as before, with the right side facing out, and pin it to the binding along the bottom ring. Place the pins so that the points face into the body of the lampshade so that you are less likely to scratch yourself. Smooth the cover up the line of the struts, keeping the grain straight, and pin at the top of each strut.

Fold away the fullness between the struts into tiny pleats and pin them (fig. 2). Repeat along the bottom ring if this is narrower than the widest part of the frame.

Start stitching the fabric to the binding on the outside of the rings using a small oversewing or hemming stitch. Work in a clockwise direction around the ring, making sure that you catch the gathers firmly in position. Use double thread and begin and fasten off securely, using several small back stitches (fig. 3).

Turn the surplus fabric back over the stitching so that the fold is level with the edge of the rings, and stitch through all thicknesses. Trim the surplus fabric close to stitching (fig. 4).

Fringe edging Fold under one end of the fringe for 6 mm (¼ in) and stick down with a spot of adhesive. Place the fold on to the bottom ring so that it is level with a seam and the top edge of the fringed section is level with the edge of the ring. The braided or solid section along the top edge of the fringe must cover the binding on the ring, the raw edges and stitching of the fabric.

Apply adhesive for about 10 cm (4 in) along the underside of the braided section and place it in position on the ring, stretching it slightly. Secure with a pin. Apply adhesive to the next 10 cm (4 in) and stick down as before.

The lining

This type of lampshade should always be fitted with an internal lining which hides the struts and gives it a professional finish. Internal linings are known as balloon linings because although they are fitted on to the outside of the frame, in the same way as the cover, when they are stitched in place inside the frame they 'balloon' away from the struts.

You will need:

Fabric to required measurements.
Lining to required measurements.
Prepared frame (with bound rings and two bound struts).
Sewing thread.
Trimming.
Clear adhesive, soft pencil.

Measuring and cutting fabric (see Fabric requirements for tailored cover).

Fitting the cover

In order to achieve a really smooth, taut cover, as well as the initial careful fitting, it is also essential to keep the grain of the fabric straight without distortion and to place the seams exactly over the struts of the frame.

Fold one of the fabric squares in half diagonally with the wrong side facing out and press the fold lightly with your fingers at each end.

Place the frame on your work surface with the bottom ring facing you and the two bound struts to the left and right. Place the fabric on to the frame so that the fold is level with the centre of the top half: if the frame has eight struts, place the fabric on to it so that the fold is in line with the centre strut (fig. 1): if the frame has six struts, place the fabric on to it so that the fold is in the centre of the two top struts.

Open out the fabric, keeping the fold in line with the centre strut or in the centre of the two top struts. Pin it to the rings at the top and bottom of the crease, keeping it taut but without stretching it.

Smooth the fabric out to the bound struts with your fingers to mould it to the shape of the frame. Pin it to the tops and bottoms of the bound struts, so that the pin points are facing in. Place more pins at about 1·5 cm (½ in) intervals down the left-hand strut, easing out any fullness in the fabric. Place the pins at right-angles to the strut with the points facing in. Starting at the top of the left-hand strut, follow the grain line of the fabric diagonally across the frame. Keeping the line completely straight and tight, pin it where it meets the right-hand strut or the bottom ring (fig. 2).

Go back to the next pin down on the left-hand strut and follow the grain down in the same way. Tighten the fabric and pin. Continue in this way, pinning and tightening the fabric away from the left-hand strut diagonally across to where it naturally falls on either the right-hand strut, or the bottom ring (fig. 2a).

Working upwards along the grain in the opposite direction, tighten the fabric from the left-hand strut to the top ring and pin at the top of the intermediate (unbound) struts (fig. 3). Remove the pin at the top of the right-hand strut, tighten the fabric in the same way and replace the pin.

Complete the pinning down the right-hand strut and along the remaining part of the bottom ring, smoothing out any remaining fullness or wrinkles with your finger by running it in the direction of the grain. Never run your finger along the bias grain or you will distort the fabric and possibly stretch it.

Using a pencil, lightly draw down the fabric in between the pins over the outer bound struts. Draw lines about 1·5 cm (½ in) long inwards from the bound struts along the top and bottom rings. Mark a dot on the rings at the top and bottom of each intermediate strut.

Remove all the pins and remove the fabric from the frame.

Marking the second section Place the marked section on to the second section with right sides together so that the edges are level and the grain, pattern or slub is running in the same direction on both pieces. Pin the sections together along the pencilled

1. Placing the fabric on the frame.
2. Following the grain line across.
2a. Tightening on to bottom ring.

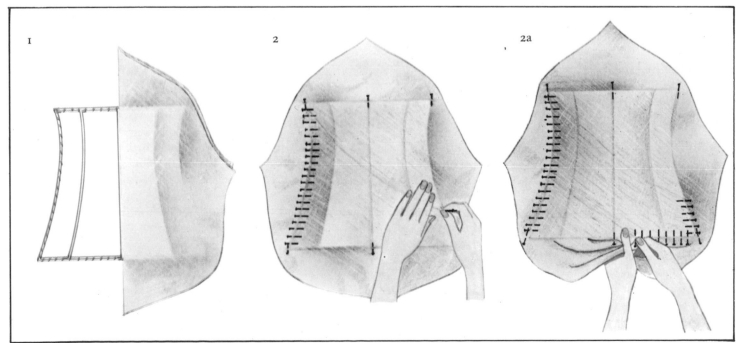

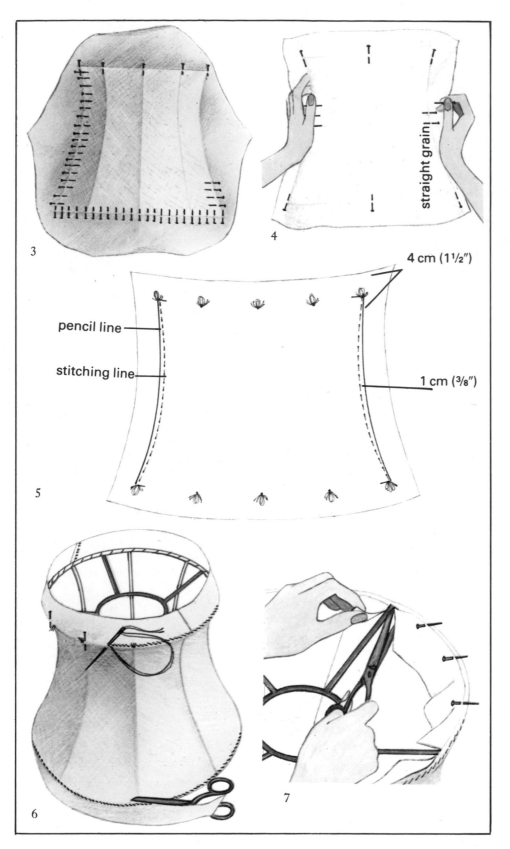

3. *Tightening fabric on to top ring.*

4. *Tightening lining horizontally between struts.*

5. *Tacking curved stitching line to form the balloon lining.*

6. *Stitching the cover to the rings and trimming the excess fabric.*

7. *Slitting the lining to fit it round the light fitting.*

open out the fabric. Press the turnings open lightly with your fingers. Spread adhesive along the turnings, press the turnings together so that they adhere and trim to within 3 mm ($\frac{1}{8}$ in) of the stitching.

Put the cover to one side while you fit the lining.

Fitting the lining

Fold one of the lining pieces in half lengthwise along the straight grain and crease the ends of the fold lightly with your fingers. Open out the fabric and place with wrong side facing upwards (with crêpe-backed satin this is usually the crêpe side) on to the frame so that the crease is level with the centre of the frame. Pin the fabric at each end of the crease to the rings and then smooth out to the side struts and pin at the tops and bottoms. Do not over-tighten at these points or the fabric will not keep to the shape of the frame. Pin the fabric halfway down the left-hand strut. Tighten along the grain and pin halfway down the right-hand strut.

Working up from these points, pin up to the top ring, tightening the fabric horizontally by pulling from the left and right, and working first on one strut and then on the other (fig. 4).

Work downwards to the bottom ring in the same way.

When the sides are pinned, pin the fabric to the rings, tightening only enough to remove any wrinkles. Check that the grain line is completely square and avoid overtightening vertically or you will lose the shape.

Mark the fabric as for the main fabric and remove from the frame.

Mark the second section of the lining in the same way and stitch the two pieces together down the sides so that the stitching starts 3 mm ($\frac{1}{8}$ in) in from the marked line at the top and bottom and curves in to about 1 cm ($\frac{3}{8}$ in) from the line in the middle (fig. 5). This forms the balloon shape of the lining.

Finish as for the cover.

Remove the binding from the struts.

Attaching the cover

Turn the cover right side out and place on to the frame so that the seams lie over the struts which were originally bound and the tailor's tacks line up with the ends of the struts and are

strut lines. Work tailor's tacks at the outer ends of the short pencil lines and at each dot.

Cut round the shape adding about 4 cm ($1\frac{1}{2}$ in) all round.

Machine stitch the pieces together down the pencilled strut lines and fasten off securely.

Cut through the tailor's tacks and

on the rings. Pin the fabric to the rings at the tops and bottoms of the intermediate struts. Do not put any pins into the fabric down the length of the struts – they must be placed in the rings only.

Check that the turnings are lying flat over the struts and are not twisted and make any adjustments needed. Working alternately on each side of one of the seams, start tightening the cover on the frame by adjusting the pins. When you make one alteration to one side of the seam go to a similar place on the opposite side and make the same alteration. Keep checking the seam and grain lines. Insert more pins into the rings between the struts so that the cover is lying taut against the frame.

Stitching the cover to rings When you are satisfied with the fit of the cover, it can be stitched to the rings. The most comfortable way of doing this is to sit with the frame on your lap with a pad of fabric beneath it to prevent your legs from being scratched.

Start stitching at a strut and work towards your free hand so that you can hold the fabric taut on to the frame with your fingers as you stitch.

Use each length of thread doubled and start and finish with two or three back stitches. Work in a close, firm hemming stitch, placing the stitches on the outer edge of the ring.

When you have stitched around both rings, cut off the excess fabric close to the stitching (fig. 6).

Attaching the lining

Place the lining into the frame and align the seams with those of the cover. Position the tailor's tacks correctly on the bottom ring and pin. Draw the fabric up the shade and pin on the inside of the ring at the top of each

strut. Roll back the excess fabric at the top inside ring and clip into it in line with the arms of the light fitting and at intervals in between if the fabric seems tight (fig. 7). Roll the fabric over the top ring, fold under the fabric at each side of the slits for the fitting, and pin all round to the outside edge so that the pins are over the previous stitching.

Stand the frame upside down (with the top ring at the bottom), check that the seams are over the struts and pull the fabric on both sides of the seams to tighten it over the bottom ring. Working alternately on each side of the seams, pin the fabric to the ring.

Stitching the lining to rings Stitch the lining in a similar way to the cover, placing the stitches on the outside of the ring (fig. 8). Cut off the excess fabric close to the stitching.

Finishing the slits To finish the slits for the light fitting, cut a bias strip for each one, 5 cm (2 in) long by 2·5 cm (1 in). Fold in the raw edges so they meet in the middle and then fold the strip in half again.

Slipstitch the folds together lightly. Place each strip loosely round a fitting so that it covers the slit and pin the ends on the ring (fig. 9). Secure with a few stitches and trim off any surplus fabric level with the raw edges of the lining.

Trimming the shade Finish the shade by trimming with braid, velvet ribbon or a bias strip.

Trimming with self bias strip Cut 3 cm (1¼ in) wide bias strip equal in length to the circumference of each ring plus 1·5 cm (½ in) for turnings. Fold each strip in half lengthwise with the wrong side facing out. Place the strip round the appropriate ring so that the raw edges are level with the turned back edges of the fabric and the

bulk of the strip extends beyond the frame. Stretch the strip round the ring slightly if the struts bow inwards. Pin the short ends together along the straight grain so that the strip fits tightly. Remove the strip, open it out and stitch with right sides together along the pinned line. Press seam open. Re-fold the strip with the right side facing out and place it on the frame as before. Oversew the double strip in place firmly all round, making sure that the outer edges of the stitches come to the outer edge of the ring. Fasten off securely and turn back the strip on to the frame so that the fold is level with the rings and the stitches and raw edges are covered. If necessary, press strip lightly with your fingers and slipstitch neatly along the inner edge.

Straight drum shapes

A straight drum frame is one which has top and bottom rings of the same size – the rings can be circular or oval. Both the cover and lining fabric should be fitted on the straight grain.

The method is similar to that previously described, but it is essential that the tightening is done vertically and not horizontally, in order to maintain the correct shape.

To do this, place the fabric on to the frame and pin it to the top and bottom rings so that it is really tight (fig. 10). Then pin it to the side struts, pulling only enough to remove any wrinkles. Finish the shade as for other shapes, but without shaping the seams on the lining.

8. Stitching the lining to the outside of the rings.

9. Pinning the fabric strip to hide the slits in the lining.

10. Tightening cover for a drum shade.

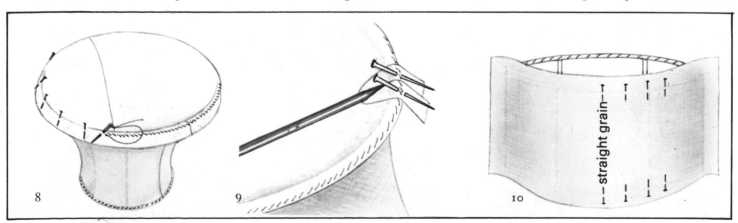

Sewing Snips

Lined picnic basket
You will need:
Wicker hamper.

Calculated amount of printed cotton fabric for lining.

Oddments of printed cotton fabrics for pockets.

2·5 cm (1 in) wide contrasting bias binding.

2·5 cm (1 in) wide contrasting ribbon or braid.

Sewing thread to match fabric.

Buttons for pockets (optional).

Making the pattern and estimating fabric requirements
Take the measurements of the inside of the basket – base, sides and lid. Add 1·3 cm (½ in) seam allowance to each measurement, and make up a paper pattern for each section. Test the paper patterns against the basket to check that they fit correctly.

Take rough measurements of your set of picnic plates (allowing plenty of ease to accommodate them) measure thermos flask, and so on, and note the measurements of the individual compartments accordingly.

The lining is made double so you will need two of each piece. For the ties you will need 14 strips of fabric, each 6·5 by 76 cm (2½ by 30 in). Work out a cutting plan to find the quantity of fabric needed. Quantities for pockets and ties will depend on individual requirements. Plan each pocket and flap on paper, then measure all round to find quantity of binding needed.

Cutting out
Cut out the pieces of lining fabric using the paper patterns.

Cut two pieces for each section.

Making the lining
With right sides facing, stitch each pair of fabric pieces together taking 6 mm (¼ in) seams and leaving an opening to turn through. Turn each section right side out, and slipstitch openings.

Plate pockets Cut out a rectangle of fabric to required dimensions, as the edges are bound, seam allowances are

Left. A wicker picnic basket fitted with a colourful lining that has pockets, ties and loops to hold picnic requirements is as attractive as it is useful for keeping things neat.

not needed. Bind the edges with contrasting binding. Position each pocket as required on the lining section and top-stitch in position along the side and bottom edges, leaving a little slack in the fabric between the two sides in order to make sufficient room for plates.

Button-down pockets These can hold paper napkins and can be made in exactly the same way as the plate pockets. Cut out a flap section to fit each pocket, bind all edges, and stitch the flap to the lining fabric just above the top edge of the pocket. Sew a little loop of binding to the centre bottom of the flap and a button in the corresponding position on the pocket itself for fastening.

Ties Use for matches, condiment

Right. Small buttondown pockets and ties made of bias binding or ribbon serve to hold even the smallest of picnic condiments and accessories, so that they do not get lost in a muddle.

Below. Pockets are made to measure to hold plates, knives and forks securely so that they do not rattle about loose, reducing the risk of breakage.

containers, corkscrew, tin opener, and thermos flask can be made from two lengths of ribbon with one end stitched to the lining fabric. The distance between each piece depends on the width of the item to be secured. Hold it in position against the lining fabric for a rough guide.

Cutlery pockets Cut out a long rectangle of fabric about half the depth of a knife and bind the edges as for the plate pocket. Sew on strips of binding vertically at intervals, where you wish to divide the pockets into individual compartments. Stitch pocket to lining fabric along side and bottom edges, and stitch along vertical strips of binding through all fabric layers to make compartments.

Fastenings Make these from strips of lining fabric. Fold each strip in half lengthwise with right sides facing and stitch together, leaving end opening for turning. Turn right side out and slipstitch opening. Alternatively, use binding.

Stitch ties to corners of each lining section. The lining sections are attached to the basket by looping the tabs through the holes in the wickerwork and tying securely.

No kitchen should be without potholders, and they need not be the usual square of padded fabric. By raiding your sewing basket and saving gloves that have lost their mate, you can make a bright imaginative collection of an everyday household article. The potholder below is made of simple patchwork triangles.

Pot holder ideas

Make sure you are never without a pot holder within easy reach by providing yourself with a collection of them in all shapes and sizes. Hang them up in convenient places where they will also provide decorative touches of colour to brighten up your kitchen.

Choose washable fabrics and synthetic wadding which does not shrink. The details are very much up to you. The simplest method is probably to sandwich two pieces of fabric together with wadding in between the layers and then to bind the edges. Add a loop in cord or ribbon with which to hang the glove up.

There are innumerable possible variations.

You could make a patchwork holder using a variety of printed fabrics, combining flowers, spots, checks, stripes – the more variety of fabrics the jollier the finished effect.

The edges can be finished with binding or ribbon, or stitched in a contrasting colour.

You might even try recycling an old woollen glove by protecting the right side of the palm and inside thumb with a layer of wadding, held in place with a piece of fabric, cut to the right

size and shape and sewn on with the edges turned under to stop them from fraying.

Similarly, patch an old sock with colourful fabric and insert a layer of wadding into it so that it lies flat. Work buttonhole stitch all round, both to close the open edge and to neaten the other edges.

Chair covers and windbreak

If you have some old deckchairs which are unused because they have torn or shabby canvas, why not give them a new lease of life? With gaily printed deckchair canvas (available from large stores) and a coat of coloured paint on the woodwork, they can be smartened up easily and cheaply – and made more comfortable if you pad the seat at the same time. All you need is your sewing skill and some simple handyman's equipment.

Deckchair cover
You will need:

Ripping chisel, mallet, hammer.
Paint, polyurethane varnish, paintbrush, woodworking adhesive, medium grade glasspaper.
Calculated length of 40 cm (15 in) wide deckchair canvas.
14 to 16 1·5 cm ($\frac{5}{8}$ in) improved tacks.

Cross-stitch an appropriate kitchen motif, or quilt a plaid potholder.

Strong needle and thread.

To prepare the deckchair

Remove the tacks holding old canvas carefully with a ripping chisel (or an old blunt wood chisel) and a mallet. To do this, place the tip of the chisel under the head of the tack and tap the handle of the chisel with the mallet. Always work in the direction of the grain of the wood – in this case it is along the length of the rail – in order to avoid splitting the wood. When the tack is loosened, lift it out with the claw section of a hammer. As you work, note how the canvas is wrapped round the rails. Stick any splintered wood in place with adhesive. Prepare, paint and varnish frame. Leave to dry.

To calculate the length of the new canvas

Lay the chair out flat and measure from the rail to which the canvas was attached at the top to the rail to which it was attached at the bottom. Keep the tape measure taut between the two.

Add 15 cm (6 in) for turnings and wrapping the canvas round the rails.

Attaching the canvas

Fold under one end of the canvas for 2·5 cm (1 in). Lay the deckchair flat, with the notches facing up. Tack the folded edge of the canvas to the inside face of the rail on the notched section of the chair (fig. 1), using seven to eight tacks placed at 5 cm (2 in) intervals. Avoid putting the tacks in exactly the same position as before. Bring the canvas right round the bar and up to the other end of the un-notched section of the chair. Pull the canvas taut and take it right over the rail, fold under the excess fabric and tack it to the underside, again using seven to eight tacks at 5 cm (2 in) intervals (fig. 2).

Padded deckchair

You can make the deckchair more comfortable by padding the canvas with foam.

You will need:

Twice the calculated amount of 40 cm (15 in) wide canvas.
Sheet of 1·3 cm (½ in) thick foam, 2·5 cm (1 in) narrower and 10 cm (4 in) shorter than basic length of canvas.

To make the padded deckchair

Cut the canvas into two equal lengths. Place the foam sheeting on the wrong side of one canvas piece, leaving a 1·3 cm (½ in) border on each side and 5 cm (2 in) border at the top and bottom. Tack in position all round the edges and at intervals across the width.
Put the canvas pieces together with right sides facing and stitch them down the long sides taking just less than 1·3 cm (½ in) turnings so that you clear the foam. Use strong thread, a heavy needle and a medium-length stitch.
Turn the canvas right side out and press the seams. Machine stitch across the top and bottom of the canvas 5·5 cm (2¼ in) from each end to catch in the foam, and then at 23 to 25 cm (9 to 10 in) intervals in between through all thicknesses.
Attach the padded canvas to the frame in the same way as for a standard cover.

Make yourself comfortable with deckchair and protective windbreak.

Incorporating a head pillow

A bolster neck cushion can be incorporated simply by adding to the length of canvas needed for recovering the deckchair. The filling for the bolster can be made from a sheet of foam.

You will need:

Calculated length of 40 cm (15 in) wide deckchair canvas, plus 45 cm (18 in).
Sheet of 1·3 cm (½ in) foam 30 by 45 cm (12 by 18 in).
21 to 24 1·5 cm (⅝ in) improved tacks.

To make the head pillow

Start to cover the chair in the same way as for a standard cover, but at the top bring the excess under the top rail. Bring the canvas up tautly and tack to the top rail.
Set the chair in its upright sitting position and bring the excess canvas over the top rail. Roll up the foam to make a bolster 30 cm (12 in) wide and secure with a few stitches. Wrap the excess canvas round the foam and try it out for size and comfort, adjusting it if necessary (fig. 3). Tack the end enclosing the foam roll, to the top rail in the same way as for the first row of tacks. Fold in the sides of the canvas neatly and stitch down.

Wind-break

On breezy days, a wind-break can make all the difference to the comfort of a picnic. The simple version shown here is easy to transport and erect. However, although you can make it as long as you like, it should not be more than about 122 cm (4 ft) high unless the stakes are driven a long way into the ground, or it might be blown over. If you are going to be using it as a wind-break for a cooker, remember to keep the cooker well away from the wind-break as a precaution against fire.

You will need:

Calculated length of 90 cm (36 in) wide deckchair canvas.
Stakes (either 2·5 cm (1 in) diameter dowelling, broom handles or 1 cm (⅜ in) aluminium tubing) at least 26 cm (10 in) longer than the height of the windbreak; sufficient for one each end and at about 45 cm (18 in) intervals in between.
Rubber caps for stakes (as used for

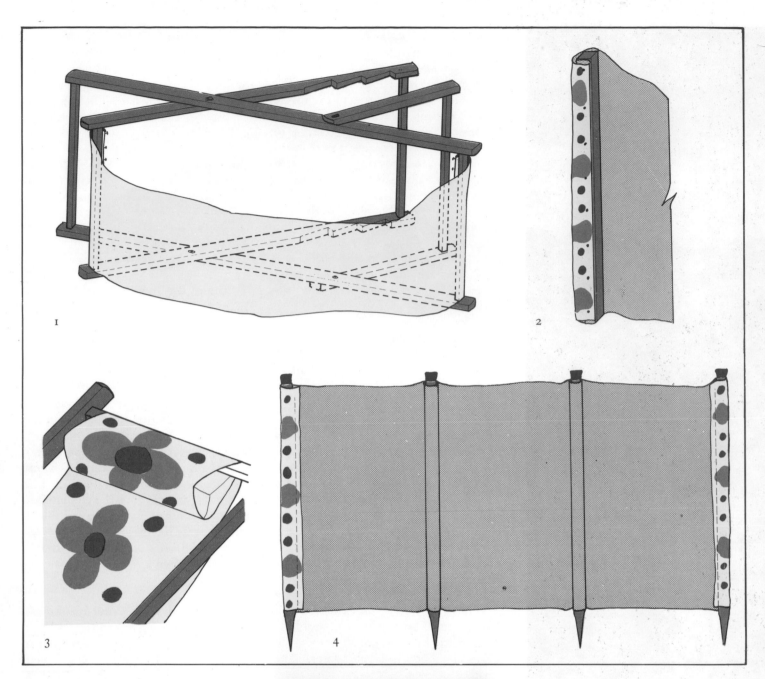

1

2

3

4

furniture feet).

Making the casings

The canvas is used sideways so that the selvedges form the top and bottom of the wind-break and do not need neatening.

To make the casings for the stakes, turn under and make double hems at each side edge (fig. 4). Check that the stakes will slip easily into the hem casings.

Divide the fabric between the end casings into equal sections, about 45 cm (18 in) wide. Make a fold at each section bringing the right sides of the fabric together. Measure from the fold the size of the casing and machine stitch through the doubled canvas along this line. Make all the casings in the samc way.

1. Tack folded edge of canvas to the rail of the section of the chair.
2. Pull the canvas to the un-notched section, fold and tack in place.
3. Make a head pillow from extra fabric tacked to the top rail and then tucked around a foam cushion.
4. For the windbreak, make casings at each end and stitch evenly spaced pleat pleats in the centre to take the stakes.

Preparing wooden stakes

If you are using wooden stakes, taper off one end of each with a chisel or handyman's knife to make a fairly thick point. This makes them easier to bang into the ground. Insert the stakes into the casings (the points should be at the bottom) and fit a rubber cap over the top of each stake.

Mob caps and sponge bags

This bathroom set is made from a graph pattern. There is a matching Dorothy bag and quilted sponge bag. The mob caps come in two sizes and have a pretty lace trim. Both caps and bags are lined with a waterproof fabric.

Making the pattern

Draw up the pattern to scale from the graph pattern given here. One square represents 2·5 cm (1 in) square.

This bathroom set would be a welcome present for a travelling friend.

You will need:

For mother's cap and bag:

90 cm (36 in) wide fabric, 70 cm

(¾ yd) for cap.
90 cm (36 in) wide quilted fabric, 50 cm (½ yd) for bag.
2·30 m (2½ yd) lace trimming.
Two cards bias binding.
Sewing thread to match fabric.
Two large press studs.
90 cm (36 in) wide waterproof fabric for lining both cap and bag, 80 cm (⅞ yd).
60 mm (¼ yd) elastic.
For daughter's cap and bag:
90 cm (36 in) wide fabric, 60 cm (⅝ yd) for cap and bag.
18 cm (7 in) square of quilting fabric for base of bag.
1·40 m (1½ yd) 6 mm (¼ in) wide ribbon to tone with fabric.
Sewing thread to match fabric.
2·70 m (3 yd) lace trimming.
70 cm (¾ yd) hat elastic.
90 cm (36 in) wide waterproof fabric for lining both cap and bag, 60 cm (⅝ yd).

Cutting out

A seam allowance of 6 mm (¼ in) has been included on all edges.

1. Putting lace trimming on mob cap.
2. Sewing binding to gusset seam.
3a. Fold raw edges to centre. 3b. Put these edges together and slipstitch.

To make the caps

For each cap, cut one piece of the appropriate size from fabric and one from lining.

Place the lining to the wrong side of the fabric and tack together. Make two rows of machine stitching round the lines indicated on the pattern to form the casing for the elastic. Zig-zag stitch the outer edges together to neaten.

Place the lace trimming to the right side of the cap edge and machine stitch in place as close to the edge of the cap as possible (fig. 1). Overlap the raw ends of the lace and neaten. Work a row of zig-zag stitching over the row of straight stitching to hold the lace secure and flat. Press the cap flat on the right side only with a cool iron. (Test waterproof fabric first.)

Cut a small hole in the lining only, between the two rows of machine stitching and insert the hat elastic using a bodkin. Pull up to fit head and secure the elastic.

Mother's bag

Cut out bag and gusset sections from quilted fabric and lining. Tack lining fabric to the wrong side of quilted fabric bag section and the two gusset sections.

Sew bias binding to the upper short edge of each gusset section. Sew bias binding to the upper straight edge of the bag. Press flat on the right side only. Clip into seam allowance of the bag section as indicated on the pattern for gussets. With wrong sides together, stitch the gusset sections to the bag, matching the clips on the bag to the corners of the gusset sections. Commencing from the bound straight edge, sew bias binding round the gusset seams and the curved flap edge of the bag (fig. 2).

Press with a cool iron on the right side of the fabric. (Test waterproof fabric first.)

Sew press studs in positions marked on bag and bag flap to close.

Cut a strip of fabric measuring 58·5 cm (23 in) by 7·5 cm (3 in). Fold the raw edges to the centre as shown (fig. 3a) and tack. Turn in the seam allowance on the short ends and tack. Fold the outer fold edges together, tack and slipstitch round the entire edge (fig. 3b). Press flat.

Sew handle to bag in position as indicated on the gusset pattern piece.

Daughter's bag

Cut out one bag section from fabric and one from lining. Cut out base in quilted fabric and in lining. Cut two casings in fabric.

Tack the lining to the wrong side of the bag side and base sections.

With right sides together, stitch the side seam. Neaten the seam edge by sewing the raw edges together with a row of zig-zag stitching. Turn under the seam allowance on all edges of the casing sections, tack and press flat. Place in position as indicated on the pattern and top-stitch in place, leaving the short ends open, with gaps on either side of bag for the ribbon ties. Neaten the upper edge of the bag with a row of zig-zag stitches. Sew on the lace trimming as instructed for the hat. With right sides together, pin the bag to the base, easing in any fullness. Stitch and neaten the seam.

Cut ribbon into two lengths. Starting at A thread one length of ribbon through the casings completely round bag and sew the ends securely together. Starting at B thread other ribbon through similarly. Pull the ribbon out at each side of the casing as shown to close (fig. 4).

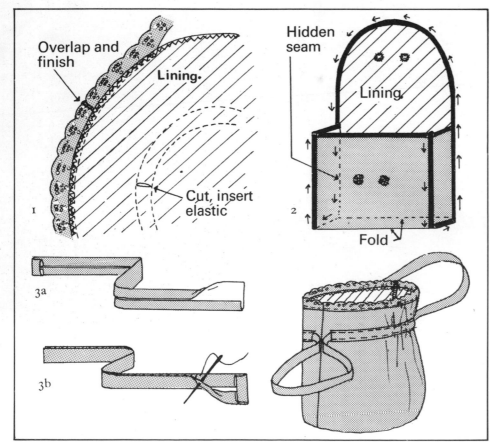

Overlap and finish
Lining.
Cut, insert elastic
1
3a
3b
Hidden seam
Lining.
Fold
2

Graph pattern for sponge bags and mob caps

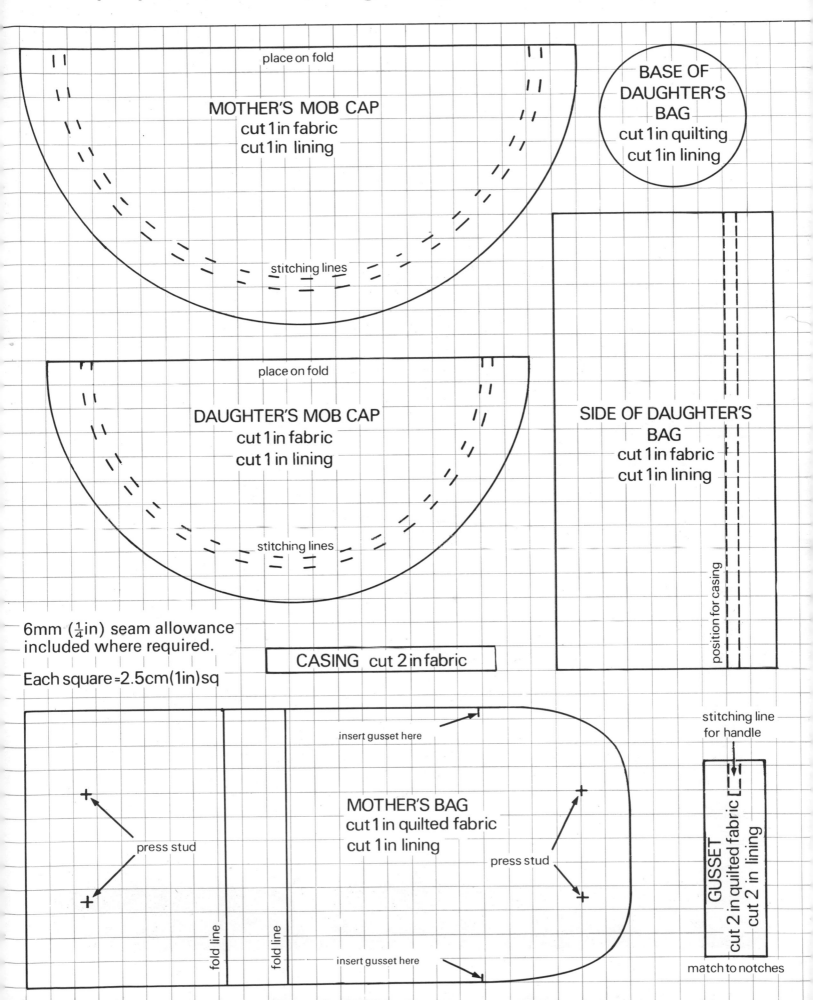

place on fold

MOTHER'S MOB CAP
cut 1 in fabric
cut 1 in lining

stitching lines

BASE OF DAUGHTER'S BAG
cut 1 in quilting
cut 1 in lining

place on fold

DAUGHTER'S MOB CAP
cut 1 in fabric
cut 1 in lining

stitching lines

SIDE OF DAUGHTER'S BAG
cut 1 in fabric
cut 1 in lining

position for casing

6mm (¼in) seam allowance included where required.

Each square = 2.5cm (1in) sq

CASING cut 2 in fabric

insert gusset here

stitching line for handle

press stud

MOTHER'S BAG
cut 1 in quilted fabric
cut 1 in lining

press stud

GUSSET
cut 2 in quilted fabric
cut 2 in lining

fold line

fold line

insert gusset here

match to notches

Basic Equipment Check List

All of these items are distributed by Coats Domestic Marketing Division and are available from the sewing sections of most large stores. The Coats brand name for the item is given in brackets.

For Pattern making

Metre stick
Pattern paper (True Sew)
Household scissors for cutting paper
Tape Measure (Pikaby)
Tracing wheel (Pikaby)

For cutting out and marking

Chalk (Pikaby Marking Chalk)
Dressmaker's tracing paper (Pikaby)
Marker pencils (Milwards)
Pins (Coats, steel)
Dressmaker's fabric shears

For sewing

Hand-sewing needles (Milwards)
Machine needles (Milwards—see machine needle and thread chart)
Pin cushion
Embroidery scissors for fine work
Thimble (Pikaby, steel)
Thread (Coats Satinised Cotton, Drima, also Drima Bold Stitch for top-stitching, buttons, buttonholes, button thread)

Notions

Bias binding (Coats)
Buttons (Pikaby)
Button-covering kit (Pikaby)
Curtain hooks
Curtain rings
Elastic (Pikaby)
Hooks and eyes (Pikaby)
Interlining (Vilene, sew in and iron on)
Petersham (Pikaby)
Piping cord (Strutts)
Press studs (Pikaby)
Seam binding tape (Coats)
Shirring elastic
Trimmings (such as beads, braids, fringe and ribbon)
Nylon touch-and-close fastening tape (Velcro)
Zip fasteners (Lightning metal zips and Opti-lon nylon zips)

Index

Pictures Contributed by:

Steve Bicknell: 126/7, 128T, 168, 176,195.
Camera Press: 159, 188, 189.
Heidede Carstensen: 148.
John Carter, 14, 73, 77, 100, 110, 114.
Bob Davidson: 47.
Alan Duns: 121, 124/5.
Jenny Franklin: 23.
Geoffrey Frosh: 157.
Nelson Hargreaves: 172/3.
Courtesy Harrison Drapes: 151, 152L.
Paul Kemp: 156TL.
Peter Kibbles: 154.
David Levin: 165.
Chris Lewis: 132L, 119T&B.
Bill Maclaughlin: 182.
Stuart Macleod: 67TL, 81.
D. Marsden: 161.
Nigel Messett: 181.

Illustrators

Suzanne Bowen-Morris 37; Michael Boyes 124BL; Rosemary Chanter 17TC/TR/BC, 20T&B, 21T; Lynette Colbert 112; Marta Czok 78/9, 117; Victoria Drew 128B, 129R, 130TL; E. Embleton/B. Firth 92R, 93BR&T, 94/5; Terry Evans 72, 74, 80, 82, 83, 84; Barbara Firth 11, 16, 17TL, 18, 19, 24, 26, 27, 28, 29, 30, 31, 32, 33, 34TR, 38, 4, 40, 41, 42, 43, 44, 49, 50, 51, 54, 55, 57, 58, 59, 60, 61, 63, 64, 66, 89, 97, 99TL, 106/7, 108/9, 136, 137, 138, 179, 180, 185, 186, 187; Angela Fishburn 132; John Hutchinson 69, 70; Janet Kirkwood 75; Janine Kirwan 134; Brian Mayors 56, 65, 86, 90, 91, 96, 98; Janet Smith 111; Lynette Stock 196; Paul Williams/B. Birth 44, 115; Paul Williams/ Chris Legee 76; Paul Williams 103, 104, 105, 139, 140, 141, 142, 160, 177B, 178.